CO-AMY-233

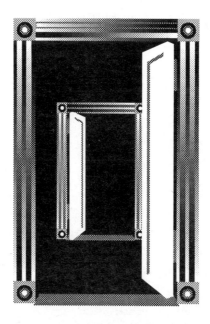

FOUNDATIONS OF ELEMENTARY AND MIDDLE SCHOOL COUNSELING

LLOYD A. STONE

Emporia State University

FRED O. BRADLEY

Kansas State University

Longman *Publishers USA*

**Foundations of Elementary and
Middle School Counseling**

Copyright © 1994 by Longman Publishers USA.
All rights reserved.
No part of this publication may be reproduced,
stored in a retrieval system, or transmitted
in any form or by any means, electronic, mechanical,
photocopying, recording, or otherwise,
without the prior permission of the publisher.

Longman, 10 Bank Street, White Plains, N.Y. 10606

Associated companies:
Longman Group Ltd., London
Longman Cheshire Pty., Melbourne
Longman Paul Pty., Auckland
Copp Clark Longman Ltd., Toronto

Acquisitions editor: Virginia Blanford
Production editor: Linda Moser/Books by Design
Cover design: Robin Hoffmann
Production supervisor: Richard Bretan

Library of Congress Cataloging-in-Publication Data

Stone, Lloyd A.
    Foundations of Elementary and Middle School Counseling / Lloyd A.
Stone and Fred O. Bradley.
        p.   cm.
    Includes bibliographical references and index.
    ISBN 0-8013-0632-9
    1. Counseling in elementary education.   2. Counseling in middle
school education.   I. Bradley, Fred O.   II. Title.
LB1027.5.S79   1994
    372.14—dc20   94-14026
                                                         CIP

1 2 3 4 5 6 7 8 9 10-MA-9897969594

Contents

CHAPTER 3 GROWTH AND DEVELOPMENT   41

CHAPTER 4 COUNSELING THEORY AND TECHNIQUE   69

CHAPTER 6 **PLAY MEDIA IN COUNSELING**   117

CHAPTER 7 **CLASSROOM GUIDANCE**   129

CHAPTER 8 **GROUP COUNSELING**   149

CHAPTER 9 THE TEACHER'S ROLE IN GUIDANCE   171

CHAPTER 10 PARENT EDUCATION AND CONSULTATION   183

Preface

One of our prime tasks has been the academic preparation and clinical supervision of students aspiring to become elementary/middle school counselors. We feel fortunate to have amassed considerable information concerning the role of the elementary/middle school counselor. We have observed firsthand what needs to be done, what works and what doesn't work, and what impact a counselor can have on an elementary or middle school. In this text we have included information, based upon our research and experiences, that will help prospective elementary/middle school counselors to understand the historical actecedents of their work and to assist the students in their schools.

Foundations of Elementary and Middle School Counseling is a blend of history, theory, and practical information that should interest anyone wishing to find out more about school counselng at this level. For those aspiring to become elementary/middle school counselors, it is intended as an introductory text.

Too often, school counseling and guidance programs have failed due to counselors' uncertainty about their role. Chapter 2 addresses this issue. Another reason for failure has been the lack of consistent program organization and evaluation. Chapter 12 contains information about these activities. The chapters on counseling theories, growth and development, assessment, consultation, and group counseling will assist the learner in obtaining essential background information for further study. The chapters on play media, classroom guidance, and parenting discuss how the counselor can function in these areas. Finally, the trends and issues chapter is intended to inform readers of current issues and to apprise them of what they can expect. We realize that none of our chapters covers everything on a given subject. Our intent is to offer the reader an overview that will lead to further study and research.

We believe that elementary/middle school counselors are pioneers in a not-so-old profession. It is our sincere hope that this book will motivate these practitioners to try new methods, to explore new activities, and to realize that they need not be mere spectators as their profession develops and their roles become further defined. Practitioner involvement is essential to our profesion. We challenge our readers to be active in professional organizations, to experiment with new applications of counseling and guidance principles, and through these activities, make their contribution. Only then can the work of the elementary/middle school counselor truly contribute to the total educational process of those we serve.

ACKNOWLEDGEMENTS

Many people have directly or indirectly contributed to the preparation of this book. Certainly our former professors, our colleagues, the reviewers, and our students—past and present—have all been instrumental in encouraging us to develop our ideas, clarify our beliefs, and gain the confidence to proceed with this endeavor. Also, the following individuals reviewed the manuscript and provided helpful suggestions:

Stewart Ehly, University of Iowa
Susan James, Western Kentucky University
Gerald Juhnke, University of North Carolina at Greensboro
Frances Mullis, Georgia State University
Sharon Robinson, Arizona State University
Eldon Ruff, Indiana University at South Bend
Bruce Shertzer, Purdue University
Rex Stockton, Indiana University
David Zimpfer, Kent State University

Our secretaries deserve special recognition for helping us in manuscript preparation. Most important, we are grateful to our wives, Twila and Nancy Jo, for their unfailing understanding, patience, time, and support as we completed this task.

Lloyd A. Stone
Fred O. Bradley

chapter 1

History, Philosophy, and Rationale

INTRODUCTION

As you read this chapter we hope you will develop an appreciation of how guidance in the schools has evolved. We believe that to facilitate future change, we need to understand the past. The purpose of this chapter is to help you become familiar with the history of guidance and counseling in the schools. We do not intend to detail the entire history of school counseling. We will discuss those aspects that appear to have had the greatest impact. This chapter also contains a brief overview of the philosophical basis for elementary school counseling, as well as the rationale for the counselor's work.

Guidance and counseling in the schools, whether at the elementary or secondary level, is still a relatively new phenomenon. It is important that people who choose to pursue a career in school counseling develop a clear understanding of how the profession has evolved, as well as the philosophy underlying the work of the school counselor.

Although this book is designed primarily as an introduction, no history of guidance could be complete without a review of events that have affected guidance programs at the secondary level. Therefore, the history of school counseling in general is covered briefly first. Since most of the significant developments in school counseling have occurred relatively recently, we will focus on the twentieth century. The intent is not to overlook or diminish contributions prior to the turn of this century, but rather to emphasize the changes since then. Following is a discussion of those events and individuals who seem to have had the greatest impact on the guidance and counseling movement.

HISTORICAL EVENTS AND CONTRIBUTIONS

The school guidance movement has been influenced by a convergence of three fields: vocational guidance, the testing movement, and the mental health movement. The gradual coming together of these areas, along with three additional factors—early writings in counseling theory, federal legislation, and recognition that school guidance programs should be based upon the needs of students—has resulted in the profession as it is known today.

Gladding (1988) observes that reviewing important events is one way to chart the evolution of counseling. Further, he cautions that names and events do not likely fit into a rigid chronology. However, to help you better grasp our evolution, we begin our historical review at the turn of the century and continue in chronological order whenever possible.

The Early Years

Vocational Guidance.   Early in the twentieth century, primarily between 1900 and 1910, the three areas mentioned earlier—vocational guidance, testing, and mental health—had their beginnings. In addition, the first organized public school guidance program was initiated. Many authors, including Gibson and Mitchell (1990), Gladding (1988), Nelson (1972), and Dimick and Huff (1970), credit Jessie B. Davis with organizing the first public school guidance program—in Grand Rapids, Michigan, in 1907. Prior to this, Davis, a school administrator, had already spent considerable time attempting to counsel students.

Davis, who was influenced by educators such as Horace Mann and John Dewey, was not advocating counseling in the modern sense but a forerunner of counseling, school guidance (Gladding, 1988). According to Aubrey (1977), Davis believed that proper guidance would help cure the ills of American society. Further, Davis seemed to believe that students should be taught about hard work, ambition, honesty, and overall good character (Rockwell & Rothney, 1961). Some of Davis's ideas and techniques may not be appropriate in today's schools, but it is apparent that he cared deeply about high school students. In 1913, Davis helped found the first professional guidance organization, the National Vocational Guidance Association (Dimick & Huff, 1970).

While Davis was making history in Michigan, Eli Weaver was introducing a similar guidance program in the New York City public schools. In his program, teachers served as counselors, and all students were required to formulate a career plan (Dimick & Huff, 1970). Weaver was credited with establishing teacher guidance committees in every high school in New York City. These committees were organized to help students discover their own strengths and use them to secure employment (Rockwell & Rothney, 1961).

Davis and Weaver have received the most attention, but there were other pioneers of the school guidance movement.

Frank Parsons, neither a counselor nor a teacher, perhaps influenced vocational education and guidance more than anyone. Gibson and Mitchell (1990); Lewis, Hayes, and Lewis (1986); Nelson (1972); and Dimick and Huff (1970) credit Parsons with being the "father of guidance," although not all his ideas were original; he expressed the thoughts of many people in his era.

Parsons was born in New Jersey in 1854. At age 15, he entered Cornell University (Gummere, 1988), where he earned his degree in engineering. But he also had acquired a legal background. He was thus able to promote social welfare among factory workers, as well as fair and kind treatment for working children (Miller, 1970). Much of Parsons's work was devoted to providing information about careers to schools located primarily in Boston and elsewhere in New England.

Because of his extensive work in vocational education, Parsons opened the Vocational Bureau of Boston in 1908. In his first report as director, Parsons urged that vocational guidance become part of the public school system (Brewer, 1942). Following this first report, he devoted much of his time to his book, *Choosing a Vocation*. The book outlined a plan for a "school for vocational counselors" (Brewer, 1942). Unfortunately, Parsons never saw his plan reach completion: He died in 1909, shortly before his book was published.

According to Gibson and Mitchell (1990), "Parsons' pioneer efforts and publications were popular, and succeeded in identifying and launching a new helping profession—the guidance counselor" (p. 7). Parsons proposed a three-step approach to working with clients: "(1) know the person, (2) know the world of work, and (3) match the man with the job" (Dimick & Huff, 1970, p. 6). Although this appeared to have merit, it was difficult to implement primarily due to the lack of techniques needed to "know the person."

At about the same time Parsons and vocational guidance were becoming influential, the testing effort was gaining momentum.

The Testing Movement.   The first general intelligence test was introduced in 1905, developed by Alfred Binet and Theodore Simon (Gibson & Mitchell, 1990). It provided the data for Louis Terman's later work at Stanford University, which resulted in an intelligence test that is still used—the Stanford-Binet (Glanz, 1974). The development of this instrument, perhaps more than any other, gave great impetus to the testing movement and paved the way for the development and standardization of other group and individual measures.

As World War I began, recruiters discovered that many draftees could neither read nor write. The military needed to determine which draftees were suitable for service and officer training (Dimick & Huff, 1970). The American Psychological Association (APA) formed a committee to develop a group instrument for this purpose. Even then, an effort was made to keep the test free from cultural bias, and to ensure that education and special training would not appreciably affect the results. Due to these pioneering efforts, the Army Alpha and Beta intelligence tests were developed. The Alpha was used to test literates; the Beta, illiterates or those with little knowledge of English. Dimick and Huff (1970) report that more than a million and a half draftees took the Alpha in 1918, and that several thousand took the Beta. These tests not only helped place recruits during World War I; they also supplied data relevant to the measurement of human ability. Recognizing the implications of this effort, Arthur L. Otis began his work on a paper-and-pencil version of the Stanford-Binet. Otis, at the time a graduate student of Louis Terman at Stanford, later published the Otis Self-Administering Test of Mental Ability, which was used by thousands of schools for many years.

Another important development in testing was the publication in 1928 of the Strong Vocational Interest Inventory (SVII). Edward Strong, its author and developer, had closely tied the SVII with the recent preparation and evaluation of occupational materials. This inventory has gone through numerous revisions. It served as the basis for the Strong-Campbell Interest Inventory (1985), still used in schools.

The Mental Health Movement.   Since ancient times, theories concerning physical and emotional health centered around mythology and superstition (McDaniel et al., 1959). For centuries, the prevailing belief was that the mentally ill were "dangerous, inferior, and should receive cruel and harsh treatment" (McDaniel et al., 1959). These unfortunates were said to be possessed by evil spirits. They were labeled as witches, tortured, and often burned at the stake. Not until the mid-eighteenth century was humane treatment of the mentally ill attempted (Zeran, Lallas, & Wegner, 1964). In 1752, the Blockely Insane Asylum was established in Philadelphia, although this hospital was not exclusively intended for the treatment of the mentally ill. A similar hospital—the Eastern State Lunatic Asylum, established in Williamsburg, Virginia in 1773—did provide exclusive treatment for them (Zeran, Lallas, & Wegner, 1964). Little else was done before the social reforms of the nineteenth century.

The leader of the mental health reforms in the twentieth century was Clifford Beers. With the publication of his book *A Mind That Found Itself* (1908), the public became aware of the harsh treatment given to the mentally ill (Miller, 1961). In his book, Beers describes his experiences as a teenager, obsessed with fear that he had epilepsy. He developed "manic-depressive psychosis" and was institutionalized following a suicide attempt. In the hospital, Beers experienced brutal treatment, including 21 consecutive days in a straitjacket (Zeran, Lallas, & Wegner, 1964). Beers's book exposed the conditions in state and private mental hospitals. In a summation of the feelings and thoughts of the mentally ill, Beers stated, ". . . they are still human: they love and hate, and have a sense of humor . . . the insane are often appreciative" (Beers, 1908, p. 248).

The book attracted so much attention that Beers, along with William James and Adolf Myer, established the National Committee for Mental Hygiene. Beers served as secretary until 1943 (Zeran, Lallas, & Wegner, 1964). His efforts with this committee, his book, and other contributions helped give birth to the mental health movement, which has had a tremendous impact upon school guidance and counseling.

Another important name, especially in the development of elementary school guidance, was William H. Burnham. In *History of Elementary School Guidance*, Faust (1968) credits Burnham with being the "father of elementary school guidance." Burnham, who did most of his writing during the 1920s and 1930s, was 40 to 60 years ahead of his time. In 1926 Burnham published *Great Teachers and Mental Health*. The book provided a rationale for the elementary school guidance and counseling movement, which would begin in the early 1960s (Baruth & Robinson, 1987). Burnham advocated understandings and activities in the elementary school that would be developmental and preventative in nature. He saw the need for assisting children to more effectively understand themselves, others, and the world. Faust (1968) wrote of Burnham's contribution,

> As it turned out . . . the momentum generated by a number of writers during the thirties, and by Burnham between 1926 and 1934 in particular, was insufficient to get elementary school counseling off to a full-fledged flight into the ultimately prevailing winds of the educative process. If the counseling vehicle got off the ground at all, the flight was no more (and no less!) than that of the Wright brothers. Counseling really went nowhere, except perhaps to the other end of the field. But the design for flight, in its unsophisticated, primitive way, had been at least sketchily blueprinted. Future, more elaborate flights into space were to be made. However little the pilots were conscious of it, those flights were to some extent based on Burnham's earlier contemplations. (pp. 18-19)

The early years of the school guidance movement were significant. Standardized testing, vocational education, and mental health were seen as significant aspects of helping people lead fulfilling lives. In those years, the groundwork was laid for the changes that were to follow.

The Middle Years

The middle years—from the late 1930s through the late 1960s—were perhaps the most important in the development of school guidance and counseling. This period saw considerable effort in the area of counseling theories; the aftermath of World War II; the founding of the school counselor's professional organization; the passage of federal legislation that would directly affect the movement; and the writing of a book that would set the stage for the counselor's role in years to come.

Counseling Theory Contributions.   With the publication of *How to Counsel Students* in 1939, E. G. Williamson made perhaps the first significant contribution to counseling theory since Frank Parsons. Williamson introduced what was to become known as the directive approach to clinical counseling, somewhat similar to Parsons's three-step model. Williamson, however, divided his approach into six steps—analysis, synthesis, diagnosis, prognosis, counseling (treatment), and follow-up. The procedure can be summarized as determining the problem through analysis and synthesis of the data, then making a diagnosis and offering a prognosis through treatment (counseling), at which time the client is given the steps needed for adjustment or readjustment. Finally, the counselor follows up to determine the effectiveness of the counseling.

Although some practitioners endorsed Williamson's directive approach, others felt that it failed to place enough responsibility on clients for solving their own problems. Among those who disagreed with Williamson was Carl Rogers.

Rogers came forth with his counseling ideas in 1942, with his book *Counseling and Psychotherapy.* Miller (1970) stated that Rogers's primary motivation for writing the book was to offer an alternative to Williamson's method. In *Counseling and Psychotherapy,* Rogers outlined what was to become known as the non-directive approach to counseling, which leaned heavily on the client-counselor relationship and was based on the belief that if given the opportunity to choose, the client would do so wisely. In effect, this placed more responsibility on clients for solving their own problems. Later, Rogers was to further refine his theory in *Client-Centered Therapy* (1951). For the next dozen years or so, Rogerian ideas would move through the counseling movement with a high degree of acceptance. His writings served to bring about the beginnings of professionalism in counseling (Baruth & Robinson, 1987). Through the next three decades, Albert Ellis, William Glasser, Eric Berne, Rudolph Dreikurs, B. F. Skinner, John Krumboltz, and Frederick Perls were to make additional contributions to counseling theory.

Testing Movement Continues.   The enhancement of aptitude tests, used to assist servicemen as well as veterans in making educational and occupational choices, could be traced to World War II—just as the Army Alpha and Beta group intelligence tests could be traced to World War I. However, for the first time, the effort was more closely tied to counseling. This came about primarily because colleges needed help implementing the G.I. Bill. As a result, counseling centers on college campuses originated.

Early Professional Organizations.   By 1950, four professional organizations had been organized, at least in part, for counselors. These were the National Vocational Guidance Association, the Student Personnel Association for Student Education, the American College Personnel Association, and the National Association of Guidance Supervisors and College Trainers (Gazda, Childers, & Brooks, 1987). In 1952, these associations formed the American Personnel and Guidance Association (APGA). The same year, the American School Counselors Association (ASCA) was organized, and in 1953 it too became a division of APGA.

Sputnik I and Federal Legislation.   In 1957 the Soviet Union launched Sputnik I. This feat probably had more impact on the growth of guidance and counseling in the schools than any other single event. There was immediate concern in the United States that our schools were not developing sufficiently competitive brainpower. To help overcome this perceived deficiency, in 1958 Congress passed the National Defense Education Act (NDEA). Two titles of the act had a direct impact on guidance programs at the secondary school level. Title V-A required states to submit a plan for group testing of students in secondary schools. This would identify talented students and encourage them to go on to college, preferably to excel in mathematics and the physical sciences. States that submitted approved plans received funds to help implement secondary school guidance programs. These funds were mostly managed by the state department of education. State departments would allocate NDEA funds to local school districts that had met certain criteria. First, the district had to have a plan that included a testing program, physical facilities to house the counselor, minimal clerical help, and a commitment to encourage talented youth to study science and mathematics. Second, the local district had to have the services of a counselor. Since there were few well-prepared school counselors at that time, Title V-B of NDEA provided funds for their training. These two titles helped bring about a tremendous increase in the number of school counselors, especially between 1959 and 1964. This growth, although viewed as positive for the most part, was not without its negative aspects.

In 1959, the majority of secondary schools did not have a counselor. Since everyone wanted to play catch-up in the space race, and since having a counselor became a status symbol, the demand for secondary school counselors was without precedent. Unfortunately, few qualified counselors were available. But because the money was there and the idea a sound one, many states encouraged schools to hire counselors who were not adequately prepared. Also, there was evidence that some individuals entered this new profession because they were "burned out" or were experiencing difficulty in their teaching. These factors, along with the fact that many school administrators had little idea of what a counselor could or should do, made it possible for the field to grow in a questionable manner. Over the past 30 years, the profession has made great strides in overcoming some of the stigma created by this rather inauspicious beginning.

In 1964, Congress amended NDEA to include elementary school guidance. Therefore, NDEA also had an impact on elementary school growth, although not to the same degree that it had on secondary programs. By 1969, states were well into implementing programs at the district level that would enhance the numbers of elementary school counselors. However, that same year the government combined NDEA and the Elementary and Secondary School Education Act III (ESEA III) into one appropriation. Although this move helped promote research in elementary school guidance and counseling, it had a negative effect with regard to the growth in numbers.

In 1962 C. Gilbert Wrenn published *The Counselor in a Changing World.* This book became an influential guide for the development of the profession in the decades to follow.

The Later Years

This was the period of refinement in the development of counseling and guidance. The profession had just gone through considerable growth. By the late 1960s and early 1970s, virtually every secondary school had access to a counselor. Elementary counseling had also grown, but nowhere near the extent of counseling at the secondary level.

Refinement of the profession took place on a variety of fronts during the late 1960s and through the 1970s and 1980s: career education, credentialing, counselor role changes, and the renaming of professional organizations and university classes to more accurately reflect counseling as a profession. What follows is a brief discussion of each of these topics and of legislation that was implemented during this period.

Federal Legislation.   In 1968, an amendment to the Vocational Education Act advocated career education, handicapped and disadvantaged programs, and extension of guidance programs into elementary schools. In 1971—as an outgrowth of this legislation, as well as the country's expanding social consciousness—career education became a priority of the U.S. Office of Education. In 1974, the Educational Amendments legislated career education, and the U.S. Office of Education initiated the Office of Career Education (Gazda, Childers, & Brooks, 1987). This brought about an expansion of elementary school counseling, in that some counselors were hired to implement career education programs in the schools. Through massive efforts of educating teachers and other school personnel, the career education concept was infused into the school curriculum at all levels, but especially the elementary. About this same time, the social ills of our country were beginning to cause a shift from the developmental approach of the career education movement to a more crisis-oriented tack. President Nixon was forced to resign after threat of impeachment; there was high unemployment, an unstable economy, and an increasingly negative attitude toward social causes. Alcohol and drug abuse were on the rise, and single-parent homes became the norm as divorce rates soared to all-time highs. These ills were to have a lasting effect on the career education movement, the expansion of elementary school guidance, and the ultimate role of the counselor at the elementary level.

Counselor Credentialing.   During the 1970s, the APGA viewed credentialing as a three-pronged process: accreditation, licensure, and certification. During the 1970s and 1980s all three steps received the attention of the profession, and considerable progress was accomplished in credentialing. It is important, in our historical review, to understand how each component is defined and the impact each has made on the profession.

Accreditation.   According to Forster (1977),

> accreditation is a process whereby an association or agency grants public recognition to a school, institute, college, university, or specialized program of study that has met certain established qualifications of standards as determined through initial and periodic evaluations. "Program approval" is another name for accreditation. In some professions, graduates of accredited preparation programs are considered credentialed. (p. 573)

Most school counselor preparation programs are accredited by their respective state departments of education. In many cases, this takes the form of program approval. Many school counselor preparation programs are found in colleges or schools of education. In these cases, the program may also be accredited by the National Council for Accreditation of Teacher Education (NCATE). In 1981, the Council for Accreditation of Counseling and Related Educational Programs (CACREP) was incorporated as an independent council by the APGA (now, after two name changes, the American Counseling Association, or ACA). The scope of accreditation by this body includes entry-level master's degree programs in community counseling, mental health counseling, school counseling, marriage and family counseling, and student affairs practice in higher education. It also accredits doctoral programs in counselor education and supervision (CACREP, 1994). Accreditation is an important aspect of counselor credentialing. It greatly increases the chances of counseling students, whether destined for school or elsewhere, of getting quality preparation.

Certification.   While accreditation credentials institutions or programs, certification (along with licensure) has historically been the common method used to credential counseling practitioners. Forster (1977) describes certification as follows:

> This is a process of recognizing the competence of practitioners of a profession by officially authorizing them to use the title adopted by the profession. Certification can be awarded by voluntary associations, agencies, or by governmental bodies, some of which are recognized by

state laws. In school counseling, certification is usually handled by an office within the state government's department of education or its branch for executing public instruction matters. (p. 573)

By 1970, all states had implemented school counselor certification. In this regard, school counseling was ahead of other areas. Over the next two decades, most states refined their requirements and in many instances adopted various versions of competency-based certification. As is evident from Forster's definition, certification can be awarded by voluntary associations as well as state departments of education.

Sensing the need for certification for their group, rehabilitation counselors began discussions in the late 1960s. According to Hedgeman (1985), the Commission on Rehabilitation Counselor Certification (CRCC) was formed in 1973. In 1974, the first examination was given, and the certification of rehabilitation counselors was initiated.

The American Mental Health Counselors Association (AMHCA) was responsible for establishing the next counselor certification credential. Messina (1985) reported that the AMHCA Certification Committee drafted an initial set of procedures in 1978, and in 1979 the first group of counselors seeking status as certified clinical mental health counselors (CCMHC) sat for the examination.

Based upon an intensive needs assessment carried out in 1980 by the APGA's Special Committee on Registry, the National Board for Certified Counselors (NBCC) was incorporated in 1982 (Stone, 1985). NBCC is a freestanding, not-for-profit corporation whose primary purpose is to certify, in a generic sense, those persons who qualify as national certified counselors (NCC). According to Stone (1985), NBCC offered three options under which individuals could become certified. One of these allowed graduates of CACREP-accredited institutions to waive the experience requirement. This encouraged institutions to seek CACREP accreditation, and thereby enabled one credentialing body to support another.

In 1983, the National Council for Credentialing Career Counselors (NCCCC) was implemented (Smith & Karpati, 1985). As the name implies, this served the purpose of certifying career counselors. In 1985, National Certified Career Counselors (NCCC) became the first specialty to affiliate with NBCC. Since then, Specialty Certifications in School Counseling (NCSC) and Gerontological Counselors (NCGC) have been formulated by NBCC. In 1993, the Mental Health Counselors (CCMHC) became the fourth NBCC specialty.

Licensure.   The efforts to credential counselors voluntarily, whether specialty or general, greatly enhanced the efforts that had already begun to pass state counselor licensure laws. Forster (1977) offers the following definition:

[Licensure] is a process authorized by state legislation that regulates the practice and title of the profession. Because of its legislative base, licensure subjects violators to greater legal sanctions than does certification. Licensure is generally considered to be more desirable when a substantial proportion of a profession's practitioners are in private practice, because of the broader coverage and greater potential for using sanctions against violators. Licensure boards are usually established with quasi-legislative power to make rules and examine applicants who seek licenses. (p. 573)

For more than 25 years the need for counselor licensure has been an issue for the profession, especially for those who are involved in private practice. Licensure is a state legislative process. The Virginia Personnel and Guidance Association began efforts to pass a counselor licensure statute in 1972. Four years later, Virginia's Governor Mills Godwin signed the first counselor licensure bill into law. Since then, a total of 39 states as well as the District of Columbia have passed legislation to regulate professional counseling.

The Era of Name Changes.   Along with credentialing, other areas were being refined during the later years. During this era, names were changed to more accurately depict the current thrust of the counseling profession. For example, some "counseling centers" became known as "centers for personal growth" or "development centers," and accrediting bodies began to look for courses that covered human development. In 1983, the APGA—the umbrella organization for counseling—changed its name to the Association for Counseling and Development (AACD). In 1992, AACD changed its name again, this time to the American Counseling Association (ACA). Several divisions of AACD/ACA also changed their names during this time to more accurately depict their current orientation.

School guidance and counseling is an outgrowth of many factors. Testing, mental health emphasis, and vocational education all made an impact upon the field. Counseling theorists, legislative activity, and societal changes also set the stage for how the profession would develop. The growth that has taken place over the last 30 to 35 years has indeed been phenomenal. With the refinement of the last two decades, and the redefining of the school counselor's role currently under consideration, a place for counselors both in elementary and secondary schools has been established.

PHILOSOPHICAL VIEWS

Activities carried out by the counselor in a developmental guidance program should be based upon fundamental philosophical beliefs. Some of these beliefs are broad and should be stated in the context of guidance, while others are more clearly associated with the belief system of the counselor. Still others best fit the activities of counselors as they go about their day-to-day task of helping students. It does not really matter whether the beliefs are broad, specific to counseling, or an attitude of the counselor. It is important that they lay a foundation upon which a developmental elementary school guidance program might be built. These beliefs make it possible for the description of a consistent, comprehensive guidance program that will be further detailed in Chapter 2.

We shall discuss several philosophical beliefs. The statements and discussions that follow encompass the primary philosophical basis needed for program implementation.

Philosophical Beliefs

A developmental elementary school guidance program should be founded upon the following philosophical beliefs. The counselor should understand these basic principles if they are to be used in such a program.

1. All human beings, including children, are unique individuals regardless of sex, race, age, ability, performance, or special status. Dinkmeyer states: "Guidance in the schools is based upon the assumption that every human being is of value and has a right to optimum development" (1968, p. 3). As such, elementary schools students should be afforded the same respect that has too often been reserved for adults. We believe that the counselor should help assure that *all* students are treated as unique individuals. Children deserve the best assistance in adjusting to their situation.

2. The counselor, as an agent of change, believes that the purpose of the counselor's activities within an elementary school is to facilitate development. Blocher (1987) offers three propositions that support this statement. He believes that these propositions help to "distinguish the process of counseling from psychotherapy, teaching, social work and other related services" (p. 11).

> The primary value commitment of the counselor is to facilitate human development by helping those with whom he or she works reach their highest level of functioning and to overcome obstacles that might hinder their further growth.
>
> Developing human beings can only be fully understood and truly helped within the context of their interactions with the physical, social, and psychological environment.
>
> The ultimate goal of counseling is to work with both the client and the environment to facilitate a dynamic and vibrant engagement, or "fit," between the developing person and environment. (p. 11)

3. The counselor must work closely with a variety of other specialists within the elementary school. In today's educational environment, a variety of specialists meet the needs of elementary school students. These include the school psychologist, social worker, nurse, speech therapist, and others. Each of these persons, in addition to the classroom teacher and building administrator, plays a part in assuring that the students' needs are met. The counselor can ill afford not to use the services of these specialists, and must cooperate with them in assisting children with their growth and development.

4. Counselors are *not* valueless. Counselors, like all other adults, have their own values. As Peterson (1970) so aptly pointed out:

> We have found growing agreement that the counselor cannot avoid bringing his values with him to the counseling relationship. He cannot avoid the consideration of ultimate values in counseling nor can he avoid operating according to some philosophical point of view.
>
> If counselors influence their clients, this presents an inescapable responsibility. The counselor is forced to ask the often embarrassing questions: Who wants to be like me? How consistent is my philosophy of life? To what degree do I embody the values to which I give lip service? (p. 224)

Many adults erroneously assume that children want to be like them, and often consciously or unconsciously attempt to impose their values on youngsters. Counselors must understand their own values, and while recognizing that these values may *influence* the people around them, be careful not to *impose* them upon the children with whom they work.

5. The term *developmental counseling* is not only acceptable terminology, but also critical to the work of the elementary school counselor. Developmental counseling is designed to produce growth within the child. This growth may lead to better self-understanding or self-acceptance. As a result of these understandings, the behavior or attitude of the child may show marked change. It is important to recognize that developmental counseling does include crisis situations and/or problem children. The developmental counselor, compared to the more traditional problem-centered counselor, uses a much broader approach in counseling, frequently consulting with teachers and other significant adults in the child's life.

6. To maximize their efforts, counselors must work with the significant adults in the child's life. The most important person in the child's school life is the classroom teacher. Therefore, a close teacher/counselor relationship is imperative if the child is to receive optimum help. Teachers, by nature of their sustained contact with children, are in a favorable position to identify those who might benefit from a counselor's expertise. In a cooperative teacher/counselor relationship, the teacher will not only make the counselor aware of the child's special needs, but also will offer to assist in any way possible.

Away from school, the parent or parents are in a position to influence not only the child's behavior but also his or her learning ability. Counselors must be aware of this influence and involve parents appropriately. In some homes the parents may not be the most influential adults. These individuals may be grandparents, live-in friends, or siblings; regardless, it is imperative that the counselor seek their involvement in attempting to help the child.

7. Counseling elementary school children is more complex than counseling young adults and adults. Perhaps one of the most obvious differences between counseling the elementary school child and a young adult or adult is that the former does not have the same freedom or opportunity for independence. A six-year-old who lives in a home where physical abuse is prevalent, and whose parents fail to show even the most basic affection for the child, has little choice but to live with the situation. However, a teenager confronted with a similar situation has a better chance of leaving such an environment. This has a significant impact upon the choices that are available during counseling. In addition, there are differences in the thinking processes of the child and the adult. Children tend to think more in the here-and-now, while older individuals are more readily able to examine the past and look into the future. These attributes make counseling the child considerably different from counseling the young adult or adult.

8. Counselors must be available and provide assistance to *all* students within the school. We believe that one of the counselor's greatest assets is availability. In some parts of the country, the counselor is required to serve many buildings and perhaps hundreds of students. Often these programs evolve into crisis-oriented activities in which the counselor spends the most time "putting out fires." It is imperative that a desirable counselor/student ratio be achieved. This may vary, based upon needs of students and the availability of other specialists within the school, but we believe that the *maximum* ratio should be 1 counselor for each 200 to 250 students.

9. Counseling and guidance programs in the elementary school should be integrated into the curriculum as part of the total educational plan. In a school where counseling and guidance are viewed as a joint approach between teacher and counselor, the guidance program will become an integral part of the curriculum. As Muro and Dinkmeyer (1977) point out:

> The counseling process is not separate from education; indeed, counseling is a vital aspect of the educational process. By the same token, the activities generally described as "teaching" are not unrelated to counseling, in that teaching, like counseling, has as its eventual goal the development of competent, healthy human beings. The counseling session and the counselor's efforts must be viewed as a logical extension of the classroom; in fact, the context of counseling is in reality just as much a part of the curriculum as social studies or language arts. (p. 7)

When teachers, counselors, and administrators work together to assure that the guidance program is indeed integrated into the total school curriculum, the chances of meeting the needs of individuals and groups are greatly enhanced.

10. Developmental guidance programs, as carried out by the elementary school counselor, should be consistent with the mission of the school and based upon the needs of students within that school. Not only should there be a philosophical statement pertaining to the guidance program, but this statement must be consistent with the total philosophy and mission of the school. In addition, programmatic activities must be grounded in guidance philosophy and based upon the needs of students. Obviously, these needs may vary from one school to another.

The field of elementary school guidance has experienced tremendous growth within the last decade. If this is to continue, and if the developmental approach is to flourish, then the aforementioned philosophical beliefs would appear to have unsurpassed importance.

RATIONALE

The question of whether counselors are needed in the elementary schools was answered many years ago, with a resounding yes. But the placement of counselors in these schools has been a relatively slow process. As with most educational dilemmas, insufficient funding has been the primary reason for lack of growth. However, it is also evident that when well-meaning administrators and others attempt to convince their respective boards of education to implement an elementary program, they often have difficulty communicating the rationale for it. In addition, finding an understandable role statement or job description often eludes them.

The purpose of this section is to offer evidence that could help schools articulate *why* a counselor is needed. Too often, in education, we attempt to implement or sell an idea because we believe it to be right or timely. Guidance programs in the elementary school are too important to rely on such nebulous justification. We must present a sound philosophical basis upon which the program will be developed, and specify areas in which the developmental approach of the elementary school counselor could make a difference. This is not to imply that the presence of an elementary school counselor will be a panacea for the societal problems we are about to address. But there is growing evidence that sound developmental guidance practices in the elementary school do help children make appropriate decisions as they enter adulthood.

In the final decade of the twentieth century, it is necessary that we recognize, and be able to articulate, the societal problems that affect our children's learning and social development.

Over the past 50 years there has been a dramatic change in family life. The number of working parents is rising; their children spend more time alone and unsupervised. There are also more single parents. If the present trend continues, two-parent families will not necessarily be the norm as we approach the twenty-first century. Cavasos (1989), in a report to the President of the United States, stated that 21.5 million, (65 percent) of women with children younger than 18 are either working or looking for work. Further, he found that 42 percent of children aged 5 to 13 whose mothers work spend time after school without supervision; of those, 10 percent are unsupervised for three or more hours. Myrick (1987) believes that lack of supervision leads to other problems:"Approximately one half of all serious crimes in the nation are committed by young people" (p. 18).

The home, in many instances, no longer serves as the place where children interact with two parents. Instead, they may need to find security, unconditional acceptance, and supervision in a single-parent home.

In 1988, the U.S. Office of Educational Research and Improvement published a study titled "Youth Indicators 1988: Trends in the Well-Being of American Youth." Following are summaries from this study.

Divorce

The annual number of divorces rose 115 percent between 1965 and 1975. While the rate has not been nearly this high in recent years, divorce is still a common happening and approximately 1.1 million children are involved in divorce each year. (p. 11)

Children of Single Parents

As one might expect, as the number of divorces increases, so does the number of children living in single-parent homes. In the past 25 years, the number of children living in single-parent homes has more than doubled. (p. 21)

Poverty

Although the proportion of children living in poverty declined significantly during the 1960s, it has risen since 1970. In 1985, about 20 percent of all children and 54 percent of children in female-headed families lived in poverty. (p. 31)

Homework and Television

In general, students spend more time watching television than doing homework. Patterns of TV viewing vary across race and age, with black and elementary school students watching the most. (p. 71)

Unemployment of Young Adults

Minority youth, especially black teenagers, have substantially higher unemployment rates than whites. The unemployment rate for white teenage males is less than one-half that of black teenage males. (p. 79)

Employment of Dropouts

Of those high school students who dropped out during a given school year, fewer than one-half were employed two years later. (p. 83)

Pregnancy and Abortion

The study indicates that teenage pregnancy has been on the increase for several years. Further, it was found that abortion among teenage women had nearly doubled in the last 20 years. (p. 97)

Alcohol and Drug Use

While the incidence of alcohol and drug use seems to go up and down over a given period of time, there has been an increase in the reported use over the past 15 years. In the latter part of the 1980s, almost two-thirds of all high school seniors reported having used alcohol within the past 30 days. (p. 99)

Arrests

For young adults aged 14 to 17 the arrest rate in 1950 was 4.1 per 1,000. By the mid-1980s the rate for this same age group had risen to 118.6 per 1,000. (p. 115)

There is much information supporting the idea that our society is in dire need of assistance. Child abuse, sexual and physical, is a problem in many homes. Teenage suicide has increased. There are more reported suicides and attempts among elementary school children than ever before. Teachers in the elementary schools must deal with far more student violence than they did even ten years ago.

The employment of an elementary school counselor is not an answer to all of these societal problems. However, with developmental guidance programs in our elementary schools, students will have a better chance of effectively deaing with society in general.

SUMMARY

In this chapter we described some of the people and events that have assisted the growth of school guidance programs. These programs developed as a result of the testing, vocational education, and mental health movements. They were helped along by such insightful people as Parsons, Burnham, Rogers, Wrenn, and others. Wars and federal legislation played an important part in the development of the field. Refinement of the counseling profession came about when professional associations defined roles and improved credentialing standards.

Developmental elementary school guidance programs are based upon a set of philosophical views and beliefs that are delineated in this chapter. These include seeing each individual as unique and providing assistance for all students within a school, not just those with special needs.

The problems of society were addressed; understanding and articulating societal problems helps promote a rationale for elementary school guidance programs and enhances the possibility of their implementation.

REVIEW

1. Why is it important to understand how school guidance got its start?
2. What single event probably had the greatest impact on the growth of school guidance programs?

3. Who is most generally known as the father of guidance?

4. Discuss the three most important areas in the guidance movement.

5. What did Clifford Beers contribute to the development of guidance?

6. Why was William H. Burnham considered to be ahead of his time?

7. Were the theories of Rogers and Williamson alike or different? Why?

8. Discuss some of the philosophical beliefs upon which an elementary school guidance program should be developed.

9. Write a short essay on the rationale for having an elementary school guidance program.

REFERENCES

Aubrey, R. F. (1977). Historical development of guidance and counseling implications for the future. *Personnel and Guidance Journal, 55,* 288–295.

Baruth, L. G., & Robinson, E. H. (1987). *An introduction to the counseling profession.* Englewood Cliffs, NJ: Prentice-Hall.

Beers, C. (1908). *A mind that found itself.* Garden City, NY: Doubleday.

Blocher, D. H. (1987) *The professional counselor.* New York: Macmillan.

Brewer, J. M. (1942). *History of vocational guidance: Origins and early development.* New York: Harper.

Burnham, W. (1926). *Great teachers and mental health.* New York: Appleton.

CACREP. (1994). *Accreditation procedures manual.* Alexandria, VA: Author.

Cavasos, L. F. (1989). *Educating our children: Parents and schools together: A report to the President.* (Department of Education). Washington, DC: U.S. Government Printing Office.

Dimick, K. M., & Huff, V. E. (1970). *Child counseling.* Dubuque, IA: William C. Brown.

Dinkmeyer, D. C. (Ed.). (1968). *Guidance and counseling in the elementary school: Readings in theory and practice.* New York: Holt.

Faust, V. (1968). *History of elementary school counseling.* Boston: Houghton Mifflin.

Forster, J. R. (1977). What shall we do about credentialing? *Personnel & Guidance Journal, 55,* 573–576.

Gazda, G. M., Childers, W. C., & Brooks, D. K. (1987). *Foundations of counseling and human services.* New York: McGraw-Hill

Gibson, R. L., & Mitchell, M. H. (1986). *Introduction to counseling and guidance.* (2nd ed.). New York: Macmillan.

Gibson, R. L., & Mitchell, M. H. (1990). *Introduction to counseling and guidance.* (3rd ed.). New York: Macmillan.

Gladding, S. T. (1988). *Counseling, a comprehensive profession.* Columbus, OH: Merrill.

Glanz, E. C. (1974). *Guidance: Foundations, principles and techniques.* Boston: Allyn & Bacon.

Gummere, R. M., Jr. (1988). The counselor as prophet: Frank Parsons, 1854–1908. *Journal of Counseling and Development, 66,* 402–405.

Hedgeman, B. S. (1985). Rehabilitation counselor certification. *Journal of Counseling and Development, 63,* 609–610.

Lewis, M. D., Hayes, R. L., & Lewis, J. A. (1986). *An introduction to the counseling profession.* Itasca, IL: F. E. Peacock.

McDaniel, H. D., Lallas, J. E., Saum, J. A., & Gilmore, J. L. (1959). *Readings in guidance.* New York: Holt.

Messina, J. L. (1985). The national academy of certified clinical mental health counselors: Creating a new professional identity. *Journal of Counseling and Development, 63,* 607–608.

Miller, F. (1961). *Guidance principles and services.* Columbus, OH: Merrill.

Miller, L. (1970, April). *History of guidance.* Lecture presented at the University of Wyoming, Laramie.

Muro, J. J., & Dinkmeyer, D. C. (1977). *Counseling in the elementary and middle schools: A pragmatic approach.* Dubuque, IA: William C. Brown.

Myrick, R. D. (1987). *Developmental guidance and counseling: A practical approach.* Minneapolis, MN: Educational Media Corporation.

Nelson, R. C. (1972). *Guidance and counseling in the elementary school.* New York: Holt.

Peterson, J. A. (1970). *Counseling and values.* Scranton, PA: International Textbooks Company.

Rockwell, P. J., & Rothney, J. W. N. (1961). Some social ideas of pioneers in the guidance movement. *Personnel and Guidance Journal, 40,* 349–354.

Rogers, C. (1942). *Counseling and psychotherapy.* Boston: Houghton Mifflin.

Rogers, C. (1951). *Client-centered therapy.* Boston: Houghton Mifflin.

Rotter, J. C. (1990). Elementary school counselor preparation: Past, present, and future. *Elementary School Guidance and Counseling, 24,* 180–188.

Smith, R. L., & Karpati, F. S. (1985). Credentialing career counselors. *Journal of Counseling and Development, 63,* 611.

Stone, L. A. (1985). National board for certified counselors: History, relationships, and projections. *Journal of Counseling and Development, 63,* 605–606.

U.S. Office of Educational Research and Improvement. (1988). *Youth indicators 1988: Trends in the well-being of American youth.* Washington, DC: U.S. Government Printing Office.

Williamson, E. G. (1939). *How to counsel students: A manual of techniques for clinical counselors.* New York: McGraw-Hill.

Wreen, C. G. (1962). *The counselor in a changing world.* Washington, DC: American Personnel and Guidance Assocation.

Zeran, F. R., Lallas, J. E., & Wegner, K. W. (1964). *Guidance: Theory and practice.* New York: American Book Company.

chapter **2**

Developmental School Guidance: What Does the Elementary School Counselor Do?

OUTLINE

INTRODUCTION

Elementary school counselors have been a part of American education for many years. Their number is small compared to that of secondary school counselors, and the need continues to be great. Considerable effort has gone into defining the elementary school counselor's work, yet a definitive role for this profession still seems to elude us. Over the years the American School Counselors Association (ASCA) has issued role and function statements, and many authors have attempted to further define what the elementary school counselor should do. Given the research and effort that has gone into this, we still hear of elementary school counselors who say they don't know what to do on the job. Are counselor education programs failing to communicate to their students? Is the subject so confusing that graduates cannot put the role into practice? We believe the situation to be paradoxically complex while at the same time being simpler than one might expect. One of the problems is definition. The terms *guidance* and *counseling* are used interchangeably. The roles of the elementary and secondary school counselors are discussed as if there were no difference in preparation or job description. Even though the term *developmental* has been around the guidance literature for decades, some authors seem to be so intoxicated with the word that they fail to describe any concrete aspects of the counselor's work. Presumably, they do so because they are afraid of really talking about specifics, thus violating the current byword in counseling—*developmental*. We too consider ourselves to be in the developmental approach corner. However, this will not prevent us from describing the elementary school counselor's role in terms that are understandable and practical.

This chapter outlines and discusses the work of the elementary school counselor. In addition, we briefly cover the work of secondary school counselors so that you can envision the counselor's work from kindergarten through grade 12.

DEFINITION OF TERMS

Four words need to be defined if our point of view is to be fully understood: *guidance, counseling, developmental,* and *comprehensive.* For many years these terms have been used interchangeably or arbitrarily. For example, we find authors using the terms *guidance counselor, developmental counseling, developmental guidance, comprehensive guidance, comprehensive developmental guidance, school counselor,* and so on. In addition, we see *guidance program, guidance services, guidance personnel, guidance materials, guidance activity,* and *guidance curriculum.* To the novice, it becomes even more complicated when *guidance* and *counseling* are used interchangeably. We say "to the novice" because most of us are so inured to this that our confusion has become part of our understanding (if this is possible!). Following are definitions as they apply to this book.

Guidance

Because of its multiplicity of meaning, the term *guidance* has always been difficult to understand. Myrick (1987) states that guidance is a force within the school curriculum that aims at the maximum development of individual potentialities. The same could be said for counseling. However, it is not our purpose to discuss the similarities between the two terms but to define each as succinctly as possible.

Dimick and Huff (1970) offer the following definition for guidance:

> Guidance from our point of view is largely a cognitive process designed to provide the individual with data external to himself—such as test data. This informative data hopefully will be assimilated by the client and made personally relevant so that the individual will be able to make the most appropriate choices for himself. Due to the specific problem-orientedness of the guidance function, it tends to be short-term in duration and relatively counselor-structured. The degree of counselor-client involvement is also minimal when compared to counseling and therapy. Such functions as advising, collecting and disseminating information, placement and follow-up, are typically considered guidance functions. (p. 26)

Although this definition indicates a difference between guidance and counseling, it hardly offers a precise definition of guidance. Some authors, such as Muro and Dinkmeyer (1977), solve the dilemma by simply not offering a definition of guidance. They do, however, define counseling in great detail. Gibson and Mitchell (1990) offer no clear definition of guidance either, even though the word is contained in one of their book titles.

Gladding (1988) offered one of the shortest definitions of guidance: "Guidance [focuses] on helping individuals make choices" (p. 5). Further, he reports that early guidance occurs in schools and as such results in a relationship between equals wherein the adult is helping the student find "direction in life." To delineate between the terms *guidance* and *counseling,* Gladding explained that "counseling [focuses] on helping individuals make important changes." The key words appear to be *choices* and *changes.* According to Gladding, guidance helps students make choices; counseling, to make changes.

Glanz (1974) undertook one of the most comprehensive attempts at defining guidance. Presupposing that education and guidance are interdependent and are designed to serve the individual in different but related fashions, Glanz wrote that guidance could "create psychological meaningfulness for the educational process as individuals are served and assisted in their development" (p. 40). As he continued in his quest for a definition, he stated:

> Guidance cannot exist without an educational foundation that permits persons to learn how to think, to learn facts, to acquire knowledge, and to create concepts; education is incomplete without guidance to focus its potential for individuals within a society. (p. 38)

> Guidance as a part of education focuses on the individual and his use of the facts, knowledge, and concepts he has obtained through education. The goal of guidance is the mature, self-directed person with the skills of critical thinking that permit him to become free and responsible.

According to Glanz, counseling is the basic process or technique of guidance. However, Glanz believes that counseling is not the *all* of a planned program to individualize educational and growth experiences. He continues:

> Guidance is the single most usable term to describe and circumscribe the varied activities and involvements that provide for the individualization of educational and personal growth experiences. *Counselor* and *counseling* are the keystone concepts within guidance.
>
> As long as professional guidance personnel do not confuse guidance or pupil personnel services with counseling; as long as counselors can be certain that in counseling they must be counselors and not wideranging guidance or pupil personnel workers; and as long as words do not interfere with meaning, the semantic confusion can be reduced. (p. 41)

The wisdom of Glanz's view concerning the interchangeable use of *guidance* and *counseling* is as timely today as it was when he wrote the preceding.

Before we move on to other definitions, let us offer the following definition of guidance as it pertains to this book. *Guidance is a planned program of experiences aimed at assisting individuals in better understanding themselves, others, and the world in which they live so that they might make informed choices, solve problems, and become responsible members of the community in which they live.*

Counseling

Defining counseling may be almost as difficult as defining guidance. Tyler (1961) notes that counseling is something that everyone seems to understand but no one seems to understand in exactly the same way. One reason for the confusion would again be the interchangeable use of *guidance* and *counseling*. Dimick and Huff (1970) attempted to shed some light on this confusion:

> Traditionally, counseling has been viewed as one of the services of the total guidance program. In other words, counseling has been only one of the things a counselor does. He has combined counseling with his other duties, including the organization, collection and dissemination of information; the conducting of relevant research; the testing and placement of students; and other duties, to form the total guidance service. Counseling, then, has been viewed as a subdivision of the broader concept, guidance. If this is the case, then it would seem confusing, if not absurd, to speak of counseling *and* guidance. One does not generally refer to one's family as "my son and my family." (p. 24)

Although we could argue with the above description of guidance services, the authors offer a clear differentiation between the terms *counseling* and *guidance*. In other words, to speak of counseling *and* guidance is to say "my family and my family" (Dimick & Huff, 1970, p. 24). Our definition of guidance allows for counseling to be a part of the total guidance program in the elementary school. Let us, then, look at some definitions of counseling.

According to Dinkmeyer (1968),

> Counseling is a personal relationship between a professionally trained counselor and a child which assists the child to communicate and meet immediate and future needs. This process facilitates growth through changes in perception, conviction, attitudes, and behavior. This process should be differentiated from therapy which puts greater emphasis on personality reorganization. (p. 221)

In our discussion of guidance, we pointed out that it emphasizes choices and that counseling emphasizes change. Note that the definition above refers to growth through changes.

McCleary and Hencley (1965) offer a further distinction between *guidance* and *counseling*:

> "Counseling" . . . refers to those activities that are conducted only in terms of the individual's interest, and *he* decides what action, if any, is to be taken. There is abundant evidence to indicate that attitudes and values are not likely to be changed by exhortation or even by objective,

intellectual analysis. What the individual student needs is a confidential, accepting relationship with someone who understands and with whom he can review his problems, express emotions, and puzzle out solutions. Under these conditions, the counselor can suggest; but, if he is to maintain a counseling relationship, he must always communicate to the student that the decisions are his own. (pp. 250-251)

Here, the authors further differentiate between counseling and guidance. This raises a serious question with respect to the use of the term *guidance counselor* (Dimick & Huff, 1970).

We hope that this discussion does not seem academic and irrelevant. We have attempted to show that there is indeed a difference between guidance and counseling and that to use them interchangeably or synonymously only adds to the confusion. After a careful search of the literature and much thought on our part, we came to the conclusion that the definition of counseling offered by Muro and Dinkmeyer (1977) most closely paralleled our own.

. . . one could describe child couseling as an interaction between an adult and a child or group of children wherein the conditions that exist between them could be characterized by mutual concern, respect, warmth, and caring. It is a process designed to produce growth. Such growth may be in the direction of greater self-acceptance, or greater self-worth, or it may involve a change in the child's perceptions, behaviors, attitudes, and convictions. (pp. 17-18)

As we look at virtually any definition of counseling, we do find common terms. Counseling is viewed as a *process;* it may be carried out almost anywhere, but it requires an environment conducive to the client's mode of learning; and it assists the individual in making changes. In contrast, guidance is characterized as a *program* (that includes counseling), which focuses on an individual's ability to make more informed choices toward a happier and more fulfilling life. We need to watch our tendency to use the terms *guidance* and *counseling* interchangeably, and to better communicate to our constituencies the differences between the two.

Developmental

The literature in our field abounds with the use of the terms *development* and *developmental,* especially at the elementary school level. A few authors make a concerted effort to define what they mean by *developmental counseling* or *developmental guidance.* We are interested only in a viable definition for *developmental* as it pertains to the total guidance program. *Developmental* in conjunction with *counseling* describes a theory of counseling, while *developmental* in conjunction with *guidance* refers to an approach for an entire guidance program—which includes counseling.

Myrick (1987) points out that the developmental approach "considers the nature of human development" (p. 32). This includes "the general stages and tasks that most individuals experience as they mature from childhood to adulthood." Thus, the implementation of a developmental guidance program should recognize the importance of human development as the basis of guidance. As Myrick states:

> First, human development is a life-long set of physiological, psychological, and social processes that begins at birth and continues until death. Second, this development involves an interaction between what a person is given genetically at birth and the different environments in which that person lives and grows. Human development is a journey from birth to death in which the personality unfolds, changes, and changes again. (p. 33)

In the developmental approach to providing a guidance program, you are not preoccupied with being a counselor. Instead, you focus on children as they grow, develop, and interact with the educative process. You will need to understand human behavior and to have had comprehensive experiences in dealing with children. The developmental program, which is organized around a guidance curriculum, requires the cooperation and help of all persons within the school if it is to succeed. Therefore, you will work with teachers and other school personnel to optimize the learning climate.

The term *developmental* as it pertains to elementary school guidance was perhaps best defined by Representative Carl Pursell of Michigan in H.R. 3970, a bill he introduced in 1990.

> The term "developmental" means . . . a systematically planned program that (A) provides appropriate counseling and guidance interventions to foster social, emotional, physical, moral, and cognitive growth for elementary school children; (B) provides direct intervention services to help children cope with family, social, and academic problems; and (C) supports and enhances the efforts of parents, teachers, and other school personnel to provide children maximum opportunity to acquire competence and skill in self-understanding and appreciation, interpersonal interaction, educational achievement and literacy, and career awareness and personal decision making. (pp. 9–10)

With the developmental approach, young people can learn more about themselves and their world. They are given opportunities to learn interpersonal skills, which will assist in the prevention of personal problems while helping them draw upon these skills to work themselves out of a problem. Through developmental guidance programs, clients learn how to interact in a more positive and effective manner and consequently take a more active part in their learning.

Comprehensive

A companion byword to *developmental* is *comprehensive*. For example, Myrick (1987)—discussing developmental guidance for all schools—states, "a comprehensive guidance program can meet the growing needs of students and the adults who work with them" (p. 30). *Webster's New World Dictionary* (1986) defines *comprehensive* as follows: "covering completely" or "inclusive"; and "having wide mental comprehension" (p. 292). Although the dictionary may adequately define the word for most uses, the editors did not intend this definition to be taken literally in regard to guidance. Yet most professionals use it without considering what it really means. Do they believe that a "comprehensive guidance program" will "cover completely," be all-"inclusive," or have "wide mental comprehension"? If we are going to use the term, we should define what the term means to us. Representative Pursell offers the best definition of *comprehensive*.

> The term "comprehensive" means, with respect to counseling services, a program in which (A) a counselor uses a range of individual and group techniques and counseling resources in a planned way to meet the personal, social, educational, and career development needs of all elementary children in a school and (B) a counselor works directly with children, parents, teachers, and other school personnel to create an optimal positive learning environment and personal growth opportunities for all children. (p. 9)

In other words, a comprehensive elementary school guidance program, using a variety of techniques, provides services not only for children but for teachers, parents, and others to help meet the needs of *all* the children.

Later, with the definitions of *guidance, counseling, developmental,* and *comprehensive* in mind, we begin to explore in more detail the activities that together comprise the work role of the elementary school counselor.

THE COUNSELOR AS A PERSON

Becoming an elementary school counselor means considerably more than obtaining knowledge, passing tests, and accumulating the necessary graduate hours to complete a degree. According to Blocher (1987),

> The development of a fully professional counselor involves coming to understand oneself in terms of personal characteristics, cherished beliefs, guiding values, and interpersonal behaviors. It means a keen and courageous sensitivity to how others react to us. It requires patience, persistence, and cognitive complexity to weigh, analyze, and consider all of the crucial elements in complicated situations, rather than seizing only upon the most salient and superficial. (p. 18)

The primary determinant of the productive or nonproductive counselor is the person who is attempting to function as that counselor. Not only must you possess personal characteristics that enhance your work, those around you must perceive these traits. What are these essential personal characteristics?

The answer is complex. Most counselor education programs rely to a large degree on the undergraduate grade point average. However, academic abilities have little to do with creative, growth-promoting relationships (Dimick & Huff, 1970). Other so-called criteria such as sense of humor, personal appearance, and ability to carry out research are frequently used to determine potential success as a counslor. There is little or no evidence that such qualities have any bearing on your ability to help children. Rogers (1969) suggests some alternatives to these criteria. He suggests that counselor preparation programs consider your problem-solving ability, spontaneous curiosity and originality, and empathic understanding. We concur with Rogers, and realize that these criteria are used sparingly by most institutions. Following are other important characteristics.

Self-Understanding

To be effective, you need a good understanding of who you are. As Dimick and Huff (1970) state:

> If [the counselor] is to have the kind of potent influence that he desires, he must know his biases, his commitments, his vulnerable spots, his weaknesses, his strengths, his fears, his defenses, and his total impact on others. Only inasmuch as he is aware of the dimensions of "self" will he be able to use his "self" to benefit others. (p. 108)

It is essential that you have ample opportunities to look at yourself. You will want to pursue avenues that produce self-understanding: seek counseling, keep journals of feelings and experiences that can later be reviewed and discussed with fellow students; attend workshops and seminars designed for personal growth. Your practicum experience should provide opportunities to get realistic feedback about both your counseling behavior and personal behavior. Although this feedback may not always be what you want to hear, it can promote personal and professional growth not otherwise available.

Caring

Being a counselor involves a deep commitment to human beings and to fulfillment of the human potential. Children respond best to those who they perceive like and care about them. Especially in the counseling aspect of the guidance program, you must communicate by word and deed that you care about the child and are there to help in any way possible. Only through a deep counselor commitment can trust, hope, respect, and the willingness to try be instilled in the child (Dimick & Huff, 1970). Occasionally we hear of a teacher who wants to become a counselor because "the kids are beginning to drive me nuts and I can hardly stand them anymore." This is hardly an acceptable reason for going into counseling. Youngsters can be just as challenging in the guidance program as in the classroom. In fact, since counselors spend more time dealing with the "total" child then does the classroom teacher, it is essential that counselors have a genuine love for children and are interested in their welfare.

Creativity and Flexibility

In many aspects of elementary school counseling there is no prescription for dealing with a particular situation. Therefore, being a creative individual who is flexible enough to discover and try new approaches is a definite asset. The counselor who is willing to change, to move in a different direction in order to find solutions, is in a much better position to meet the needs of the child than one who adopts a rigid approach.

Knowledge

Developmental school guidance has its roots in an understanding of human growth and development. You must also be knowledgeable in a variety of other areas. These include cultural differences and likenesses; individual and group counseling approaches; ethics; career development theory; classroom management techniques; consultation skills; assessment; school and community resources; and many others. It is not enough that you care and be a nice person. To truly arrive at a level of professionalism, you must *know* and be able to communicate this to others.

Ethics

The most important professional consideration for the counselor is ethical and moral behavior. Not only must you be knowledgeable about counselor ethics, but you must act in terms of beliefs and commitments arrived at through self-examination. Only then can you take a stance with regard to client confidentiality, referrals, and the behavior of professional colleagues. Confidentiality can become a difficult issue in counseling small children. You need to maintain confidentiality, while at the same time being aware of what may be best for the child who may not be mature enough to understand all of the ramifications of a particular situation. Belonging to a professional association such as the American Counseling Association (ACA) and/or the ASCA, both of which have a code of ethics, is one way to assure currency when it comes to ethical considerations.

Other Characteristics

In addition to self-understanding, caring about others, and being knowledgeable and ethical, you need to be a good listener, spontaneous, emotionally stable, and able to refrain from imposing values upon clients. During a crisis, you must be sensitive to the needs of others while at the same time remaining objective. Being a competent, caring professional is not easy. It takes a team player who is committed to helping others reach fulfillment. Not everyone possesses such attributes to the same degree; this is as it should be. However, you must understand the degree to which you do possess these desirable characteristics, and develop as best you can those that may fall short.

THE ELEMENTARY SCHOOL GUIDANCE PROGRAM

Elementary school counselors are frequently asked by parents or others in their community, "What does an elementary school counselor do?" Often the answer is either so general or so technical that the inquirer leaves with the feeling that counselors don't know what they do. It is important that you articulate as clearly as possible the activities in which you engage. Only through clear communication to students, parents, teachers, other school personnel, and the community can a true understanding of the elementary school counselor's work be achieved.

The next part of this chapter covers some of the elementary counselor functions as found in the literature. We list and briefly discuss the activities of the counselor's work that can be translated into a brief statement regarding the makeup of an elementary school guidance program.

Goals and Objectives

There appears to be a consensus among authors concerning the objectives of a developmental elementary school guidance program. While some may choose different words, or place more emphasis on one area than another, a common thread is to state goals that help facilitate the total educational process for all students, with emphasis on personal growth. Myrick (1987) lists eight goals he believes are appropriate for all schools.

Goal 1: Understanding the school environment
Goal 2: Understanding self and others
Goal 3: Understanding attitudes and behavior
Goal 4: Desision-making and problem-solving
Goal 5: Interpersonal and communication skills
Goal 6: School success skills
Goal 7: Career awareness and educational planning
Goal 8: Community pride and involvement

Stone and Peer (1970) state that elementary school guidance goals should be consistent with, and complement, the overall objectives of the school in which the guidance program is being implemented. They add that elementary school guidance programs should function as a part of the total school curriculum, and serve

1. to develop optimal conditions for learning and growth;
2. to help children develop socially and to mature in their relationships with others;

3. to help children better understand the role of education in their lives;

4. to help children better understand themselves;

5. to help children with their goal-seeking, choice-making, and life planning;

6. to help teachers and parents better understand the child as an individual;

7. to help teachers individualize the instruction in accordance with each child's abilities;

8. to provide information about individual pupils or groups of pupils that would be useful for curriculum planning to meet the needs of pupils;

9. to assist in providing principles of good mental hygiene to pupils, teachers, parents, and administrators; and

10. to identify those pupils with special needs.

Both lists share a common theme: that developmental elementary school guidance programs should serve to help children better understand themselves, others, and the world. What, then, are the activities or functions of the elementary school counselor that will help meet these objectives?

Four Guidance Program Approaches

Four program approaches can be implemented in an elementary school: preventive, remedial, crisis, and developmental (Myrick, 1987). We have already stated our preference for the developmental approach. However, we don't think the others should be ignored. True, an elementary school guidance program should be developmental in nature and should help satisfy the needs of *all* students. However, you must maintain sufficient flexibility within the program to deal with crises. Likewise, you must be prepared to perform remedial actions and occasional prevention-oriented activities to keep a crisis from developing. Therefore, although the following discussion includes developmental activities, we recognize the need for those procedures that are remedial, preventive, or crisis oriented.

DEVELOPMENTAL GUIDANCE PROGRAM ACTIVITIES

Your role can best be delineated by looking at the groups of people with whom you work. The following outline points out for whom the counselor provides a particular activity and offers a brief discussion of the activity as it pertains to that group.

Activities Provided Directly for Students

Individual and Group Counseling.   Counseling can be done individually or in small groups. Sometimes it is carried out at a time of crisis, sometimes to prevent a problem from escalating, and sometimes to remedy an existing situation.

But *always,* the counseling should be developmental—dealing with the "whole" child. Its primary purpose is to help children understand or adjust to different situations. If as a result of counseling children learn that it is acceptable to seek help, the long-range impact of this on society could be far-reaching. Too often, adults avoid psychological help until it is too late. Counseling in the elementary school will help alleviate this problem.

Classroom Guidance Curriculm.   An important part of your work is determining the needs of children, and organizing and implementing a classroom guidance curriculum that will assist in satisfying those needs.

Student Assessment.   You need to take an active role in coordinating the individual and group assessment within a school. This is not to imply that you are totally responsible for this process. The key word here is *coordination.* A well-executed assessment program will help identify students with special needs and assure that activities can be organized to help satisfy those needs.

Providing Resources.   Given the complex society in which we live, it is imperative that you make available to students the latest information on a variety of topics. Although certain materials may be more relevant to upper elementary students, virtually all young people who can read are potential users of these resources. Some materials should be made available in the library, while others are more likely to be found in the counselor's office. You should have reading materials, videos, computer programs, and the like that will help students in the areas of educational information (e.g., how to study), career information, and information of a personal or social nature.

Making Referrals.   Occasionally, children have problems for which you will have neither the expertise nor the time. Therefore, it is incumbent upon you to make appropriate referrals in these cases. You need to be familiar with the referral resources available, and know how and when to refer.

Activities Provided Directly for Teachers

Orientation Concerning the Elementary School Guidance Program. Teacher orientation is an ongoing process. Counselors need to find ways to continually involve teachers in guidance. One of the best ways to accomplish this is to assure that teachers are involved in selecting the program's objectives and to continually update them on counselor activities. Teachers who understand what the guidance program is attempting to accomplish will be much more supportive and involved in carrying it out. Proper orientation is a means to this end.

Consultation.   You can be tremendously helpful to the classroom teacher through consultation. Usually this is provided to assist the teacher in dealing with students who have special concerns or needs. Consulting with teachers is one of the most significant functions of the elementary school counselor. Teachers who take the time to consult with you regarding individual students, or strategies for the whole class, will likely be more successful in their efforts to reach and educate the "whole" child. Chapter 11 will go into greater detail about the counselor's role in consulting with teachers.

Observation of Students.   Sometimes teachers feel they are too close to the forest to see the trees. You can assist the teachers through observation. Sometimes this can best be accomplished in the classroom; sometimes it is more meaningful to observe the child in a less formal setting, such as the lunchroom or playground. Regardless, you can provide objective observation, which can assist the teachers in helping the student. Teachers, because of the hectic classroom environment and the need for constant classroom observation, many times avail themselves of this service. It is frequently used to help identify those students who have special needs and to find alternative ways to meet those needs.

Assisting with Referrals.   It is not uncommon for students to need special services or educational experiences. By utilizing available information or by helping to gather additional information, you can assist the teacher with referrals. Counselors, by nature of their training and position, should know of referral possibilities within a given educational system or community. Through this knowledge and appropriate consultation with the teacher, students are more likely to receive referrals that will best satisfy their needs.

Serving as a Sounding Board.   Teachers come up with some unique and creative ideas on how to improve the learning atmosphere within a classroom or school. You should be receptive to these ideas and offer constructive suggestions and/or opinions as to their workability.

Activities Provided Directly for Parents

Parent Education and Consultation.   A parent or parents are, without a doubt, more important than anyone else in a child's life. Societal problems have become school problems, and parents are expected to raise their children in a society of unprecedented complexity. Many parents feel the need for information on how to deal more effectively with their children. This can best be provided through an organized program of parent education. You are in a favorable position to provide this, and we therefore see the provision of parent education as a part of your role. You should also be available for parent consultation. You are the primary person for providing consultation to parents since teacher consultation is also a vital part of the elementary school counselor's function. We believe that parent education and consultation are of significant importance; therefore, we have devoted an entire chapter of this book to it.

Assisting with Parental Understandings.   You should assure that parents are well informed in a variety of areas. You can help parents understand the objectives of the school. Parents who take the trouble to understand the school's objectives are usually more supportive. Also, parents need a clear understanding of the objectives and expected outcomes of the guidance program. This can be accomplished through parent meetings, talks at service clubs, news releases, newsletters, home visits, and the like. Since elementary school guidance is still a relatively new program in many schools, you must find ways to clearly communicate the program's goals. You also need to help parents understand their children's social, emotional, and academic strengths and weaknesses. Parents who do so are in a better position to adapt their own behavior to better meet the needs of their children. Your willingness to assist parents with their understandings of the school, the guidance program, and their children is of paramount importance to children's growth and development.

Assisting Parents with Referrals.   Your first step is to be familiar with referral sources in the school and community. With this information, you can put parents in touch with other specialists within the school or community. In addition, You can serve as a resource person for parents in a variety of areas, including drug and alcohol abuse, child abuse, and the effects of divorce on children.

Activities Provided for Administrators and Other School Personnel

Assisting in the In-Service Training of Faculty and Staff.   Although in-service education is *not* your responsibility, it is imperative that you be available to assist in any way possible. Sometimes, because of the day-to-day contact with students, teachers, and parents, you will have good ideas regarding needed in-service. This knowledge should be made readily available to the administrator or other school personnel in charge of this activity.

Consulting.   Your role includes consultation with administrators and other school personnel, such as the school psychologist, social worker, speech therapist, nurse, or other support staff. This consultation centers around the special needs and concerns of students, as well as guidance interventions.

Serving as a Resource Person.   You should be able to provide information about referral agencies, field trips, evaluation techniques, and any activity that will promote children's growth and development. This is not to imply that any of this is your responsibility. Instead, you serve as a resource for all school personnel in these as well as other areas. However, you should accept major responsibility in providing information concerning students' social, economic, and academic background. This information is valuable not only in determining guidance curriculum but in assisting the administration and other school personnel.

Summary of the Elementary School Counselor's Role

Most counseling activities can be classified under three categories: counseling, consultation, and coordination. You should strive to balance the time spent in these activities. Usually recommended is approximately 30 percent to each category. We have found, however, that it is easier for parents, teachers, and others to understand your role if we talk about the groups of people whom you help—students, teachers, parents, school administration, and others. Ultimately, it is the individual student who should benefit from the activity. Carrying out activities for students, teachers, parents, and others in an organized and comprehensive fashion will assure that a developmental guidance program has been implemented.

GUIDANCE PROGRAMS AT THE SECONDARY LEVEL

Individual and Group Inventory

One of the procedures counselors use in the secondary school is individual and group inventory. This involves accumulating, organizing, and interpreting data pertaining to a particular student or group of students. The standardized test is included in this aspect of the counselor's work and is perhaps the most frequently used method of collecting data. There are several kinds of standardized tests. The most frequently used in the secondary school are intelligence, achievement, and aptitude tests; personality inventories; and vocational interest inventories. Another way of collecting student data is through teachers' records, such as anecdotal notes and work samples. School records, including parent information, family background, attendance records, health information, and grade point average are also helpful. Inventory is paramount in helping students better understand their academic strengths and weaknesses as well as their interests and personalities.

Educational, Personal, and Career Information

The secondary school counselor is responsible for having available, and helping students find and use, information that might assist them with a variety of decisions. High school students can profit from a wide array of information, including post-secondary educational opportunities, job descriptions, working conditions, employment outlook, educational requirements, and income. In addition, students frequently need information of a more personal nature—regarding alcohol and other drugs, sexuality, date rape, personal hygiene, and leisure activities. This may be provided to the student via field trips, career kits, occupational outlook materials, career days, audio and video cassettes, interviews, brochures and leaflets containing personal information, college and vocational school catalogs, financial aid books and flyers, Armed Forces publications, and computer-generated programs.

Counseling

Counseling is at the heart of the secondary school guidance program. Through counseling, students have an opportunity to understand the data that have been collected through inventory and appraisal, and to integrate this with information that has been made available to them. Through counseling, students can review the choices that are available to them and make informed decisions that will result in positive changes. Counseling may be done individually or with groups, depending on what is best for the individual. Most important, counseling provides a setting in which the student is free to explore ideas and attitudes within the security of a confidential relationship.

Placement and Follow-up

A secondary school counselor must be concerned with the success of students while they are still in school as well as when they graduate. It is important to help them choose the proper curricula to best satisfy their educational and career objectives. By using data available through individual and group inventory, and by reviewing information made available through the information service, the counselor can help the student find appropriate placement. This could be placement in a class; part-time job; or job, college, or vocational school after graduating. The student makes choices based upon information that is pertinent to his or her situation, interests, and abilities. Regardless of when or where a placement is made or how a student is helped, the counselor needs to be vigilant in following up. This will help assure that the student is carrying out decisions made during counseling, and is not being discouraged by real or perceived hurdles. Follow-up of graduates is also a necessary part of the counselor's work. Determining graduates' success or failure is an important indicator of the effectiveness of a secondary school curriculm. In addition, the counselor and school can use follow-up data for making other needed programmatic changes.

Research and Evaluation

Appropriate research gives the school a basis for judging the extent to which it meets the needs of its students. Meaningful research is important to the success of a guidance program as well as the entire school, and the counselor should devote time to organizing and carrying it out.

Evaluation, especially of the guidance program, is essential if the program is to succeed and be flexible enough to meet the needs of the students. At times, follow-up studies could be construed as a part of the evaluation of a guidance program. The secondary school counselor must recognize the need for program evaluation and develop a comprehensive plan for its implementation.

Summary of the Secondary School Counselor's Role

The counselor spends time and effort consulting with other professionals and keeping them informed of all aspects of the guidance program. No school guidance program could function without the assistance and cooperation of teachers, administrators, and other personnel. Teachers should be directly involved in the secondary school guidance program. An innovative approach to meeting this need has been to designate teachers as student advisors and assign them a group of students. Usually this is called a teacher-as-advisor program (TAP), and is designed to provide continuous guidance from an adult within the school (Jenkins, 1977). TAP programs have proven very useful in secondary schools. Counselors are instrumental to the organization of such a program. Another program that is becoming increasingly popular, and probably best fits under the heading of information service, is providing classroom guidance activities. This has long been a part of the elementary school counselor's work, and is now becoming much more prevalent at the secondary level. For additional information on the role and function of the middle school counselor, refer to chapter 13.

SUMMARY

The terms *guidance, counseling, developmental,* and *comprehensive* were defined to better distinguish between various aspects of your work. An important part of the definition of guidance is that it helps one make choices, whereas counseling helps one make changes.

We've discussed several personal characteristics that are desirable in a counselor. These include self-understanding; caring about others; being knowledgeable and ethical; having good listening skills; and being spontaneous, emotionally stable, and able to refrain from imposing values upon clients.

We discussed the overall goals and objectives of an elementary school guidance program, and listed the eight developmental goals that Myrick (1987) believes to be appropriate for all schools. Stone and Peer (1970) reminded us that program goals must be consistent with and complement the overall mission of the school, and that elementary school guidance programs should function as a total part of the school curriculum.

We pointed out that the elementary school counselor provides activities directly for students, teachers, parents, administrators, and other school personnel. We discussed several functions under each group but reminded you that regardless with whom the counselor is working, the benefit should ultimately go back to the student. Finally, we pointed out that virtually all of the elementary school counselor's role could be classified under counseling, consultation, and coordination.

We briefly outlined the work of the secondary school counselor. At this level, the counselor will devote time to individual and group inventory; educational, personal, and career information; counseling; placement; follow-up; and research and evaluation. We briefly discussed the organization of a teacher-as-advisor program and the trend toward increased time spent in classroom guidance activities.

REVIEW

1. Why is it better not to use the terms *guidance* and *counseling* interchangeably?
2. Define the following: *guidance, counseling, comprehensive,* and *developmental.*
3. What are some personal characteristics the counselor should possess?
4. What groups of people are served by a comprehensive elementary school guidance program?
5. What are some important goals of an elementary school guidance program?
6. List the four most common guidance program approaches. Discuss each.
7. Prepare an outline for a short speech on the role and function of the elementary school counselor.
8. Briefly describe a secondary school guidance program.
9. Why is counseling considered to be the heart of a guidance program?

REFERENCES

Blocher, D. H. (1987). *The professional counselor.* New York: Macmillan.

Dimick, K. M., & Huff, V. E. (1970). *Child counseling.* Dubuque, IA: William C. Brown.

Dinkmeyer, D. C. (Ed.). (1968). *Guidance and counseling in the elementary school: Readings in theory and practice.* New York: Holt.

Gibson, R. L., & Mitchell, M. H. (1986). *Introduction to counseling and guidance* (2nd ed.). New York: Macmillan.

Gibson, R. L., & Mitchell, M. H. (1990). *Introduction to counseling and guidance* (3rd ed.). New York: Macmillan.

Gladding, S. T. (1988). *Counseling, a comprehensive profession.* Columbus, OH: Merrill.

Glanz, E. C. (1974). *Guidance: Foundations, principles and techniques.* Boston: Allyn & Bacon.

Guralnik, D. B. (Ed.). (1986). *Webster's new world dictionary of the American language* (2nd college ed.). New York: Prentice-Hall.

Humes, C. W., & Hohenshil, T. H. (1987). Elementary counselors, school psychologists, school social workers: Who does what? *Elementary School Guidance and Counseling, 22*(1), 37–45.

Jenkins, J. M. (1977). The teacher-advisor: An old solution looking for a problem. *National Association of Secondary School Principals, 61,* 29–34.

McCleary, L. E., & Hencley, S. P. (1965). *Secondary school administration.* New York: Dodd, Mead.

Muro, J. J., & Dinkmeyer, D. C. (1977). *Counseling in the elementary and middle schools: A pragmatic approach.* Dubuque, IA: William C. Brown.

Myrick, R. D. (1987). *Developmental guidance and counseling: A practical approach.* Minneapolis, MN: Education Media Corporation.

Rogers, C. R. (1969). *Freedom to learn.* Columbus, OH: Charles E. Merrill.

Schmidt, J. J. (1986). Becoming an "able" counselor. *Elementary School Guidance and Counseling, 21*(1), 16–22.

Stone, L. A., & Peer, G. G. (1970). *Implementing a functional elementary school guidance program.* Topeka, KS: State Department of Education.

Tyler, L. E. (1961). *The work of the counselor.* New York: Appleton.

U.S. House. (1990). *To improve counseling services for elementary school children.* (H. R. 3970, 101st Congress, 2nd session). Washington, DC: U.S. Government Printing Office.

Wilgus, E., & Shelley, V. (1988). The role of the elementary-school counselor: Teacher perceptions, expectations, and actual functions. *Elementary School Guidance and Counseling, 35*(4), 259–266.

chapter 3

Growth and Development

OUTLINE

INTRODUCTION

Keeping up with children's seemingly endless changes is quite a task, both for parents and those who work with children in the elementary and middle school. As youngsters move from the earliest school years toward adolescence, the changes are dramatic. Therefore, a knowledge of human growth and development is crucial for the elementary and middle school counselor. The ages of 5 through 14 are times of distinct and rapid change; and developmental differences are apparent from year to year. You, as a counselor, need to monitor children's developmental levels to determine their adjustment difficulties, and to consider the most effective manner in which to work with the child.

There are numerous approaches to development, from Freud's psychosexual schema to Kohlberg's conception of moral development. The material presented in this chapter is based primarily on work done at the Gesell Institute (Gesell, Ilg, & Ames, 1956, 1977; Ilg, Ames, & Baker, 1981). Since development is relatively constant, the years when these writers formulated their material are not crucial. Supplemental material is provided from the work of Elkind (1978; 1981; 1984), Erikson (1963), and Youngs (1985). Where a contemporary issue comes into play, we include specific material related to that issue.

Material is presented by school grade level, from kindergarten through eighth grade, to provide you with a basis for organizing your guidance and counseling activities. As we consider each school grade, we note particular considerations for counseling and guidance. We recognize similarities and overlap between grades as well as from the end of one level to the beginning of the next. At the conclusion of the chapter, we provide a summary of the guidance and counseling high points.

As an entree to the grade-level material we explore briefly the contributions of four noteworthy scholars in the area of growth and development: Freud, Piaget, Kohlberg, and Erickson. We have included these scholars because they are well known and because each places emphasis on a different aspect of the child's development. The approaches selected represent either a specific point of view or a particular aspect of development. Our intent is to provide various ways of thinking about development—not to endorse the theorists' point of view.

THEORIES OF DEVELOPMENT

Psychosexual Development: Freud

The likely beginning for an overview of approaches to human growth is Freud's psychosexual developmental schema, based primarily on the emotional development of children in the early years. Freud's model emphasizes sexual gratification, in which the child's efforts are focused on resolving conflict at each stage of development.

The *oral* stage, which begins at birth and continues through the first year, emphasizes gratification through the mouth. Infants focus all of their attention around that orifice, from sucking on the breast or bottle to mouthing almost anything within their grasp. Since newborns are completely helpless, they depend on others to provide sustenance and meet oral needs. Freud believed these dependent feelings could return later in life, particularly during moments of stress.

In the second year of life, the child's *anal* region becomes an area of conflict when impulses of retention and expulsion are experienced. This conflict can be heightened by toilet training. Gradually, children recognize a sense of power through their capacity to manage anal impulses. Freud thought that when parents are strict in their training procudures, children will withhold not only their feces but also facets of the personality. Therefore, the expression "children will become potty trained when they're ready" suggests a path to better adjustment.

Following the anal stage is the *phallic* stage, during which children become preoccupied with their sexual organs and with gratification received from genital manipulation. One of the primary adjustment tasks for the child is to overcome a desire to replace the same-sex parent with the opposite-sex parent as a love object. The phallic stage begins around age three; the struggle over the opposite-sex parent's love appears at about age four. This concept of the *oedipal* and *electra* complex—in boys and girls, respectively—is the central focus of controversy in Freud's theory of personality development. Freud considered the resolution of the conflict over the love for one's parents to be the sign of healthy adjustment.

Freud believed that between the ages of 5 and early adolescence (approximately age 13) the child enters a stage of *latency,* when sexual interests are dormant. Freud did not describe the development and behavior of the child during this time, other than to indicate that this is a period of relative calm, when the child's energies are focused on general sociocultural development.

With the onset of puberty the child enters the *genital* stage, at which time the emphasis is on the development of heterosexual characteristics and interests. The child seeks to develop balanced relations with both sexes.

Freud's theory addresses personality formation more than development. Further, he does not provide uniform emphasis on all phases of the developmental schema, since the latter stages receive rather shallow attention.

Cognitive Development: Piaget

One of the most influential scholars on children's thinking and reasoning processes was Jean Piaget, who identified four stages of cognitive development. Piaget believed that children's knowledge of the world and their function within it were a product of their interaction with people and objects. Piaget's four stages—*sensorimotor, preoperational, concrete operational,* and *formal operational* (Stewart & Koch, 1983)—correspond roughly to the elementary and middle school years. Piaget believed that these stages were sequential and that the child must complete one stage before successfully undertaking the next.

During the first two years of life the child's growth centers on *sensorimotor development.* The child is exploring his or her world through the senses. The main focus of development is in motor skills, where infants first react to and later act upon their environment. Somewhere toward the end of the first year, children will start to show coordination between sensory and motor activity. This coordination is the primary learning task of this stage of development. Between the end of the first and second years of life the child's environment is broadened vastly by learning to crawl and walk, and to speak a little. The child is now ready for the second, or preoperational, level of development.

The period from ages two to seven is occupied with *preoperational development.* Piaget breaks this stage into two parts: *symbolic functioning* and *intuitive thought.* In general, this stage is concerned with language development and the ability to manipulate objects and events. The child can begin to consider quantities and similarities among objects.

Between ages two and four, the child operates in what Piaget calls symbolic functions. The child can create images and symbolically represent something for something else. This level of functioning is well represented through imagery play. Language development is rapid.

During the intuitive subset of this second stage of development, children can see relationships and identify classes of objects or ideas. Note that children can only think in terms of one class at a time and cannot see relationships between two classes (e.g., they know their mother but do not see that they are a daughter or son).

The third stage, *concrete operational,* occupies most of the elementary school years, from ages 7 to 11. The child begins to understand principles and applies them to concrete objects. Addition and subtraction are examples of this level of functioning. Also, the child gains the ability to classify objects (e.g., fruits and vegetables). This is a fascinating time as the child learns to mentally organize and plan a sequence of events. From an interpersonal aspect, the child can appreciate the perspective of another person.

The final stage of Piaget's developmental schema is called *formal operational.* Most meaningful at this time is the child's advancement toward more adult thinking. From age 11 on, the child begins to think abstractly. Adolescents can clearly think in terms of the "ideal" situation—their idealism is well noted. They can draw relationships between two statements or events, deal with analogies, and manipulate variables in school-based learning activities. Multiple alternatives to problems become possible to the developing adolescent; thinking becomes more deductive in nature. As children grow into adolescence, they become very involved in their own reflective thought and the ideas of others. With continued growth, adolescent thinking becomes more systematic and rational.

Piaget's contributions to children's cognitive development have been far-reaching, and his formulations have been incorporated into learning methodology. If we can view Piaget's stages as a gradual transition from one level to another rather than an abrupt change, his ideas can be useful in considering how children learn and interact with their world.

Moral Development: Kohlberg

Probably the best-known writer in the area of moral development is Lawrence Kohlberg. Piaget examined the issue of moral development, but Kohlberg advanced the scholarly consideration of how children approach issues of morality, right and wrong, and reward and punishment. Kohlberg built on Piaget's earlier work, in which the latter had formulated two stages of moral development: external constraint and internal autonomy (Stewart & Koch, 1983). Using these two stages of development as a departure, Kohlberg formulated a six-stage model (Kohlberg, 1976). The work of both Piaget and Kohlberg is based on the cognitive development of children and their increasing maturity as the basis for more advanced moral judgment.

Kohlberg's approach consists of three broad levels of moral reasoning: preconventional, conventional, and postconventional. The *preconventional* level is usually associated with children under the age of nine. The predominant aim of the child is to receive rewards and avoid punishment. There are two stages at the preconventional level. In the first stage, the child believes in the omnipotence of superior people such as parents and teachers. In the second stage, the basic principle governing moral behavior is the fair exchange: It is acceptable to behave in a certain way if it can be justified. Children in both stages are primarily selfish and concerned with their own gratification.

The second level, *conventional* morality, is represented by adherence to the rules established by society. Conformity is the general moral mode of behavior. Children become motivated to fulfill their obligations to family and others, and develop a general concern for people and their welfare. Adolescence through adulthood is the age range most frequently associated with this level of moral reasoning, or between ages 10 and 20. In the first stage of this level, children become sensitive to how others will view their behavior, and to doing the right thing. The individual is very much interested in pleasing others and being regarded as a good person. In the second stage, morality is dictated by social order. The adolescent is interested in doing the legal or socially proper thing for the benefit of society, which in turn protects the rights of the young person.

The third level of Kohlberg's moral development model, the *postconventional*, is based on a mode of functioning in which people behave according to their own moral tenets and typically takes place after age 20. At this level, they can think abstractly and are capable of considering multiple alternatives to any given dilemma. Kohlberg suggests that only 20 percent of the adult population operate at this level of moral reasoning before age 20. In the first stage of this level, people recognize how laws are established, that these laws may be arbitrary, and that they provide for the social order. The individual's role in society is to obey societal laws unless they are destructive to individual rights. The last stage of this level, the highest in Kohlberg's model, is the point at which people reason through universal ethical principles. These principles represent the highest ethical standards and reflect equality, justice, and respect for human rights and life. Moral behavior at this level is directed by conscience and may not be in concert with the views of the general public.

At least in the earliest levels, Kohlberg's formulations about moral development provide interesting material for consideration regarding how children view their own behavior and their relations with others.

Traditional Development: Erikson

Erikson (1963; 1968) created an approach that he regarded as a theory of identity and life-span development. Although his early formulations were influenced by Freud, Erikson's concepts of development were primarily influenced by his work with Native Americans and military veterans. Erikson (1963) divided the life span into eight stages:

1. trust versus mistrust;
2. autonomy versus shame and doubt;
3. initiative versus guilt;
4. industry versus inferiority;
5. identity versus role diffusion
6. intimacy versus isolation;
7. generativity versus stagnation; and
8. integrity versus despair.

Typically stages 2 through 5 or 6 are pertinent to school-age youngsters. Because a small number of children may be either developmentally delayed or advanced, the first five stages will be outlined in this section. Stage 1, *trust versus mistrust,* is most directly related to infants and small children. The primary focus of this stage is readily apparent and important to establishing security in young children during the first two years of life.

The second stage, *autonomy versus shame and doubt,* relates to ages two to four. The key feature of this stage is the parents' supporting role as their children develop mastery of their bodies and begin to provide minimal self-care.

Stage three, *initiative versus guilt,* covers ages four to six. This is a time of increased activity. The primary responsibility of parents is to allow children to explore their curiosity in a safe manner, enabling them to obtain a sense of self-direction. Without this exploration, children may develop a sense of guilt from being constantly restricted in their movements.

The fourth stage, *industry versus inferiority,* covers the elementary school and beginning of the middle school years—ages 7 to 12. Children begin to establish contact outside the home. They learn in school and through relationships with both adults and peers. Therefore, success is vital to their sense of well-being and confidence. Erikson places tremendous emphasis on the role of parents and other meaningful adults in the development of children's feelings about themselves.

The fifth stage, *identity versus role diffusion,* typically takes place between ages 13 and 18. This is the last stage that concerns the elementary and middle school educator. Children display increased mobility and autonomy; they establish a sense of identity that is important in the transition from childhood to adulthood. The later middle school years form the beginning of this quest. This is a time when many adults, particularly parents, experience great confusion and concern over the rapid changes in young people. Indeed, this may be a time of considerable turmoil for all.

Comparing the grade-level progression with Erikson's schema reveals obvious and interesting parallels. Erickson's third stage, *initiative versus guilt,* correlates to the kindergarten year, when the importance of parents predominates. Erikson's fourth stage, *industry versus inferiority,* correlates to the remainder of the traditional elementary school years, grades 1 through 6. The overriding concern here centers on success and acceptance at school as the basis for the child's healthy adjustment. The fifth Eriksonian stage, *identity versus role diffusion,* covers the later middle school or junior high years through high school. For our purposes, the developmental issues of the eighth-grader relate nicely to Erikson's propositions that the young person is beginning to build a sense of personal identity and is moving toward greater autonomy. Although Erikson approaches development from a broad perspective, we can see at each elementary and middle school/junior high grade level distinct parallels to his task functions.

The remaining stages of Erikson's schema relate to the adult years and therefore are not germane to our discussion. Although each stage spans a broader age range than we will consider in our discussion, the concepts are pertinent to the relationships children have with others, particularly adults. Even though the first two stages provide the foundation for a child's self-view and his or her relationship with significant adults, the most relevant here are stages 3 to the beginning of 5. The concepts of adult/child relationships presented in these stages are meaningful to the counselor's work both with children and parents.

Figure 3.1 provides a comparison of the major theorists discussed here. This figure correlates the major stages of each theory and the age of the child. Although the theorists represent differing approaches to human growth and development, it may be of interest to view the relationship among their various stages and the child's chronological growth.

GRADE-LEVEL DEVELOPMENT OF ELEMENTARY AND MIDDLE SCHOOL CHILDREN

The typical approach to development has been to discuss the changes children experience in terms of *age-level* development. Characteristics of children at various ages are based on general categories of behavior derived from extensive observation. Since counselors and teachers are accustomed to thinking of children's *grade level,* however, we intend to discuss the changes in those terms. Notably, these characteristics are modal for children in any given grade level and represent a broad range of attributes. We condense these broad behavioral trends to provide key issues in development for each grade level. Because each level covers two ages, behavioral contrasts may exist from one age to the next. We discuss the younger age briefly, to avoid repeating the more extensive discussion included at the end of the previous grade level.

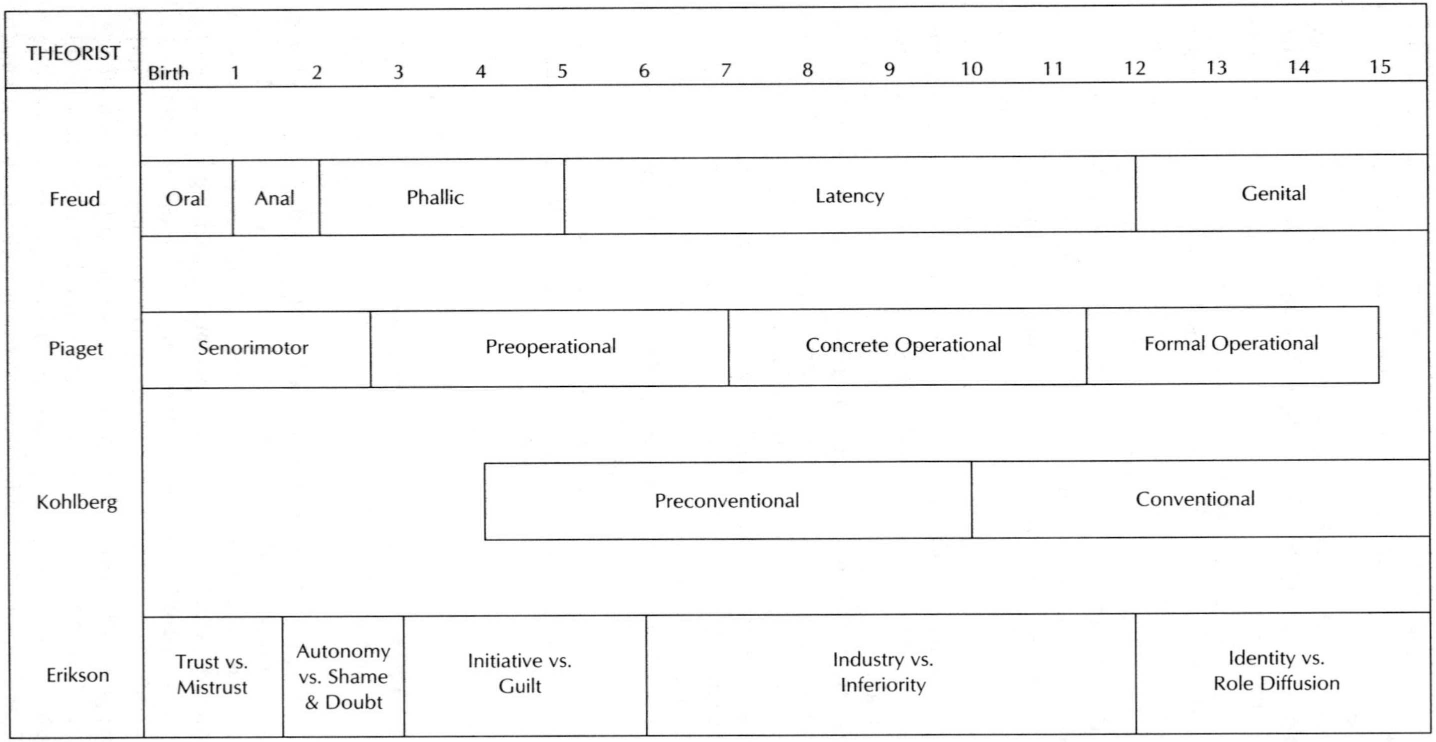

FIGURE 3.1 A comparison of developmental approaches, from birth to age 15

NOTE: These age-level separations are not finite.

Our emphasis is on social and emotional adjustment, since counselors typically focus their efforts on the child's development in these areas. In some cases, physical and intellectual development will be addressed, but only as these areas have a distinct impact on the child's social and emotional adjustment. Most important, the developmental considerations presented here represent normal or typical behavior, and you should keep in mind that children differ greatly from one another. Therefore, any observed deviation should be examined closely before judgments are made. The degree of variation will be greater in the earlier grades than the later, as children advance in age and through the educational system.

The general patterns presented here are intended to assist you in developing an appropriate guidance program for the children in your school. Since kindergarten and seventh grade are typically transitional points where children enter a new setting, these will be discussed in greater depth.

The material presented here has been adapted from the collective works of Gesell, Ilg, and Ames (1956; 1977); Elkind (1978); and Dinkmeyer and Muro (1977). The terms *generally, typically,* and *usually* have been purposely chosen because human development is not uniform and young people do not conform to standards by age or grade. Where a characteristic of a particular age is closely associated with a particular group of scholars, we will reference that source. Where behavior described represents the consensus of the writers in the field or has been identified by the teachers in the field whom we have interviewed, we will not provide citation because the characteristic appears to be commonly recognized. Also, since stress is an ever-increasing issue in the lives of children and adolescents, we will draw upon the work of Betty Youngs (1985) and David Elkind (1981; 1984) to highlight some of the more stressful occurrences in the child's life at each grade level. Finally, general guidance suggestions will be presented for each grade level. The source of these suggestions is our own experience and the work of Dinkmeyer and Muro (1977).

Kindergarten

Although maturity may vary from ages three to seven, kindergarteners are typically five to six years old. This may be their first venture away from home for any period of time. It marks the beginning of their formal education, which will last from 11 to as much as 21 years. The general developmental activities at this time include adjusting to separation from parents, adapting to learning activities, and engaging in cooperative play (Elkind, 1978; Gesell, Ilg, & Ames, 1977).

Five-year-olds generally have been regarded as pleasant children (Dinkmeyer & Muro, 1977). This is a "good" age, when children are relatively stable and content with themselves. Parents are the center of their world, at least until they get to know their kindergarten teacher; then both teacher and parents are significant (Gesell, Ilg, & Ames, 1977). At times, parents may feel that the teacher has become the most important person in their child's life.

An increasing number of children spend a significant amount of time in day-care centers prior to entering school. This experience may cause their relationship with either parent to differ from that of children who spend a greater amount of time with mom and dad.

Children at this age generally try only those tasks that they can complete successfully (Gesell, Ilg, & Ames, 1977). With this built-in sense of what they can do, five-year-olds are usually successful in their activities. Just as they are content with their world, they are responsive to adult direction and therefore relatively easy to manage (Elkind, 1978). Although they like to be with adults and can be quite helpful, they prefer to play with children their own age.

Five-year-olds are egocentric and want to be centrally involved in what is happening around them (Dinkmeyer & Muro, 1977). They will interrupt an adult conversation to force their inclusion. At school, show-and-tell is an extremely important activity because it grants them center stage and affords an opportunity to gain approval from the teacher (Elkind, 1978).

Most children at this age like school and look forward to attending. Early in the year they may tire easily and have some difficulty getting through the school day (Elkind, 1978). Although they are more calm now than they were at age four or than they will be at age six, five-year-olds may have some difficulty sitting still (Gesell et al., 1977). They may move about as they work or play and even stand while completing a task. Their attention span is usually about ten minutes (Elkind, 1978; Gesell et al., 1977). Guidance and counseling activities should be planned with these developmental constraints in mind.

As the child moves closer to age six, the calm, cooperative behavior begins to deteriorate. The earlier developing egocentrism is now full blown (Elkind, 1978). Having assumed their place at the center of the universe, the children have become rigid and exhibit difficulty with change (Gesell, Ilg, & Ames, 1977). Any alteration in the structure of the day is upsetting. Also, when they have made up their minds, they will resist tenaciously any effort to change (Elkind, 1978). Their response to peers and parents, particularly the mother, can be decidedly negative, rude, and argumentative (Gesell, Ilg, & Ames, 1977). Sixes often do not share very well. This generally difficult disposition shows through in response to any direct command.

Six-year-olds tend to think they are ready for almost anything, even though they may not be ready at all (Dinkmeyer & Muro, 1977). Just as with age five, they have great difficulty accepting blame and criticism (Elkind, 1978). The best approach is to be tentative and speculative. Children at this age respond to encouragement. Because they have to be right, they also have to win, and will resort to lying, cheating, or thievery if necessary to get what they want and think they deserve (Elkind, 1978). This does not mean they recognize their behavior as inappropriate. In the case of lying, children will act to protect themselves from any wrongdoing and may actually believe their own stories (Elkind, 1978; Gesell, Ilg, & Ames, 1977). If you really need to know the reason for the child's behavior, you will need to be indirect and creative in your questioning technique.

Bibliocounseling—the use of reading materials—(see chapter 7) is a good approach in these situations, because stories can promote lively discussion about lying, stealing, and cheating (Dinkmeyer & Muro, 1977).

Where the five-year-old was relatively calm, the six-year-old is active and animated (Gesell, Ilg, & Ames, 1977). She has tremendous energy and almost never seems to wear down (Gesell, Ilg, & Ames, 1977). In school she cannot sit still and must touch everything. As a tension outlet, she keeps her hands, arms, and legs in motion much of the time (Elkind, 1978). She may develop the annoying habits of nail biting, chewing on school supplies and clothing, and producing unusual sounds (Elkind, 1978).

On the positive side, the six-year-old is beginning to grasp the concept of time. She is developing a rudimentary understanding of past and future, and of time as it relates to today—morning, afternoon, and evening (Gesell, Ilg, & Ames, 1977). She may not yet understand the concept of week, month, or year.

At age six, children look to the teacher as an increasingly important person (Elkind, 1978). By the end of kindergarten, teachers are regarded as a primary source of information and knowledge, particularly over and above the mother.

Sources of Stress.   The primary source of stress in kindergarteners' lives is any threat to their security (Youngs, 1985). Children's sense of security initially lies with their parents, but later in the year the teacher becomes a significant source. Home and classroom are havens, and children will react to disruptions in the stability of either. Because teachers become so important, and because five- and six-year-olds are concerned with not being a problem, criticism or disapproval by the teacher is feared. Other fears may include being distinguished in school in a negative light and being regarded by others as a baby. Peer approval is already a significant issue.

Guidance Activities.   Because children at this grade level are slow to warm to strangers, you may wish to visit the classroom frequently and interact with them. This promotes familiarity before guidance and counseling activity begins. Teachers and counselors can learn a great deal about kindergarten children by simply observing their unstructured play and show-and-tell items. Some kindergarten teachers regard the latter as a unique window to the child's life. Classroom group guidance activities will work well with kindergarteners because the classroom is a comfortable, familiar place. Having the teacher remain in the room is helpful, at least at first, because she or he is a source of security. Group guidance activities such as *Developing Understanding of Self and Others* (DUSO) (Dinkmeyer & Dinkmeyer, 1982) and *Pumsy: In Pursuit of Excellence* (Anderson, 1987) are good programs to use with kindergarteners. Take care, though, to keep all activities relatively short—no more than ten minutes. Beyond this time children's attention span will rapidly disappear.

Kindergarteners do not want to be considered problem children and may staunchly refuse to acknowledge themselves as being difficult. To label someone a problem child will likely prompt denial and withdrawal. Avoid singling out children so that others view them as different. You can do this by treating *all* children as though they were special and initially becoming acquainted with all of them. Later, you can meet with problem children without making them feel conspicuous. This proactive posture will take the stigma out of later visits with disruptive children.

Kindergarten children clearly live in the here-and-now. Therefore, issues that arise should be addressed as soon as possible, both to help the child cope more effectively and to reduce denial and avoidance. Since kindergarteners want to be seen in the most positive light, positive reinforcement techniques such as encouragement are most effective in stimulating behavior change. These techniques can be presented to parents and teachers as well.

Counseling techniques should vary, but typically should include some aspect of play, since this is a readily understood medium of interaction to kindergarteners. (Play as a form of counseling activity will be addressed in chapter 6.) Since children's verbal skills at this age are limited and their attention span is short, brief sessions with limited verbal interaction are more effective. Finally, since kindergarteners have few tension outlets, the counseling session may be used to burn up some excess energy.

Small-group activity should be limited to no more than four children; three is the optimal size to ensure inclusion of each child. It is important for kindergarteners to feel that they belong in the group. They are already seeking peer approval, and exclusion is a sensitive point. Also, as children advance through kindergarten they become increasingly competitive. They want to be seen in a good light by their teacher and will seek her or his attention.

First Grade

Most first-graders begin the year as six-year-olds. They are typically self-centered and view themselves as the hub of all that is around them. (Elkind, 1978). They are volatile; where the kindergartener is rather calm and compliant, this child may show periodic signs of rebellion. At age six, the first-grader wants to be seen in a good light and will avoid blame and criticism (Elkind, 1978). He is at times difficult and demanding. The best approach to helping the troubled six-year-old is through positive supportive techniques.

Age seven brings a more settled time. Children at this age are less argumentative and demanding and even appear to withdraw, not only from conflicts, but in general (Elkind, 1978; Gesell, Ilg, & Ames, 1977). They may isolate themselves at home, preferring to be alone. With this distancing from others they may not respond very quickly to comments, questions, and directions from adults. Frequently, when given a task, they need to be given advance warning, reminded, and then checked on to see that they have completed the assignment.

Seven-year-olds need defined limits because they may demand too much of themselves and therefore take on tasks they cannot complete (Dinkmeyer & Muro, 1977). In school they have ups and downs; some days their learning activity is high; others they can barely accomplish the minimum required (Elkind, 1978). They can be self-critical and self-pitying. They may think others are picking on them—including teachers and parents. At times their expression and manner communicate a general dissatisfaction. Children at this age seem more serious and intense. They may be moody, complaining, and have a tendency to worry (Elkind, 1978). Where sixes will tackle anything, sevens are more tentative and often lack self-confidence.

In school, sevens can reason through situations and arrive at conclusions to a greater degree than before. They can concentrate better and are quieter than sixes. They establish a more personal relationship with their teachers and may compete for the teachers' attention (Gesell, Ilg, & Ames, 1977). Children at this age want to belong to the group and do not like to be singled out for criticism— or praise. Moreover, like kindergarteners, they do not want to be seen as problems and will resist direct correction for inappropriate behavior.

Sources of Stress.   Children at this age react stressfully to teacher disapproval and fear of ridicule by classmates or other children in the school (Youngs, 1985). Sevens may experience fears related to insecurity and conspicuousness in school. Their lack of self-confidence shows through in a fear of not doing well in school and not being promoted to the second grade.

Guidance Activities.   The play media and group guidance approaches used at the kindergarten level also are effective with first-graders (Dinkmeyer & Muro, 1977). In addition, because first-graders are developing their reasoning power, more verbal-based approaches can be used. First-graders can think through a situation and arrive at a conclusion if the issue is not too complex or abstract. However, verbal-based, one-to-one counseling should not be the foundation of your approach with children at this age. Like kindergarteners, first-graders are inclined to project blame away from themselves because they do not recognize themselves as a problem. The use of stories (bibliocounseling) will be even more effective at this age. Also, first-graders like to relate their own stories, which may be in large part fantasy. Children's imagination is quite active at this point. Therefore, you will need to sort out fact from fiction and look for general themes as a basis for the child's concern or fear. Finally, the first-grader is developing a tendency toward self-criticism and defeatism. You would be wise to employ genuine encouragement as a means of bolstering the child's self-confidence.

Second Grade

Most children start second grade in a relatively subdued fashion as seven-year-olds. Although they are unsure of themselves, concerned about what others think, and frequently worried, they are relatively cooperative with parents and teachers (Elkind, 1978; Gesell, Ilg, & Ames, 1977). They can remain calm and quiet for reasonable periods of time. They can concentrate better then ever and work fairly well in groups. In general, seven-year-old second-graders are becoming more verbal and rather enjoyable.

As children move from age seven to eight, however, distinct changes take place. Where the seven-year-old was concerned with the self and with how others viewed him, age eight is a time of increased focus on relationships (Elkind, 1978).

Eight-year-olds are beginning to value involvement with their peers. They want a two-way relationship and are concerned both about how people treat them and what others think of them. Although eights have more to give to relationships, they want more as well. Most noteworthy in their system of wants are strong relationships with parents—particularly the mother—and with their teacher (Gesell, Ilg, & Ames, 1977). Teachers frequently become personal and individual in children's lives during this grade, and children may take a great interest in their teachers' lives.

Working with eights is in some ways easier then working with sevens. Eight-year-olds are better at carrying out requests from teachers and parents (Gesell, Ilg, & Ames, 1977). They often delay acting on the request and may argue, but they will eventually comply. Often, eights feel they are growing up and do not need full and complete instructions, but just a brief word or phrase.

In their approach to school and other activities, eights are expansive—they think they can handle anything (Elkind, 1978). No task is too great for them. Not only can they accomplish anything, they can do it quickly. Children at this age are constantly active and busy. They relish trying new things and taking new challenges. Unfortunately, their judgment about how much they can handle is a bit faulty. Therefore, they may often experience feelings of failure. As children mature they acquire an improved sense of self-evaluation. With this increased sensitivity, they heap criticism on themselves (Elkind, 1978; Gesell, Ilg, & Ames, 1977). There is a tendency for eights to overdramatize their failures with statements such as "I can't do anything right." You need to help insulate children from their sense of failure through planning and tempering their self-expectations—they need protection from themselves. Adults can be the antidote for overly ambitious and immature children of eight by helping them to manage their tasks more reasonably.

Sources of Stress.   Second-graders are anxious about fitting into the group, relationships with significant adults, and self-conscious regarding achievement (Youngs, 1985). They are concerned about being seen as different from their peers in any way. Since parents and teachers are taking on increased significance, second-graders may feel lonesome for one of their parents. Also, they are fearful of their teacher's disapproval and discipline. Finally, second-graders are concerned about how they are doing in school—getting the problems right in math, making a mistake in spelling, or passing a test (Elkind, 1981).

Guidance Activities.   Second-graders respond well to classroom guidance. Unlike earlier grades, second-graders can engage in small-group counseling. Their increased verbal and reasoning ability enables them to benefit effectively from direct counseling. As the school year progresses, second-graders will demonstrate improved self-control and a developing self-discipline. Because these children display greater self-control and are beginning to understand cause-and-effect relationships, verbal-based counseling is more appropriate. Also, cognitive approaches (e.g., that of Ellis) can be used meaningfully. A here-and-now focus is still important, but second-graders are starting to make sense of the purpose of their behavior.

Third Grade

Eight-year-old third-graders seek praise and encouragement from significant adults. These include teachers, parents, Little League coaches, scout leaders, and the like. But relationships with other children are increasingly important, and therefore group play is very much in evidence (Gesell, Ilg, & Ames, 1977). As youngsters move toward age nine, peer relations begin to stabilize. Children focus less on the self and begin to recognize the needs of others. Also, they develop fluid speech, greater articulation, and increased curiosity.

When they reach age nine, children move toward the kind of calm and reserve that we observed in ages five and seven. They become more sure of themselves and their relationships with others, gain a sense of right and wrong, and assume greater responsibility for their actions (Elkind, 1978). Nine-year-olds seem to exist in a state of contentment with the world around them. They also can be independent and seek to be regarded as mature; as a result, they may resist direction from parents and teachers. But there is less arguing with a nine-year-old than an eight-year-old. Nines react to what they regard as adult bossing more passively than before, and may respond to requests from adults with disgust or resentment.

Nine-year-olds tend to be more interested in friends than family. They may withdraw somewhat from adults, particularly parents. The importance of parents and possibly teachers lies in what they can do for the nine-year-old. Mothers in particular may feel somewhat alienated because of the children's disinterest in family and extended interest in peers (Gesell, Ilg, & Ames, 1977). Parents may need assistance in not imposing themselves on their children and in providing them with space. The distance that children place between themselves and their parents is part of a developing quest for greater independence (Gesell, Ilg, & Ames, 1977).

The activity level of nine-year-olds is very high. They approach everything with great zeal, frequently playing and working every waking moment of the day. They enjoy games and sports and the competitive aspects of each. They refine skills and experience accomplishments (Gesell, Ilg, & Ames, 1977). Although nines want to fill each day with activity, they are more realistic about what they can manage.

Age nine is a time of developing language skills, when children begin to rely on their ability to communicate. They can think and formulate ideas and critically evaluate these thoughts (Elkind, 1978). This is also a rather neurotic period: Children complain a great deal about perceived hurts and ailments. These may be imaginary, but the youngsters "honestly" believe they exist (Elkind, 1978).

Sources of Stress.   Third-grade stresses center primarily around acceptance by peers and teachers. Third-graders are concerned about being the last one selected for a group activity, which they see as peer disapproval (Youngs, 1985). Particularly early in the year, they worry that they will not measure up to their teacher's expectations. Therefore, failure to perform well on a school assignment or test, having to stay after school, or being the subject of a conference with the parents can be particularly stressful.

Guidance Activities.   Since third-graders are becoming quite verbal, individual and small-group counseling are both appropriate. The group focus gains utility because of the importance of the peer group. Group activity can comprise either classroom guidance or small-group counseling. It is particularly noteworthy that third-graders are developing an ability to understand and express their feelings. Similarly, they are beginning to take responsibility for their own behavior. Nonetheless, they need positive support because they still lack self-assurance (Elkind, 1978). You may find that establishing rapport with children in this grade is a little more difficult than before, as they are developing reliance on the peer group. Also, since third-graders are gaining independence and believe they are more mature, play techniques start to lose some of their value. Stimulus stories (bibliocounseling) can still be used effectively, because these children can manage a greater level of abstraction and are better at understanding cause and effect.

Fourth Grade

Of all the grades in elementary school, fourth is likely to be one of the most enjoyable (Gesell, Ilg, & Ames, 1977). The reason for this pleasant school year is the relative calm of the nine-year-old and the delightfully cooperative nature of the ten-year-old. Nines usually show some independence but are still typically responsive to requests made by significant adults. Although the peer group is becoming important, nines still need support from adults to aid their developing self-esteem (Elkind, 1978). Thought processes are prog ,sing rapidly for nines, who are becoming effective verbal communicators.

The transition from age nine to ten is unlike the usual changes from one age to another. Ten-year-olds continue what the nines have begun—a calm and relatively cooperative manner. Actually, age ten is often considered the nicest age of all (Gesell, Ilg, & Ames, 1977). Tens regard the word of parents and teachers to be absolute law. Tens want to do the right thing, be good, and have parents and teachers approve of them. By obeying their parents and teachers, they feel a sense of acceptance.

Not only do ten-year-olds get along well with adults, they are generally satisfied with other family members and peers. They are pretty much at peace with the world. This is not to imply that tens do not have some rough moments. They can display outbursts of temper, but the anger is generally short lived. They generally roll along through life with considerable flexibility and casualness. Probably at no other point in their lives will children seem so pleasant and enjoyable to parents.

Ten-year-olds are stable, pleasant, dependable, and generally good-humored. They are capable of forming good relationships with parents, teachers, and other meaningful adults. Since they recognize their mistakes and are aware of elements of time (past, present, and future), they are inclined to engage in meaningful self-disclosures to teachers and counselors. They also engage in self-referrals to the counselor. Tens are beginning to demonstrate true responsibility.

Sources of Stress.   Because peers have become very important to fourth-graders, most stresses surround friendships and acceptance by age-mates (Elkind, 1981; Youngs, 1985). Fourth-graders fear lack of approval by their classmates and exclusion from peer activities. They do not want to be singled out by the teacher or ridiculed by their peers. Finally, they are starting to develop particular friendships and may worry about the permanence and reciprocity of the relationship.

Guidance Activities.   By fourth grade, children have become highly verbal, are capable of understanding and expressing their emotions, and by the latter part of the year are developing a sense of insight that enables them to work through problem situations. Given this increased sophistication, both one-to-one and small-group counseling are effective (Dinkmeyer & Muro, 1977). Biblio-counseling can also be productive. Play activities, however, will not work very well because fourth-graders find them childish. These youngsters have not developed a strong sense of self-confidence and need support from both teachers and counselors. Overall, fourth-graders are comfortable sharing in class, so that large groups are appropriate media for developmental guidance. Finally, self-referrals are in order, because children at this level are becoming increasingly sensitive to their place in the world. Because of their increased mobility and increased time away from home, material on alcohol and drugs should be presented at this grade level.

Fifth Grade

This school year begins with delightful ten-year-olds and ends with intense 11-year-olds. Tens are becoming more mature and can engage in verbal interactions, assume more responsibility, understand right and wrong, and reason through problems. They generally have good dispositions, feel good about themselves, and are at peace with those around them. The emotional outbursts at this age are short and easily forgotten. Tens like their teachers, providing they are fair and impartial. Tens like routine and prefer the teacher to establish a schedule and stay with it. Overall, late tens are responsible and cooperative in school. But as the year advances they become increasingly restless and reduce their focus on schoolwork.

The importance of the peer group increases, with emphasis primarily on same-sex mates, but there is developing interest in the opposite sex. Now the children wish to interact with grownups in a more mature manner, including adult conversation. Conflicts with significant adults become more apparent.

Age ten is a time of comfort and stability. This is the period when youngsters have mastered childhood tasks, and the tensions and frustrations of adolescence have not yet begun. This equilibrium fades late in this year and disappears with the onset of eleven.

At 11, distinct changes start to take place. Elevens are rapidly moving toward adolescence, both physically and socially. Today, young people of this age are typically more advanced and exposed to much more than were elevens a decade ago. This is the beginning of what has been called the storm-and-stress period (Gesell, Ilg, & Ames, 1956). Children undergo a growth spurt that propels them toward adolescence. The physical growth is apparent to virtually all who are around elevens, while the accompanying emotional and psychological changes are only apparent through the increased activity level. Elevens have almost boundless energy. They can be loud, boisterous, and apparently without manners. They are not particularly sensitive to others; they simply move headlong into whatever seems to get their attention. Young people of this age can take foolish risks, just for the sake of excitement.

Eleven-year-olds clearly think they are gowing up, or already grown up, and this brings them into natural conflict with parents and teachers (Gesell, Ilg, & Ames, 1956). Fifth-graders need to challenge and criticize as a means of testing their own authority. They are just plain argumentative, although they do not like others to argue with them. This is an emotional age that comes as a surprise to those who are unprepared, particularly because of the sublime nature of ten-year-olds. Elevens can be moody, withdrawn, or prone to outbursts of rage. In short, they are unpredictable and delicate to handle. Most of this extreme behavior is reserved for home or other familiar environments. With strangers, elevens can be very cooperative, belying what parents and teachers really know.

Because elevens are such a contrast to tens, they can be discipline problems and a source of frustration to parents and teachers. This adult reaction brings forth cries of persecution. Elevens are all of a sudden full of self-doubt and highly sensitive to criticism. The confidence displayed by tens is gone. In an almost antithetical manner, elevens seek to gain notice and bolster self-confidence by challenging adults, particularly parents and sometimes teachers. They will act out to get a response—any response. If they can't get attention in a positive way, they'll get it in a negative way. There is a general defensiveness associated with elevens. This is the beginning of the real move toward independence from parents and other adults. Although this will intensify later, the early signs clearly appear during the eleventh year. Young people of this age are beginning to consider the future and may fantasize about their adult life.

With the changes in self-concept and overall reaction to the world, eleven-year-olds generally struggle in their relations with parents, and in some ways with teachers. Elevens are much more inclined to challenge adult authority. With other children their reaction is quite different. In fact, elevens invest much more heavily in their peers. But for the first time their choice of friends is not based on proximity or common participation in some activity. They select their friends based more on mutual interests and personality. Boys and girls are not quite involved with one another, but are much more aware of each other. Because of maturational differences, girls are more inclined to be interested in boys than vice versa.

School also changes. Eleven-year-olds do not necessarily dislike school, but are much more particular about what they do like (Gesell, Ilg, & Ames, 1956). Overall, they prefer straightforward material and areas of learning where they can excel. Because they are so active and divide their time among many interests, learning can be tiring. Also, because of their activity level and argumentative nature, they can be a problem in the classroom. These young people, who heretofore have experienced no difficulty in school, may now become an occasional headache to their teacher.

Sources of Stress.   The stresses faced by fifth-graders are similar to those of fourth-graders. Being negatively singled out in school is still a concern (Youngs, 1985). Peer approval is important, as before, but a new issue arises: the fear of losing one's best friend to a different friend. Fifth-graders also fear that they will not move on with their class. This is particularly acute if sixth grade is the highest grade in the school (Elkind, 1981; 1984).

Guidance Activities.   Since fifth-graders in general can reason through situations and understand cause-and-effect relationships, classroom guidance, bibliocounseling, and both individual and small-group counseling are all appropriate. Because of physical development and movement toward adolescence, issues surrounding peer relations and sexual development—particularly for girls—are pertinent topics for classroom guidance. In the case of sexual development, segregation of the sexes may stimulate more interaction. Both sexes may be more comfortable with a same-sex counselor.

Ten-year-olds will work well in most guidance settings and will respond to most activities. By contrast, elevens need to be treated more carefully. They require firmness through understanding, which is difficult at times, particularly for parents. Because parents may become frustrated, it may be appropriate to counsel them as well. Also, because of elevens' quest for greater independence, career development activity can be meaningful.

Sixth Grade

The turmoil of eleven-year-olds begins this school year. Their high activity level and seeming inability to sit still is very much in evidence. Also, due to puberty, mood swings are frequent and dramatic. Parents and teachers need the same patience they exhibited when this age began. They also are competitive, both in the classroom and on the playground. Noteworthy at this time is a tendency for young people to begin selecting areas in which to excel—some in school subjects and others in music and sports. They will also pursue out-of-school activities, including youth organizations. On a positive note, elevens can readily label and discuss their emotions, if they are so disposed.

The most important thing to elevens, particularly late elevens, is their social world (Elkind, 1978; Gesell, Ilg, & Ames, 1956). Peers and socialization predominate over almost everything else. Most such activity is of the gang variety, although both sexes may have a preferred friend. Within the group elevens can tease each other incessantly, at times cruelly. Their targets are usually fringe members of the group. Toward the end of this year elevens mellow somewhat, so that their emotions and activity levels are not quite so dramatic.

Twelve-year-olds are clearly in limbo (Gesell, Ilg, & Ames, 1956). They are moving away from childhood and toward adulthood, but are firmly in neither camp. They may indeed be more like children, but they feel they are more like adults. A twelve-year-old may feel indignant that a parent or teacher would treat him like a child. Frequently this is a difficult time for adults, because earlier behavior guidelines must be adjusted. The difficultly lies in what kinds of freedoms children can handle, both in the classroom and at home. Young people develop a greater sense of self-reliance, but they—and we—still harbor some doubt about this. In general, twelve is a time for experimentation with independence.

Twelve-year-olds, particularly later in the year, are outgoing and gregarious. They enjoy the company of others and can relate well to both peers and adults. They are beginning to form friendships outside the family. They are less self-centered than elevens and can display increased insight and intuition. Overall they are more sensitive to others and more responsive (Elkind, 1978). Noticeably, they demonstrate more adult behaviors, even though they are not yet adults. By late in the year, twelves have become more self-assured and self-accepting. With this more settled nature, they are more lighthearted and humorous, less moody, and much less disagreeable than elevens. Continuing what began at age eleven, twelve-year-olds become more future-oriented and start to think about the years after high school.

Sexual development is a prime issue for both boys and girls (Gesell, Ilg, & Ames, 1956). This is more pressing for girls because of their earlier start, but boys become more self-conscious as well. For some girls and a few boys, physical development is near adult. For others the process is delayed. These developmental extremes require special attention by teachers, parents, and counselors. For all, there is concern with body functions and physical appearance.

Although dating is not the typical thing to do, each sex is becoming increasingly interested in the other. Most interaction is in the mind rather than through face-to-face contact. Boys can have "girl friends" and girls can have "boy friends," but the "friend" may not even be aware that he or she is the object of someone's affection.

In school, twelves are more settled than elevens (Elkind, 1978). They sit still more easily and their concentration is improved, but do have moments of restlessness and daydreaming. Because of their outgoing nature and sense of humor, twelves are inclined to fool around. Extending the pattern that began with age eleven, twelves exhibit distinct likes and dislikes in school. Because of their exuberance, they will fare better under a strong teacher who maintains clear guidelines for acceptable behavior. Inexperienced teachers and those with a loosely structured approach may lose control of sixth-graders.

Sources of Stress.   The stresses that sixth-graders face are similar to those of fifth-graders. They are concerned about being popular with their peers and not appearing in a negative light. Appearance is now taking on increased significance, and conformity in dress is the rule. Sixth-graders fear acting and looking different; this is aggravated by sexual development (Youngs, 1985). Girls who have begun to menstruate need assistance in properly understanding this phenomenon, or they may be fearful of their own biology. Finally, sixth-graders may fear not moving on to the next level. This is particularly stressful to students who struggle academically and who attend schools where sixth grade is the last.

Guidance Activities. A broad range of activities can be used with sixth-graders. With the right language level, most of the approaches used with adults will be appropriate with this grade level. Either small or classroom-size guidance groups will be well suited for most sixth-graders. Unlike earlier grade levels, both sexes can participate in the group. Most guidance will be verbally based, but because sixth-graders are physically active, they will respond well to situations that call for movement rather than sedentary interaction.

Young people at this grade level are entering a most difficult period. Never before have they experienced such pressure. Topics pertinent to sixth-graders include peer relations, self-concept, coping with increased pressures of growing up, educational and career development, sexual development, and alcohol and drug use.

Seventh Grade

For most young people, seventh grade is a time of transition. Physical changes have already begun for many, and the rest are not far behind. Many school districts use seventh grade as the point of separation between elementary and secondary school. Seventh-graders will thus experience a new environment and structure—with many teachers rather than just a few. When they enter middle or junior high school, young people experience personal change as a result (Elkind, 1984). To add to the chaos, they are rapidly moving toward greater autonomy from parents and other adults.

Twelve-year-old seventh-graders are an active bunch. If allowed unbridled freedom, they will destroy a classroom or burger joint. The explosive nature of this age is punctuated by moments of eerie calm. Because young people at this time are so social, the peer group is almost irrationally important, and relationships with friends can be life-and-death matters. By the end of the school year the pressures of growing up are dramatic (Elkind, 1984). With this pressure comes the twelves' false sense of maturity and capability. Late twelves and early thirteens are quite sure of themselves and their ability to care for themselves. This is the beginning of that omnipotent phase wherein young people believe that nothing can hurt them. They naively take chances and make judgments that would terrify an adult.

Toward the latter part of this age young people become more self-assured, possibly because they are settling into the school and relatively satisfied with themselves. They are a bit more self-accepting than earlier in the year and are correspondingly more self-reliant. Late twelves will display less self-centered behavior.

Twelve-year-old seventh-graders are sensitive to themselves and their peers (Elkind, 1984; Gesell, Ilg, & Ames, 1956). They can understand emotions in themselves and others, and are more responsive to the feelings of close friends. They may indulge in serious introspection, with much effort given to considering who and what they are. Seventh-graders are beginning to assert themselves in a more adult fashion. They also can be less flighty than before, although they are still capable of strong emotional responses to criticism—real or imagined. Toward the end of the year there may be less rapid emotional fluctuation.

Developmentally there are distinct differences between girls and boys at age 12. Girls are more advanced physically than boys, and may be taller, with some nearly reaching their adult height. Girls also may be more advanced sexually, but some boys are demonstrating sexual development as well. For both, this condition creates a concern with the body.

Although each sex shows some interest in the other, girls are more romatically interested in boys than vice versa (Elkind, 1978). With boys, the interest is more curiosity mixed with anticipation, because that's what older kids do. In either case, one sex may not even be aware of the other's interest.

School inspires strong feelings in twelves: They either like it or they hate it (Elkind, 1978). Even though most twelves would not openly acknowledge this, school is an important place. For seventh-graders it is the exciting center of social interaction. Teachers have a real task on their hands because of the activity level of twelves, and a sense of control and structure is important in managing this restless and mentally peripatetic group.

Emotionally, twelves are less moody than before and can be agreeable and familiar with adults and peers. Toward the end of this age they may even demonstrate improved self-control. Admittedly, this is more evident in public than at home.

As young people reach age 13, subtle changes appear. Most notable is an increasing preoccupation with self (Elkind, 1978; 1984). They spend more time alone, behind closed doors, deep in introspection. They seem to be searching for answers to the questions of who and what they are. Thirteens may even appear to close out most of their family and friends. Friendships are narrower and more intense, with a close sharing of private thoughts. Girls appear to establish closer ties than boys. Also, girls are more interested in boys than vice versa. They find older boys more appealing; girls consider their male age-mates childish. By this time the telephone is an indispensable instrument.

In school, thirteen-year-olds are more settled. They are better adjusted to routine and can handle the less controlled school day better than during the early part of the year (Elkind, 1978; Gesell, Ilg, & Ames, 1956). They may be slightly better organized than before and manage their schoolwork more effectively. Privately, they still give credence to the teacher's knowledge and authority, but begin to clearly establish likes and dislikes for teachers. These preferences are based on the way particular teachers interact with them and their peers.

These young adolescents see themselves as mature and are sensitive to this issue. They think they are capable of making their own decisions and establishing their own directions. It is important that parents and teachers carefully and clearly set limits at this age, because thirteens' confidence in self-managment is naive.

Sources of Stress. The general stresses faced by seventh-graders surround peer relationships and greater independence in school and community (Elkind, 1981; 1984; Youngs, 1985). It is commonly believed in the child guidance field that ages 12 to 15 are the most vulnerable because of the pressures that young people face. Seventh grade begins a period when youngsters are directly faced with the issues of alcohol, drugs, and emerging sexuality. They are susceptible to peer pressure to experiment in each of these areas. The interest and guidance of parents and teachers are very important during seventh grade. Many parents begin to distance themselves from their children because they feel that the youngsters do not want them involved in their lives. However, contrary to their actions, young people very much want and need adult guidance.

Guidance Activities. Seventh-graders' involvement with their peers creates a need to focus on relationships with age-mates. The group setting is thus particularly attractive. You can also organize coed groups for some guidance activities. In particular, because of the emerging adolescents' intense concern with self, group activity can focus on who and what they are. Also, groups that examine heterosexual relations will ultimately be well received if you can solicit the youngsters' involvement. Seventh-graders may not appear very interested in male/female relationships and therefore may be reticent to participate in such groups; but they will be keenly alert to the material presented.

There is a distinct need to keep lines of communication open between young people and the adults in their lives. The youngsters' increased autonomy becomes very confusing to parents. You can make excellent use of your time by creating support groups that will help parents communciate more effectively. You also can help them learn how to renegotiate the rules that govern the child in the home and community.

Most guidance and counseling approaches will be verbally based and can involve discussions of cause-and-effect relationships. The key may be to solicit the ideas and opinions of young people at this time, as they are capable of reasoning through situations and determining socially appropriate behavior.

Eighth Grade

Many educators regard eighth grade as the most difficult school year for young people (Elkind, 1984). The transitions that were beginning in the earlier years are now clearly in motion. The quest for autonomy is increasing, and parents may experience further confusion and frustration. In all likelihood, young people are equally confused. For many teachers it is a time to just hold on.

Older thirteen-year-olds seem unusually hypersensitive, reacting to almost anything that questions their ability or independence (Elkind, 1984). They may be unwilling to accept the fact that mistakes are natural. To thirteens, making a mistake is a sign of diminished capacity and acceptability. Therefore, they may enjoy the mistakes of others, particularly parents and teachers. Because this is a time of intense introspection and agonizing over questions of self, thirteens seem angry and generally unhappy (Elkind, 1978 & 1984; Gesell, Ilg, & Ames, 1956).

They are concerned about physical appearance—height, weight, and attractiveness. Fitting in with the group is extremely important because it can prevent being singled out as odd or undesirable.

The isolation that began with the onset of age 13 continues into eighth grade. Youngsters set aside time to think about themselves. It is not uncommon for older thirteens to seclude themselves from their friends. Some thirteens begin to read more, selecting materials that address meaning in life.

Relationships with the opposite sex vary considerably. For some this a period of disinterest; for others the seventh-grade fascination continues. In either case the typical thirteen-year-old eighth-grader is not overly involved with the opposite sex. The developmental differences between boys and girls at this age may have something to do with the level of interest each holds for the other.

The reclusive and introspective nature of thirteen-year-olds, paired with their intense effort at self-understanding, give rise to the difficulty of the age. The youngsters are trying hard to put into perspective their place in the world and to differentiate themselves from their parents. There is a great deal of confusion and fear of the unknown. Thirteens' temperament is a function of this inner quest for understanding. However difficult, this struggle calls for a demonstration of patience by parents and teachers.

As young people enter their fourteenth year, changes in emotional makeup and social interaction begin to appear. Fourteen-year-olds seem to settle and come out, although not immediately. They gradually give up their reclusive nature and are generally happier. The latter part of the eighth grade will provide some more pleasant times for the fourteens and the adults around them.

At some level, fourteen-year-olds have worked through the initial struggle about their growing independence and can now meet life with a renewed enthusiasm. Although emotional flare-ups still occur, they are not as intense and subside more quickly. As children move further into age 14, they take themselves less seriously. This does not mean they lose their intensity; they just do not consider so many things as life-or-death propositions.

As fourteens acquire greater emotional maturity, they enter a time of increased self-acceptance and healthier self-evalution. They come to recognize favorable qualities in themselves and start to show greater pride in their accomplishments—academic, athletic, artistic, peer-oriented, or extracurricular. Because fourteens are more settled, friendships flourish again. Same-sex group activities are the order of the day for both sexes. Girls begin to focus on interpersonal qualities in their friendships rather than choosing friends merely on the basis of proximity or common activity. With boys the ties with friends seem less close knit. They may gather in loose gangs, each of whom has a role (e.g., leader, brain, jock, or clown). Roles in boys' friendship groups seem to complement one another, so that everyone has a place.

Relationships between girls and boys begin to change during the fourteenth year. Social interaction between the sexes increases, primarily through group gatherings such as parties. Particularly for girls, some dating is in evidence. It is still typical for girls to show interest in older boys, who are closer to the girls' level of maturity. In all likelihood, girls are more inclined to go on dates than are boys. Parents take a definite stance on whether girls date, and if they do, the kinds of dates they have.

In general, fourteens engage in socialization as their primary pastime. The telephone is the most important means of arranging activities; it also allows them to carry on this pastime when getting together is not possible. Young people have a tendency to identify with a particular group. At school, social activity is equally important, and fourteens like to work in groups so that the social atmosphere can be extended. Social activity may well get in the way of classroom work, much to the consternation of the teacher. Fourteens tend to be interested in school subjects that relate to social issues, because they have a great concern for fair play. They have great energy, and frequently parents and teachers need to temper the youngsters' expansiveness. Fourteens do not quite equate what they can do with the time available to accomplish their objectives.

An aspect of fourteens' developing maturity and differentiation from their parents is their desire to work and learn on their own. They may make a big issue of taking responsibility for their actions and insist that they can handle any outcome. Although they can tolerate failure, particularly if it is not brought to their attention by their parents, they are not necessarily prepared for it. By the end of eighth grade, fourteens are truly becoming more adult and can engage in a mature conversation with parents and teachers. As eighth grade ends, the struggle that began the school year has subsided somewhat.

Sources of Stress.   First, eighth-graders are concerned about their popularity and about being singled out in school in a way that would make them different from others. Second, because they possess fragmented information, they are concerned about their own sexuality. They have not yet defined their sexual identities. Third, they are beginning to worry about their emotional health. Happiness is a concern because eighth-graders are becoming more sensitive to the unhappiness they see around them. Fourth, they are sensitive to and con-cerned about their developing bodies. There is a general self-consciousness about appearance and physical development. Finally, they wonder what the next year will hold. Since eighth grade frequently signals the end of school at one level, the impending move to the next level causes stress (Elkind, 1984; Youngs, 1985).

Guidance Activities.   Since eighth-graders' verbal skills are generally in place, and they are already aware of cause-and-effect relationships in their behavior, most guidance and counseling will be based on verbal interaction. Both individual and group activities are appropriate. Most students can even profit from classroom-size discussions, even if their experience is vicarious. A variety of media can be used to stimulate discussion. By eighth grade young people can assume responsibility for the direction of guidance, and teachers or counselors may take on more of a facilitative role.

SUMMARY

This chapter has reviewed children's development from the perspective of their social and emotional maturation at each grade level of elementary and middle school. This should prove useful to you in planning developmental guidance activities and defining the nature of counseling activity.

In general, children seem to follow a developmental pattern wherein an "up" year is followed by a "down" year. This cyclic rhythm is fairly consistent, with even/down years until age ten, when the pattern alters and the cycle shifts to the odd/down years. With knowledge of this alternating pattern, parents and teachers can better anticipate their children's emotional condition.

Table 3.1 provides a capsule of the main features of adjustment at each grade level. The table highlights the children's adjustment issue, the primary stressor, and the most relevant guidance activity. (Shown in this table are the typical adjustment issues, rather than exteme behaviors. We clearly recognize the variation among young people at any grade level.)

TABLE 3.1 Grade-level development and guidance issues

Grade	Adjustment Issue	Stressor	Guidance Activity
Kindergarten	Separation from home	Threats to security	Familiarity and work in the classroom
First	Self-centered, want to be seen as good	Teacher disapproval	Play media and groups
Second	Cooperative with adults, peer involvement	Fitting in with others	Classroom guidance
Third	Seek encouragement, later some with-drawal from adults	Acceptance by peers and adults	Classroom guidance and small-group counseling
Fourth	Enjoyable age, a period of calm	Friendships and peer acceptance	Individual and small-group counseling
Fifth	Challenging year starts calm and becomes intense	Peer approval and not being seen in a negative light	Bibliocounseling, individual, and small-group counseling
Sixth	High activity level, social world is all-important	Popularity with peers	Language-based activities
Seventh	A time of transition, distinct gender differences	Independent functioning and peer pressure	Group activities
Eighth	Difficult year for many, transition and differentiation from parents	Peer acceptance and developing sexuality	Verbal-based activities

We have suggested the types of guidance activities that are most appropriate for each grade level. A close review of this material will indicate that the guiding principles are based on children's verbal fluency, reasoning ability, and the pertinent issues at hand. During the primary grades (kindergarten through third), youngsters' limited verbal skills will dictate more action-oriented techniques. Also, during these grade levels children have a limited understanding of cause-and-effect relationships, and therefore find it difficult to assume responsibility for their behavior. Finally, during the primary grades children are adapting to new people and a new environment, and much of their development is affected by this adaptation.

In the intermediate grades (four through six), young people have developed better verbal skills, can reason through problem situations, and have focused on developing peer relations and coping with the outside world. Therefore, verbally based guidance and counseling is the mode.

The middle school/junior high grades (seven and eight) are a continuation of what began in the intermediate years. The differences lie in the youngsters' abilities to take more responsibility for their behavior. The focus of this period is on learning to manage young people's increased independence and the ramifications of such freedom.

REVIEW

1. Consider the major differences between primary-grade level and intermediate-level developmental issues.

2. What distinguishing characteristics of the fourth grade make this grade level the ideal of the elementary school years?

3. To work with first-graders, design a classroom guidance activity to address the developmental tasks of Erikson's third stage.

4. What are the major issues that distinguish kindergarten and seventh grade as traditional transitional grades?

5. Select a grade level between one and six and describe the features that relate to Erikson's fourth stage of development.

6. How do the developmental characteristics of eighth-graders correlate to Erikson's fifth stage?

7. From a guidance perspective, how would you work differently with a second-grader and a fifth-grader?

8. In what ways can knowledge of development aid the delivery of guidance and counseling services?

REFERENCES

Anderson, J. (1987). *Pumsy: In pursuit of excellence.* Eugene, OR: Timberline Press.

Blocher, D. (1974). *Developmental counseling* (2nd ed.). New York: Ronald Press.

Dinkmeyer, D., Sr., & Dinkmeyer, D., Jr. (1982). *Developing understanding of self and others.* Circle Pines, MN: American Guidance Services.

Elkind, D. (1978). *A sympathetic understanding of the child: Birth to sixteen* (2nd ed.). Boston: Allyn & Bacon.

Elkind, D. (1981). *The hurried child: Growing up too fast, too soon.* Reading, MA: Addison-Wesley.

Elkind, D. (1984). *All grown up and no place to go: Teenagers in crisis.* Reading, MA: Addison-Wesley.

Erikson, E. (1963). *Childhood and society* (2nd ed.). New York: Norton.

Erikson, E. (1968). *Identity, youth and crisis.* New York: Norton.

Gesell, A., Ilg, F., & Ames, L. (1956). *Youth: The years from ten to sixteen.* New York: Harper.

Gesell, A., Ilg, F., & Ames, L. (1977). *The child from five to ten* (Rev. ed.). New York: Harper.

Ilg, F., Ames, L., & Baker, S. (1981). *Child behavior: Specific advice on problems of child behavior* (Rev. ed.). New York: Perennial Library.

Kohlberg, L. (1978). Moral stages and moralization: The cognitive-developmental approach. In T. Lickona (Ed.), *Moral development and behavior: Theory, research, and social issues.* New York: Holt.

Muro, J. J., & Dinkmeyer, D. D. (1977). *Counseling in the elementary and middle schools: A pragmatic approach.* Dubuque, IA: William C. Brown.

Stewart, A. C., & Koch, J. B. (1983). *Children: Development through adolescence.* New York: John Wiley.

Youngs, B. (1985). *Stress in children: How to avoid and overcome it.* New York: Arbor House.

chapter 4

Counseling Theory and Technique

OUTLINE

INTRODUCTION

Theory provides practioners with a guide to help them make sense out of the
helping process (Brammer, 1988). It always enters into counseling, and individual
counselors gravitate toward certain theoretical ideas because they seem to fit.

The broad questions then become: Which theory is best for me, and which theories better address the needs of children? This chapter will outline an orientation to the theory and process of counseling, provide you with an overview of the theories most frequently associated with elementary and middle school counseling, and discuss the development of a personal theory of counseling.

What, then, is the difference between theory and technique? Simply stated, *theory* is the philosophical basis for how we perceive behavior, and *technique* is the manner in which we work with the people whom we counsel.

To be effective, you must have a theoretical basis for your approach. But the development of a theory is a process that takes time. First and foremost, we base our approach to others on how we view ourselves and how we consider our life experiences. The material contained in this chapter is designed to help you sort through your own thoughts about theory and move a step closer to formulating your own approach.

Most textbooks on theory organize their presentations around common categories. To give you a standard reference point, we have selected much the same categories that many others have used (Burks & Stefflre, 1978; Corey, 1988; Corsini, 1973; George & Cristiani, 1990; Patterson, 1980). For our presentation, the following categories are used: the nature of the human being, growth and development in an adaptive state, maladaptive behaviors, the predominant techniques used in applying the theory, and the application of the thoretical approach to the school setting.

There are more than a hundred different theories, points of view, or approaches to theory in counseling. How can you select the ones that best represent you? This question is not easily answered. The best fit likely results from the introspective pairing of an understanding of the self and an examination of a variety of theories. The theories we have included are consistent with our perception of theory in terms of your work as an elementary and middle school counselor—the receptiveness of children to counseling activity, the amount of time you have to work with the children, and the depth of your involvement with them. We use the term *child* or *children* rather than *client* to refer to individuals being counseled. We find it more appropriate, considering the subject matter.

All the theories presented here originate in the beliefs and values of the individuals most closely associated with them.

Before we begin our review of counseling theories, we briefly discuss our view of the counseling process, to which all of the theories can be applied.

Counseling Process

Carkhuff (1987) outlines the helping process as a three-step sequence comprising exploration, understanding, and action. We also propose three phases: the *three A approach.* The first A is *awareness,* in which you establish rapport with the child and gain a sense of what is happening in the child's world. Some theoretical approaches extend this to include children's self-awareness. We regard this phase as a process wherein much of the early work in counseling consists of building a relationship with children and gaining a broad understanding of their lives and the significant adults with whom they interact.

The second *A* is *acceptance*. This can occur at two levels: first, acceptance of children and their situations; and second, children's acceptance of self and of their circumstances. This phase is reached through the first *A,* awareness, and is often reconsidered as counseling continues and new issues are examined.

Our third *A—action—*corresponds to Carkhuff's. The focus here is on behavior change, based on the strategies you formulate as a result of the first two phases. In some cases the successful completion of the second phase eliminates the need for the third. That is, if children become more self-accepting, then there may be no need for further action. This is a form of *passive action.* (An example of passive action is when a child accepts being taller or shorter than his or her peers, and recognizes that being different does not mean being inferior.) Because you may work with children or adults over a period of time, you may cycle through these three phases repeatedly, depending on the number of issues to be considered.

You might think this process model is simplistic. Perhaps; but we do not feel a model has to be complex to be practical. Our concern is to provide you with a means to intuitively appraise your progress in counseling. A more complex model might give rise to confusion and concern about where you are in the process.

We endorse the developmental approach to guidance and counseling. We also recognize that there are other modes, which can be utilized while embracing a developmental view. The theories presented are organized more or less alphabetically; no one theory is given distinct preference.

ADLER'S THEORY OF INDIVIDUAL PSYCHOLOGY

The Adlerian point of view has been advanced most notably by Dreikurs and associates (Dreikurs & Grey, 1968; Dreikurs & Soltz, 1964) and Dinkmeyer and associates (Dinkmeyer & McKay, 1976; Dinkmeyer, McKay, & Dinkmeyer, 1980; Dinkmeyer, Pew, & Dinkmeyer, 1979). Dreikurs has been most closely identified with the articulation of Adler's theoretical beliefs.

Alfred Adler was one of Freud's early disciples, initially influenced by the psychoanalytic point of view. Adler was the first to break with Freud, in 1911. Their disagreement centered on Freud's theory of the sexual etiology of neuroses. Freud believed that people develop neurotic behavior because their psychosexual development is incomplete. Adler proposed that neurosis is caused by an individual's lack of social involvement—a striving for superiority, an upward drive to improve oneself at the expense of others.

Adler believed the behavior of the child is goal-directed and purposive, the main purpose of which is to have a place in the social environment—to belong.

Alder posited that everyone possesses feelings of inferiority. In striving to overcome this inferiority, the child seeks perfection and adopts maladaptive behaviors. The child's lifestyle, which is developed by age five or six, is influenced by these feelings of inferiority and the efforts to overcome them. The child's self-perception in the social environment determines how he or she compensates for this inferiority. Adler defined the well-adjusted individual as one who embraces social interest and can give and take in the social arena.

Dinkmeyer and his associates have promoted Adler's views in the schools. As a result, Adler's Individual Psychology has gained a measure of support in elementary and middle schools.

Nature of the Human Being

Adler takes a holistic view of the human being. The individual is acted upon by the environment, at the same time acting upon it. At birth, children are neither good nor bad but have the potential to behave either way. Therefore, human beings are morally neutral. As children grow, they form a lifestyle, a conception of themselves in the environment. Lifestyle is goal-directed and the goals selected indicate relative healthy adjustment or maladjustment. For the most part, Adler had an optimistic view of human nature.

Adaptive Behavior

According to Adler, the individual is first and foremost a social being, and all behavior can be explained in terms of the social meaning attached to it. Also, all behavior has a purpose. Linking these two principles provides the basis for Adler's view of how children develop. They strive toward *social interest*—what Adler calls *Gemeinschaftsgefuhl*—to exist in a cooperative give-and-take with others. As children grow, their primary task is to overcome feelings of inferiority in pursuit of that goal. The most exemplary form of purposive behavior is to serve the interests of others over and above one's own self-interest. This develops from a healthy assessment of the self in relation to others. Because children are both actors in the environment and are acted upon by it, when they have a healthy perspective about themselves and how others view them, they can embrace social interest. Adler contends that the striving for social interest is innate and develops consciously over time.

Maladaptive Behavior

Dysfunctional behavior results from feelings of inferiority. These feelings arise when children doubt their place in the social environment. Although from birth, children may naturally feel inferior because they are smaller, weaker, and less well developed than virtually everyone around them, it is their misinterpretation of this condition that creates maladaptive behavior. In attempting to overcome this inferiority, children compensate by striving for perfection and superiority. This results in selfish behavior, which is clearly counter to the cooperative give-and-take of social interest.

Counseling Techniques

The Adlerian approach focuses on children in their social environment. Therefore, many of the techniques are aimed at providing you first and then the children with an understanding of children's behavior. Although a variety of techniques are used, the initial emphasis is on the relationship between you and the child.

You make use of verbal techniques, such as restatement and reflection, to gain an understanding of children and their world and to enhance the relationship.

Other techniques increase your awareness and that of the child. The first is to "guess in the right direction." This approach is to help you gain information about the child's lifestyle. Guessing is open-ended to allow the child to validate or refute your hunch.

Once you have begun to develop a picture of how children relate to their environment, you will interpret the children's view of themselves. This is an extension of guessing in the right direction.

You will comment to the children about their behavior. This might take the form of an overt confrontation designed to point out discrepancies between how children see themselves, their mistaken beliefs about what they need to do to fit in, or the goals of their dysfunctional behavior.

More direct assessment or diagnostic techniques emphasize lifestyle investigation. Some of the more frequently used techniques include early recollections and reviewing the family constellation. In examining children's early recollections, early memories are used to discover how children may see themselves in relation to others.

A review of the family constellation is an investigation of the children's birth order. This review helps you to formulate assumptions about how children see themselves in the family, which may reveal how they view themselves in the broader environment. (Exploring the family constellation is an assessment technique.)

Behavior change techniques are built around helping children feel accepted in their social environment. One of the most powerful of these techniques is encouragement. This goes beyond simply praising children, because it is not dependent on success.

Another technique intended to influence behavior is the use of consequences. This arranges the logical results of children's behavior. In the case of deviant behavior, the result is something that is logically related to the misbehavior. By contrast, with socially appropriate behavior comes the pleasure of a sense of belonging.

Counseling Process

Adlerian counseling, in its purest form, includes four stages: (1) establishing the relationship, (2) diagnosis or assessment, (3) development of insight, and (4) reorientation and action. The means of delivery may take many forms. One is Adlerian family counseling—wherein the counselor works with the entire family in a structured group interview (Christensen, 1983; Dreikurs et al., 1959). A different form is the individual interview, which may follow the numbered sequence identified above. A middle ground between the two would be the use of structured programs such as DUSO (Dinkmeyer & Dinkmeyer, 1982).

The first stage is fundamental to the Adlerian process and involves the establishment of the child/counselor relationship. This is important because it provides the climate for both of them to consider the child's maladaptive behavior. The counselor's behavior is, in effect, a modeling of social interest.

The second stage involves investigating the child's perceived lifestyle. This is designed to uncover maladaptive self-perceptions and begin the movement toward the third stage, insight.

The fourth stage involves behavioral change: The children try out new behaviors and try to integrate them into their daily lives.

The first and second stages of the Adlerian process correspond to our awareness phase: Insight leads to greater awareness and self-acceptance. The last two Adlerian stages overlap with our acceptance and action phases.

Application to the School Setting

The primary appeal of Individual Psychology lies in its positive nature. Since this theory emphasizes valuing the child, many professionals find it to be compatible with the counselor's role.

The Adlerian approach has been effective with parents and teachers. In particular, some of the work of Dinkmeyer and his associates (Dinkmeyer & McKay, 1976; Dinkmeyer, McKay, & Dinkmeyer, 1980) focuses on the parent/child and teacher/child relationship. The two programs that address this are Sequential Training for Effective Parenting (STEP) and Sequential Training for Effective Teaching (STET). Both programs identify problem behavior by using the "four goals of misbehavior": attention seeking, power struggles, revenge seeking, and assumed disability. One of the concerns regarding the Adlerian approach is that when used with elementary school children there is a tendency to focus on discipline problems rather than on the healthy development of children (George & Christiani, 1990).

BEHAVIORAL THEORY

The behavioral approach is associated with either classical conditioning, as advanced by Ivan Pavlov, or operant conditioning, as developed by Skinner. Pavlov, a Russian psychologist, began the behavioral movement with his research on classical conditioning in the nineteenth century. This form of learning involves generating a new stimulus by pairing it with a natural stimulus, both conforming to produce the same response. This generalized approach was continued in the United States with John Watson (1930). The movement achieved true popularity—and notoriety—with B. F. Skinner's (1953) work and has been furthered by a number of individuals, including Wolpe, Bandura, Krumboltz and Thoresen, and Patterson. Krumboltz and Thoresen (1976) and Patterson (Patterson & Gullion, 1968) are among the more influential behaviorists in the school setting. The behavioral approach found most often in educational and therapeutic settings is operant conditioning. It is frequently used with institutionalized and behaviorally disturbed school children.

Nature of the Human Being

The behaviorist believes that the child is neither good nor bad at birth, but essentially neutral, with potential to go in either direction. The development of children is based on a unique interaction between them and the environment (usually defined as society). Children are influenced by the people in their environment, and they influence others. Crucial in the development of children is that they are products of their experiences; therefore, behavior—both adaptive and maladaptive—is learned. Behaviorists are not concerned with feelings or insights, but with goals and methods that will ensure repeated behavior. Depending on experience and reinforcements, children will respond predictably to a given stimulus. This is operant conditioning, which posits that a reinforced behavior is likely to recur. We are more likely to repeat the pleasant results of our behavior and less likely to repeat the unpleasant results. Both adaptive and maladaptive behavior are learned.

Adaptive Behavior

Adaptive behaviors are those that society deems appropriate. In the adaptive state, children not only experience pleasure, but that pleasure is reinforced by people who are important to them. This is the pairing of social reinforcers—words of praise and support, along with more concrete results (e.g., receiving a good grade in school or scoring points in a game). These are the principles of reinforcement simplified. Children experience a meaningful interaction between themselves and others. This interaction underscores the foundation principle that individuals influence and are influenced by their environment.

Maladaptive Behavior

An important difference between adaptive and maladaptive behavior concerns the response of the environment. Because the response is negative, maladaptive behavior is regarded as inappropriate by society. The same principles of learning and reinforcements apply, but in the maladaptive case, children engage in behaviors that create problems. They are reinforced for their inappropriate behaviors by incurring a negative reaction from significant others.

Counseling Techniques

The goal of counseling is to change learned maladaptive behaviors with operant conditioning. This has been identified as consisting of six steps (Blackman & Silberman, 1980):

1. operationally define the behavior to be changed;
2. collect baseline data to determine the magnitude or nature of the behavior;
3. design the counseling or learning situation;
4. identify the potential reinforcers;
5. reinforce the desired behavior; and
6. record or document the reinforced behavior to demonstrate the change.

Counseling involves unlearning the ineffective behaviors and assuming new, more effective ones. Counselors are less concerned with the process of counseling than with establishing goals and creating new learning patterns. The client chooses the goals with your assistance.

To facilitate learning, a number of techniques are employed. They can be divided into two groups: those that influence the unlearning of behaviors and those that promote new learning. Following are the more frequently used techniques associated with these processes.

Unlearning

Extinction.   This consists of progressively weakening negative behaviors by removing the reinforcement. An example of this would be for a teacher to ignore a child who acts out in class. To eliminate all reinforcement, the teacher would avoid any recognition of the behavior. There are times when we can withhold reinforcement and unintentionally extinguish a desired behavior. In this case effective behavior would be eliminated.

Satiation.   This is the opposite of extinction, removing an undesired behavior by requiring children to continue it until they tire. This has proven successful in smoking clinics, where participants are required to smoke until they become sick of it.

Incompatible Alternative.   Here, a behavior diametrically opposed to the undesired behavior is adopted. The alternative may take three forms: the opposite of the undesired behavior, an alternative that cannot be performed at the same time as the undesired behavior, or an alternative that distracts the child from the undesired behavior. You might, respectively, place problem children in a position of leadership, structure the activities of children who waste time and have difficulty organizing themselves, or divert attention from emotionally provocative situations.

Systematic Desensitization.   This is used with anxiety-producing situations, such as school phobia. Desensitization breaks down the anxiety with an incompatible response—relaxation. This involves three operations: (1) relaxation training, (2) developing a hierarchy of anxiety-producing situations, and (3) working through the hierarchy.

New Learning.   Behavioral contracting, modeling, positive reinforcement, and shaping are new learning techniques wherein you provide support for socially acceptable behavior.

Contracting.   Children enter into an agreement with one or more adults, specifying a performance level to meet predetermined goals. Through the clear language of a contract, which specifies behavior, time allotted, and performance levels, children can learn new behaviors while receiving adult support. The strength of this approach lies in children's knowledge of exactly what is excepted of them.

Modeling.   This technique, associated with behavioral theory, is used in a variety of theoretical approaches. The basic premise is that a person will imitate the behavior of others. This is particularly useful with children, who can acquire a great deal through imitation, particularly of the significant adults in their life. The process is quite simple. The adult repeats the desired behavior; over time, the child assimilates it. (A caveat: Modeling can also provide children with undesirable behavior. If you believe in modeling, the principle of "do as I say, not as I do" does not work.) Among the most powerful models in children's environments are parents, teachers, and other adults who work with them—coaches, youth leaders (e.g., dance instructors and scout leaders), and counselors.

Positive Reinforcement.   This versatile technique is intended to improve a child's performance by rewarding each successful attempt. Whatever behavior immediately precedes the reward is likely to recur because of that reward. The key, then, is to identify and provide reinforcement immediately after each desired behavior. Reinforcement may be tangible (e.g., candy, tokens, points, or stickers) or intangible (e.g., praise). What is crucial in this approach is to properly identify the reward to a child and then apply the reward as soon as the desired behavior is demonstrated.

Shaping.   This reinforces successive approximations of the desired behavior (Krumboltz & Krumboltz, 1972). It is designed to help the child develop new behaviors by reinforcing *efforts of improvement* toward the end result—the desired behavior. Shaping is a meaningful technique because the child does not have to demonstrate the finished product.

Counseling Process

Traditionally, the behavioral approach has been dependent on the control and manipulation of behavior by the counselor. The child's role here is more passive than in other approaches. Therefore, the process of awareness, acceptance, and action may better relate to your involvement as counselor than the child's as client. Recently, a view of the behavioral model has emerged that emphasizes a positive relationship between client and counselor and a more active role on the part of the client (Watson & Tharp, 1981). Self-management is an essential feature, and the three-phase process we have outlined is more in evidence.

Application to the School Setting

Behaviorism is attractive to school personnel because it is a learning-theory approach that can influence children's adaptation to their school environment. Similarly, it appeals to school personnel because it is action-oriented and under the control of adults. Many professionals in the schools feel more comfortable when they are in charge of the relationship with children. Two distinct strengths of this practice are reinforcement and shaping, both of which are meaningful in the school setting. Finally, specific, observable behavior change is apparent.

With regard to limitations, some feel that this approach gives the adult too much control over the child. Also, there is concern that the behavioral approach is sterile and cold, because children's behavior can be manipulated with little direct interaction.

CLIENT-CENTERED THEORY

Over the past three decades, the theoretical approach referred to as client-centered, nondirective, and (more recently) person-centered counseling has been synonymous with Carl Rogers. Rogers's (1942) formulations were a departure from the two primary approaches of the day—trait factor, associated with E. G. Williamson, and traditional Freudian psychoanalysis. Rogers's approach was humanistic and far different from each of these popular viewpoints. His primary focus is on the relationship of the self-concept to experience. When Rogers published *Client-Centered Therapy* (1951), he developed a more complete theory of personality in which he outlined the counselor's empathic endeavor to identify with the client's experience. More recently, Rogers's principles have been extended beyond therapy to other settings, such as education. As a result of the increased adaptation of the Rogers approach, it is currently referred to as person-centered theory.

Nature of the Human Being

The term *self-actualization* (Maslow, 1970) is often used to represent the human evolution toward a greater level of functioning. Rogers (1951) called it a "state of becoming." In all likelihood Maslow never foresaw his concept of self-actualization to be used in this manner. Rogers intended to view the human being as engaged in an actualizing process whose goal is self-enhancement. This is possible because Rogers and his followers conceived of the human being as rational, realistic, and self-directed. Appropriately, another term for the Rogers person-centered approach is *self-theory.*

Adaptive Behavior

Adjustment is a state of congruence between an individual's perceptions and experiences. When people experience adjustment they possess a realistic view of themselves and can accept both flaws and strengths. Their view is developed through integration and differentiation. *Integration* is the blending of external experiences with self-perception; *differentiation* is the translation of experiences and ideas into behavior. It is the latter that moves the individual toward actualization. The well-adjusted child possesses a healthy self-concept, which results from the realistic perception of self and a healthy perception of the view that important people hold.

Maladaptive Behavior

Maladjustment occurs when children are in a state of *incongruence*—the degree of disparity between self-perception and reality (e.g., children acting on a sense of self-depreciation, thus making it the reality). This dissimilarity makes children feel vulnerable and anxious about their identity, "the who and what am I." In children, vulnerability and anxiety may be apparent, but confusion they may possess about their identity may be rather subtle.

Counseling Techniques

The goal of early contact is the development of rapport between children and counselor. Rapport creates trust, wherein children will risk increased exploration of their feelings. This is referred to as the *client perspective* (Gilliland, James, & Bowman, 1989). Essential to progress in counseling is the relationship between child and counselor. Overall, the emphasis is on the child's here-and-now. Therefore, techniques become means or methods to enhance the relationship and increase the focus on the child's present experience.

Fundamental techniques are the counselors use of the *therapeutic triad*— warmth, empathy, and congruence. *Warmth* is also called *unconditional positive regard* for the child. The meaning is obvious. *Empathy* is the counselor's effort to relate to the child's internal frame of reference—"what it must be like to be this child, right now." *Congruence* is twofold: On the one hand, it is the counselors' state of homeostasis and, on the other, a genuineness in the way they relate to the child.

Counseling Process

Since client-centered counseling requires insight, there is a good match between the process Rogers identified and ours. The awareness phase is the relationship-building process that enables both counselor and child to understand the child's life dilemmas. Acceptance is essential to change, since the child must arrive at this point to overcome incongruence between experience and perception. Finally, new perceptions and behavior are demonstrated in action-oriented steps that promote and reinforce congruence in the child.

Application to the School Setting

The most attractive features of the client-centered approach are the relationship-building aspects. To many, warmth and empathy represent the epitome of counselor behavior. This environment has been adopted by a number of theoretical approaches and regarded as fundamental to all helping relationships (Patterson, 1980).

Questions have been raised about children's willingness to participate in client-centered counseling and the slow progress resulting from strict emphasis on the child's insight to bring about behavior change. Children who enter counseling against their will may blindly resist it, and progress—if any—will be almost imperceptible.

DEVELOPMENTAL THEORY

This approach is best considered a point of view rather than a theory, as it does not possess the conventional characteristics that we associate with theory; moreover, it has interdisciplinary qualities that could be attributed to a large number of scholars. Blocher (1974), one of the leading proponents of developmental counseling, views the personality of the individual as unfolding through healthy interaction with the environment. Developmental counseling is proactive, stressing educative-preventive goals. This is in contrast to those theories that are reactive, focusing on the remediation of existing problems. The approach is anchored in human development theory and based on the premise that specific behaviors are simply a part of life stages through which the child moves. Counseling helps children manage their lives within the various stages of development.

Nature of the Human Being

The primary goals of developmental counseling are to enhance freedom and improve human effectiveness (Blocher, 1974). The child is viewed in a positive light.

Further, human beings are responsible for their own actions and must make their own choices (Blocher, 1974). Children have their own unique heredity and experiences, and react holistically and subjectively to reality.

Adaptive Behavior

Children are emotionally healthy when they have mastered the developmental tasks for a particular life stage. This mastery further provides them with a means to function effectively in the environment. When children function effectively, greater levels of achievement are possible. Therefore, behavior change is viewed as maximizing effectiveness and enabling children to increase achievement.

Maladaptive Behavior

Maladaptive behavior is present when developmental tasks have not been mastered. Children who have difficulty getting along in the environment are considered to be maladjusted, as are children who possess faulty self-perceptions and do not accept themselves.

Counseling Techniques

Counseling focuses on the present. Clients are not mentally ill, but in a state of development; the child is a client, not a patient (Blocher, 1974). Therefore, the counselor functions as a teacher and supportive agent as the child progresses toward specific goals. This approach embraces the client-centered principle of increased insight, but also extends beyond as the counselor endeavors to assist in the behavior change.

Some techniques are based on Blocher's human effectiveness model, wherein

1. children are in a process of constantly changing roles and relationships, and adapt differently to the demands placed on them;
2. the counselor needs to understand the wide range of coping behaviors available to children and help them acquire new behaviors;
3. children are helped by the counselor to master developmental tasks that enable them to function more effectively and meet the demands of the next stage of development; and
4. the counselor helps children to consider the question "who am I" in the formation of a unique, all-embracing identity.

These four points provide the foundation upon which particular techniques are based.

Techniques are based on the developmental interview (Blocher, 1974), which consists of three parts: formulation of goals, dimensions of the counseling process, and perceptual skills.

Goal formulation involves both counselor and child: The counselor brings a conceptual frame of reference regarding human development and a personal value system. The child has a perception of his or her situation. These two elements provide for the mutual formulation of counseling goals, leading to a developmental contract (Blocher, 1974). The contract changes as counseling progresses.

The technique used to establish goals is called *structuring*. At its simplest, structuring is the communication of expectations about counseling. The counselor assumes the primary role. As the direction of the counseling changes, restructuring takes place. It is essential that clear communication between counselor and child exists so that each may share in the process.

Counseling is structured along three *process dimensions*. The first, *responsibility,* may be shared by counselor and child. Division of responsibility represents a continuum along which you move from time to time with the child. It is desirable to instill responsibility in the child; but there are times when you, because of your experience and wisdom, must assume a greater share.

The second dimension, *ambiguity,* refers to the uncertainty in the minds of the child and you about what is transpiring in the counseling session. Greater ambiguity for the child prompts more free-flowing responses; less ambiguity creates more stilted responses, epitomized by close-ended yes/no statements.

The third dimension, *cognitive and affective material,* relates to the balance between intellectual and emotional emphasis determined by the counselor's and the child's needs at the time.

These three dimensions impact the relationship between counselor and child and the progress of counseling. All three dimensions are managed by the nature of the communication that exists in the child/counselor relationship.

The third technique identified concerns *perceptual skills* (Blocher, 1974). Over and above what counselors say is what they understand about children. The counselor's perception is largely a function of listening skills. Ability to truly listen is rare. More frequently, counselors engage in selective listening, based upon their own values and the intensity of their focus. The aim of all counselors should be to improve their listening skills.

The techniques that Blocher has outlined are very much process-oriented and rely on effective communication. The overriding concern in developmental counseling is the relationship between counselor and child and the mutually shared commitment to the counseling activity.

Counseling Process

The process movement in the development model of counseling has not been explicitly delineated. But, when consideration is given to the emphasis placed on the relationship, communication, mutual responsibility, and human effectiveness model, the developmental model relates well to our three-phase model. What is most noteworthy is that the counselor usually precedes the child in the first two phases (awareness and acceptance). The counselor understands the children's circumstances before they do, and will likely accept these situations before they do. But children do experience these first two phases because their active involvement is necessary to master the developmental stage. The third stage (action) is a mutual effort between child and counselor.

Application to the School Setting

The developmental approach maintains a positive view of children and therefore appeals to school personnel. The developmental features are meaningful to intermediate and middle school educators. The emphasis on children's assumption of responsibility is also favored by school professionals. The attention given to the healthy growth and development of children is the strongest drawing card of this approach.

One limitation however, is the lack of clarity in the process and outcome goals. The counselor is left to work generally with children to aid their growth through the various developmental stages.

RATIONAL-EMOTIVE THEORY

The most popular cognitive approach to counseling, rational emotive therapy (RET), is the creation of Albert Ellis (Ellis, 1962; 1973; 1979; Tosi et al., 1987). This form of counseling considers the human being as capable of either rational or irrational thought and behavior. Fundamental to Ellis's theory is the statement of Epictetus, a Stoic philosopher of the first century A.D., who wrote, "Men are disturbed not by things, but by the view which they take of them." Ellis professes that emotions are based on thought, and that a change in thinking can bring about a change in feeling. The purpose of RET counseling is the reorientation of the client's thoughts to produce more rational behavior.

Ellis (1962; 1973) has readily acknowledged the relationship of his theory to that of Adler. He has drawn from Adler the notion that experiences alone are not the causes of success or failure. This supports the premise that people are self-deterministic. The counselor's role is to assist the child in developing a more rational view of life. RET employs active-directive, cognitive methods to address self-defeating behaviors. The counselor functions much like a teacher, and the child is viewed as a student.

Nature of the Human Being

People can choose their own path—how they will live with others, experience daily life, and accept their own human frailty (Ellis, 1979). They are morally neutral—inherently neither good nor bad. The interpretation attached to experiences is what creates behavior. The patterns of behavior the child adopts are reinforced by significant adults. Therefore, the unique interaction between the child's perception of life experiences and the responses from meaningful adults form the basis for behavior, rational or irrational.

Adaptive Behavior

According to Ellis (1962), rational behavior is effective and productive behavior, wherein children think of themselves as worthwhile. Maultsby (1984) has identified five points that describe a healthy, rational human being:

1. More rational people tend to accept the world in which they live.
2. They try to live reasonably in the social environment.
3. They establish intimate relations with a few people around them.
4. They are involved in productive educational or vocational activity.
5. They participate in meaningful leisure or recreational pursuits.

Ellis (1973) believes that healthy rational behavior is relative; therefore, the reasonable approximation of these five criteria constitutes adjustment. Thus, well-adjusted children have a high degree of self-acceptance.

Maladaptive Behavior

Irrational behavior is based on the child's negative perceptions of experiences and corresponding self reinforced by significant people in his or her life. This negative view results in emotional problems, and adversely affects interactions with others. Ellis has cleverly explained the development of maladaptive behavior through his A-B-C model (Ellis, 1962; 1973; Tosi et al., 1987). *A* represents the *activating* event, *B* is the *belief* system, and *C* is the *consequence* of this belief. This system explains irrational behavior through the child's perception (point *B*), experiences (point *A*), and the resulting emotionally upset reaction (point *C*). Ellis indicates that the relationship between *A* and *C* lies only in the child's thoughts and self-talk at *B*. Ellis (1962) listed 11 irrational beliefs. Tosi (1974) adapted them for adolescents, providing an excellent illustration of ineffective self-talk. These beliefs, with our application to children and middle school-age youth through the use of examples, are outlined as follows:

1. People have an absolute need to be approved and loved by the significant adults and peers around them. ("If you don't love me, then I'm no good.")
2. People can only be worthwhile if they are perfect in everything they do. ("If I don't do things just right, you won't like me.")
3. Some people are evil and should be severely punished. (If children are allowed to establish discipline for misbehavior, they will create draconian punishments: "If they don't finish their social studies on time, make them stay in from recess for the rest of the year.")
4. When things don't work out exactly the way the should, it is a catastrophe. ("I forgot my books. I don't know what to do. My teachers will never forgive me.")
5. External events cause behavior. ("It's not my fault; Johnny made me do it.")
6. People should be extremely concerned and anxious about unknown or potentially dangerous events. ("I'm so scared of storms. I just think a tornado's going to hit our house every time it rains.")
7. Responsibilities and difficulties in life are less trouble if they are ignored. ("If I don't think about my schoolwork, then I don't feel bad.")
8. The past makes an important difference in how people act in the present. ("I guess I'm just no good. I always screw up.")
9. There is a right way for the world to be, and it's terrible if one cannot change things now. ("He shouldn't talk like that, it's wrong.") Or, ("That's not fair, everybody should get to play the game.")
10. People will be happiest if they leave things alone. ("If I don't do anything, then I won't get upset and I'll be happier. To try isn't worth it.") (pp. 37–55)

Children who behave irrationally adopt a set of absolutes—*should, ought,* or *must* statements. These may be turned either toward themselves or others. The preoccupation with irrational beliefs and the self-talk that centers around the absolutes create emotional disturbance and maladjustment.

Counseling Techniques

The primary technique is changing the belief system and challenging the child's self-talk. How the counselor goes about this depends on the goals that have been established. Ellis (1962; 1979) has identified ten possible goals for the counselor: (1) self-interest; (2) self-direction; (3) tolerance toward others; (4) flexibility and receptivity to new ideas; (5) adapting to uncertainty; (6) increased use of reasoning; (7) establishing a commitment to people and things outside oneself; (8) adopting a reasonable risk-taking attitude; (9) self-acceptance; and (10) developing an appreciation of human flaws, in oneself and others.

These goals are not mutually exclusive, and the counselor may wish to address more than one. Most important, the goals are aimed at producing a more self-reliant and self-accepting child.

Techniques designed to meet the goals you identify are discussed in the following paragraphs. Since the primary intent of counseling is to alter the belief system of the child, you become an active teacher. Techniques fall into three categories: cognitive, emotive, and behavioral.

The *cognitive* technique involves your restructuring children's self-talk by first teaching them to recognize their absolutist statements—*should, ought,* and *must.* This cognitive focus disputes children's irrational beliefs. The approach is largely didactic, using a variety of media, from books to videocassettes.

The *emotive* technique exposes the way in which children's irrational beliefs interfere with their relations with others. You can use dramatic activities such as role play to help some children to better understand their irrational beliefs. Other emotive techniques may employ visual methods, including mental imagery or photographs. Other techniques in this area are modeling and role reversal.

The *behavioral* techniques make liberal use of homework and reading material (bibliocounseling). You may use relaxation techniques and desensitization to assist children in understanding their irrational beliefs.

These three techniques are not mutually exclusive. Ellis (1973) felt that your approach should focus directly on demonstrating children's irrational beliefs and self-talk. Unmasking the irrational continues with an ongoing effort to replace the illogical beliefs and behaviors with more logical ones.

Counseling Process

RET is carried out in three stages. In the first, children acknowledge their irrational beliefs and assume responsibility for these beliefs and related behaviors. In the second, children understand that their irrational beliefs can be challenged and their behavior altered. In the third stage, children develop more rational thinking and behavior patterns.

This three-stage model parallels our own. The first stage—actively focusing on the irrational beliefs—creates awareness in children of their dysfunctional beliefs and behaviors. The latter part of this stage, which focuses on the assumption of responsibility, blends into our second phase of acceptance. The second stage completes the acceptance process by emphasizing the understanding of irrational beliefs. The latter part of the second stage blends into our third phase (action) because efforts are made to help children understand that behavior can be changed. This action phase is completed when the third stage is carried out through the development of more rational/logical thought and behavior. Essentially, the two processes are the same. The difference lies in where the elements separate from one another.

Application to the School Setting

Highly important to the success of this approach are the counselors' skills and their own rational functioning. Particular skill lies in knowledge and application of the principles, interpersonal relations, and persuasiveness. Significant strengths of the theory lie in meaningful, logical pairing of cognition and emotion. Ellis's explanation of irrational beliefs appeals to school personnel, as negative self-talk is a construct that these professionals can effectively use to help children who have a strong defeatist attitude. Also, RET involves reeducation, demonstrating how children can reorient their thinking and subsequent behavior. Its action-oriented nature is viewed as a strength, because this can help children see the results of their efforts.

The most noteworthy limitation of RET is the reliance on language mastery. Younger children may have difficulty because of limited cognitive development and a possible lack of understanding of the A-B-C model. Also, in some ways RET deemphasizes the interpersonal relationship between counselor and child. The counselor's persuasiveness is viewed by some as pressuring children into behaving differently.

REALITY THERAPY

Another contemporary theory that has gained attention in recent decades is William Glasser's reality therapy. Like RET, reality therapy is a cognitive approach. The two depart on points of emphasis and methodology. The publication of Glasser's *Reality Therapy: A New Approach to Psychiatry* in 1965 marked the beginning of this theory. *Schools without Failure* (Glasser, 1969) provided an early stimulus to the use of Glasser's concepts in educational and institutional settings because it emphasized children's success. Reality therapy helps children view themselves as worthwhile and encourages them to assume responsibility for their actions. Much like RET, Glasser's theory is a teaching approach that views the counselor as a role model and focuses on present behavior.

Recently, Glasser (1986) has emphasized control theory, wherein children behave to control the world around them, rather than being controlled externally. Counseling is an effort to help children manage their internal world, thus becoming emotionally stronger and more stable.

There is striking similarity between Glasser's postulations and those of Adler. Even though Glasser (1984) has indicated that his thoughts were independently developed, he does acknowledge the parallel between his concepts and those of Individual Psychology.

Nature of the Human Being

In reality therapy, people are fundamentally self-directed, evolving into autonomous, responsible individuals. Individual behavior is internally motivated, and people are viewed in terms of their present behavior. This behavior is measured against objective criteria (reality), which may be of a social, practical, or moral form.

Glasser (1965) thinks that human behavior is oriented toward fulfilling basic needs. Initially he thought the individual had two basic needs: to love and be loved, and to feel worthwhile. Glasser (1984) combined these two needs into the need for identity, which can be translated into a feeling of belonging. How clients meet their needs determines whether their behavior is healthy or maladjusted.

Adaptive Behavior

Healthy, well-adjusted children are those whose identity needs are being met. These children possess a success identity, and hence feel they belong. Similarly, well-adapted children assume responsibility for themselves. Glasser (1965) defines responsibility as the ability of children to meet their needs while not interfering with others' ability to meet their own. In this regard, the more responsible children become, the more healthy and effective they are in our society. Also, there is congruence between perceptions and behavior. The adjusted children have control over their perceptions, which in turn reflect a realistic view of themselves.

Maladaptive Behavior

Maladjusted children possess a failure identity; they lack a sense of belonging. They engage in behaviors that dramatize their separation from others—isolation, withdrawal, self-criticism, and irrationality. They have lost control of their effective perceptions. These children are irresponsible and are frustrated in their efforts to be loved and feel worthwhile.

Children with negative self-identity are likely to give up easily and feel that they cannot succeed—what Glasser (1972) calls *negative addiction.* When they become absorbed in protecting themselves from the pain of feeling rejected, they demonstrate negative addiction. They may deny failure, project blame (avoid responsibility), or even take pleasure in their failure.

Counseling Techniques

Because of the cognitive basis of reality therapy, learning is a fundamental process in behavior change. The counselor functions as a teacher, providing children with instruction regarding irresponsible behavior. Through persuasive communication, children learn to avoid ineffective behaviors and to enhance responsible ones. At times, it is necessary for you to directly confront children about their irresponsible behavior. This compels them to acknowledge their acts. Your emphasis is on the use of *what* questions rather than *why* questions. Your aim is to help children confront the reality of their behavior and not to make value judgments.

Counseling emphasizes positive counselor responses for responsible child behavior. Irresponsible behavior is either confronted or ignored. This is much like the Adlerian focus on encouragement, but with confrontation added. In general, you try to create an atmosphere where children feel accepted. This supportive atmosphere suggests Rogers's principles of warmth and empathy.

Since adjusted behavior is based on children learning to be more effective in their daily life, problem solving is a significant part of counseling. This extends beyond the application of a problem-solving model. You endeavor to teach children to approach areas of difficulty with reasoning and logic. In addition to providing children with a model for solving problems, you may also make use of contracts to further the adoption of new behaviors. Contracts become action plans to enable children to better understand present behavior and consider future actions.

Throughout the interaction, you serve as a positive role model for responsible, effective behavior. It is through this modeling that you continually reinforce behavior change.

Counseling is a brief but intense interaction that utilizes seven principles (Glasser 1972), which represent the nature of the counseling activity beyond specific interaction techniques already discussed.

1. *Get involved.* You need to demonstrate to children that you are concerned and care about them. This is the basis for the work that is to follow.
2. *Emphasize behavior.* The focus of the counseling is on helping children be more aware of what they are doing, not how they are feeling. In this regard you should quickly point out the child's irresponsible behaviors.
3. *Consider the present.* The focus of reality therapy is on the present. This is intended to compel children to evaluate whether their current behavior is fulfilling needs. This is an important part of the child's learning.
4. *Initiate responsible behavior.* This principle builds from the preceding, in which children are encouraged and assisted in developing a specific plan for more responsible behavior. Your role is to guide children to develop a reasonable, manageable plan for behavior change.
5. *Gain a commitment.* You can better assure the effectiveness of the behavior change if you solicit a commitment from children to change.

This commitment may be verbal, but is often contractual. Children can always look back on the commitment and judge their progress, thereby learning to appraise the success of their efforts.

6. *Accept no excuses.* Accept no excuses from children for inaction failure. Since failure will occur, help children construct a new plan; and do not dwell on the failure.

7. *Replace punishments with consequences.* Since punishments do not help children develop a sense of responsibility—indeed, they free them from it—you and the child set consequences for unsuccessful efforts. The establishment of consequences is best if determined prior to the child's effort to take on a new behavior.

Counseling Process

The relationship of Glasser's approach to our model lies in the counselor's role. Glasser's process is sequential, and blends across our three phases. It is through the counselor's efforts that children gain an awareness of their ineffective behavior. The first four steps are aimed at developing that awareness. The fourth step initiates the acceptance phase. The completion of acceptance should take place with the establishment of the commitment in step 6. Similarly, steps 5 through 7 are a blend from one phase to another, with some initial focus on acceptance and action simultaneously. Clearly, these steps are action-oriented; but without acceptance on the part of the child, success cannot occur.

Application to the School Setting

Since reality therapy is a learning-based, cognitive approach, it is well suited for use in the schools. Glasser's emphasis on the present, problem solving, and responsible behavior have broad appeal to school and institutional personnel. Particularly attractive is the fact that Glasser's theory is positive and action-oriented as well.

One possible shortcoming is the reliance on effective verbal communication and necessity for children to understand cause and effect. With children in grades K–2, the approach would be restricted because of their limited language skills and their level of development.

TRANSACTIONAL ANALYSIS

In the mid-1950s Eric Berne began to organize the transactional analysis (TA) approach. TA gained popularity during the 1960s with the publication of *Games People Play* (Berne, 1964) and *I'm OK—You're OK* (Harris, 1969). As a result of these works, TA became the psychological self-help fad of the age.

Berne, a psychoanalytically trained therapist, carried elements of this classic model into his newly formed approach. Here, past experiences—primarily childhood relationships with significant adults— are important to the individual's present functioning. Similarly, Berne's (1964) concept of ego states (see Adaptive Behavior below) has overtones of psychoanalytic theory. Transactional analysis is largely a cognitive approach, but it emphasizes the transactions among people and employs behavioral methods such as contracting.

Nature of the Human Being

Transactional analysis has deterministic qualities, as demonstrated through the life script concept. Berne (1966) proposed that early in childhood a life script is chosen as a means of meeting the child's needs. Further, without any therapeutic intervention the individual would move throughout life following this script, regardless of its functional or dysfunctional nature. The four possible life positions that can be chosen are

I'm OK, you're OK;

I'm OK, you're not OK;

I'm not OK, you're OK; and

I'm not OK, you're not OK. (Berne, 1964)

Berne does not view children as passive, but as capable of making choices regarding the life position they adopt. This choice factor moderates the deterministic aspect of the theory. Also, once the life script is chosen, the pattern is not impervious to change, because change can be stimulated by the therapeutic process.

Adaptive Behavior

To function well, children must call upon appropriate *ego states* when they interact with others (Berne, 1966). The *parent state* represents the identification and assimilation of the values, attitudes, and impressions of the biological parents (Dusay & Dusay, 1984); the *adult state* incorporates the rational problem-solving process; and the *child state* covers the gamut of childlike behaviors, from spontaneous free expression to conformity to rebellion.

The early experiences children have with significant adults, particularly with parents, influence children's ego states and behavior. If children's attention and recognition needs are met, healthy, adjusted behavior is more likely. This is where the "strokes" enter in children's healthy ego state formation (Dusay & Dusay, 1984). The most positive strokes come about when significant adults, notably parents and teachers, accept the children more frequently than not.

Maladaptive Behavior

This develops when children adopt a negative life script. Three of the life scripts have these connotations. The likelihood of selecting a negative life position is increased when children receive insufficient or disapproving strokes. Therefore, early patterns of parental stroking are important to the development of the ego states and the selection of a positive life script.

Fundamental to maladaptive behavior is the adoption of "games" in children's transactions and life scripts (Berne, 1964). Counselors and other adults should not assume children are aware of the games they play. These games signal dysfunctional behavior and a reduction of the potential for intimate relations with others. Ironically, children often adopt games to "arrange" more meaningful, closer relations. Berne asserts that maladaptive behavior is learned through children's interactions with others and the subsequent decisions children make about themselves in the environment.

Counseling Techniques

As maladjustment is learned, so it can be unlearned. This is the essence of behavior change involving *redecision* (Berne 1964). The overall goal of TA counseling is to help the child attain autonomy. To become more autonomous the child must rewrite the script to adopt the "I'm OK, you're OK" posture. Accordingly, TA is an active form of counseling wherein the counselor functions as a teacher or trainer of the child.

Berne conceived his approach as predominately suited to group rather than individual therapy (Berne, 1964; 1966). However, within the group, TA counselors do engage in frequent individual dialogue with participants. Berne's rationale for the use of the group medium was that the group allows the counselor to observe the child interacting with others. This observation assists in the counselor's analysis of the child's personality, interactions with others, and the maladaptive behaviors that are assumed.

Initially the counselor engages in relationship-building techniques to facilitate contracting. (The early interaction also gives the counselor an opportunity to collect analytic information.) The contract identifies what the children want out of counseling, what the counselor will do to help them, and some criteria for success in counseling. The contract provides structure and imposes a sense of responsibility on the child.

When the contract has been established the counselor takes on an active teaching role. The first elements that may be taught are ego states and life scripts. Once children have learned the primary concepts they can gain a broader understanding of ego states and transactions. Later, children may be taught the concept of games and their role in life. Homework may be used to further illuminate behavior patterns. Once children have discovered the ineffective nature of their behavior, they can begin to redirect their life patterns. Close examination of children's life scripts and games can begin to provide insight to their behavior. This examination provides a springboard to designing new patterns and eliminating games.

To help the child assume new behaviors, role play is often used. One prominent variation is the empty chair technique, wherein the child can dialogue with someone outside the counseling setting by speaking to that person as though he or she were in the chair. It can be used to examine existing patterns or practice new behaviors.

Another technique frequently used is bibliocounseling. By assigning or reading aloud reading material, you help the child understand life patterns or games, and the child can begin to learn new behaviors. (Homework as a practice experience with new patterns of behavior is common in transactional analysis.)

Counseling Process

A detailed TA counseling process has been provided by Woolams and Brown (1979). It consists of seven steps: motivation, awareness, the treatment contract, deconfusing children, redecision, relearning, and termination (pp. 228-233).

The motivation and awareness steps blend together, since TA posits that, to desire change, children must experience discomfort with their current status. You aid this process by prompting children's awareness of their maladaptive behavior. These two steps roughly correspond to our first phase, awareness.

The third step is the contract. This is not a single agreement, but may be a series of agreements that are negotiated throughout counseling. This step shares elements with our awareness phase because children are still acquiring a sense of their present behavior. But it could also move toward our acceptance phase because to enter into the contract, children must acknowledge current disruptive patterns of behavior.

The fourth step brings awareness into focus because it condenses the information that has been collected regarding children's maladaptive behavior. Since children are assisted in feeling comfortable with themselves, this is also a bridging step to the acceptance phase. Children need to be more comfortable with themselves to move to the next step.

Redecision is the fifth step and corresponds to the beginning of our action phase. At this time children make a commitment to change some aspect of their life pattern. This comes about because children now understand their counter-productive ways and have gained some insight into alternative behaviors.

The sixth step is relearning. It supports the redecision made in the previous step. When children falter, you bolster them and work through the relapses. This is still an action-oriented step because new behaviors are constantly being integrated into children's life scripts.

The final step is termination. The goals of counseling have been met and children are able to function in a more effective manner. You now reinforce what has been learned and support the children in their accomplishments. This step is simply the end of our action phase.

Application to the School Setting

To school personnel, the most salient feature of the TA approach is the concept of strokes, particularly positive ones. This provides a strong positive support system for children.

Contracting also has interested many professionals in the schools. TA contracts clearly spell out who will do what, and when. Also, contracts help children assume responsibility for their own progress.

Life scripts and games are readily understood by many, and most people can identify with these concepts and their attendant behavior. In the school setting these concepts can lead the child to avoid assuming responsibility.

One of the limiting factors in this approach is the use of labels to describe behavior. The naive and uninformed can easily use them without understanding the theory behind them.

Professionals using this approach need to be very careful that termination is not premature. Children's understanding of their ego states, life scripts, and games is not developed enough to improve functioning. The implementation of new behaviors is a process, not an event; and the counselor needs to make careful, thorough use of the relearning step.

DEVELOPING YOUR OWN THEORY

Part of every counselor's development is the struggle to formulate a personal theory or point of view. This is your roadmap to the art of counseling. Admittedly, developing your own theory is not easy. You must weigh the positive and negative aspects of each theory you examine. When you consider a theory you should evaluate it in terms of the aspects you like—those that make sense—and the aspects that you do not like—those that do not seem to fit you. It is the equal consideration of both the pro and con that will provide you with a highly personalized appraisal of each theory. Once you have examined a number of theories you are in a position to start developing your own approach. Your theory and approach to counseling will be influenced by a wide array of factors, including your own experiences. Spend some time considering your upbringing: What important lessons did you learn from the significant adults who influenced your growing years? Next, reflect on how you think people develop—both well adjusted and maladjusted. Consider how you think people best manage the problems they face. Finally, think about the young people with whom you work and give some thought to your hopes for them.

All of these thoughts can initially be recorded at random. Once your ideas have been collected, you can tentatively draw them together. As you endeavor to make sense out of the disarray of thoughts, look for common threads—recurring themes that cut across the theories you have examined, your thoughts on how people develop and cope, and your hopes for young people. These common threads become the basis for your counseling theory. Many practitioners believe that theory is fine for the classroom, but not for the "real world." We believe the areas we have asked you to consider represent *you* and what *you* believe about people and the purpose of counseling—whether these ideas and beliefs come together in the orderly manner of theory textbooks or appear as a highly personalized collection of impressions and reflections. In other words, be yourself—while being thoughtfully consistent.

After you have formulated your theory the process of refinement begins. Each counseling experience and each exposure you have to a theoretically based activity or program will provide an opportunity to validate your theory. These experiences should be considered in terms of your likes and dislikes. After you have appraised a particular experience, add this information to the body of knowledge you have already established.

Appraising your didactic and experiential activities is in the interest of establishing congruence and consistency in your theory. *Congruence* means that you act according to your beliefs; *consistency* means that your behavior will not radically change across situations. This is an ongoing process, which builds a theoretical approach that clearly fits you and ultimately benefits your work with children.

SUMMARY

Theory is the foundation of your work with others. Therefore, your effectiveness is in large part dependent on the extent to which you have a clearly articulated theory. This chapter provided an overview of the major theories relevant to the counselor's work in the elementary and middle school. Each theory was described in a uniform manner to enable you to compare its salient points with others' and determine its fit with your own ideas. We covered major techniques because if theory is the base of your professional operation, technique is the method or means by which you interact to provide assistance. Each theory was then discussed in terms of its appropriateness to the elementary and middle school.

We concluded with a section on developing your own theoretical approach. However brief, this is the capstone for the entire chapter because it brings into focus the fundamental reason for examining theory in the first place. We strongly encourage you to think through this chapter. From time to time, review the material and "ground test" it against your developing ideas. Theory development is not a finite process. We urge you to take your time—indeed, a lifetime—in this pursuit.

REVIEW

1. What is the relationship between theory and your personal style of working with children?
2. How are theory and technique related?
3. Give several reasons why not all theories are appropriate for working with children.
4. How does the general process of counseling presented in this chapter provide a structure for you in your counseling?
5. Select the two theories that make the best sense to you, and then describe the features you find most appealing.
6. Which theory did you find least meaningful? What were the aspects that you disliked the most?
7. What do you see as the primary value of developing your own theory?

REFERENCES

Berne, E. (1964). *Games people play: The psychology of human relationships.* New York: Grove Press.

Berne, E. (1966). *Principles of group treatment.* New York: Oxford University Press.

Blackman, G. J., & Silberman, A. (1980). *Modification of child and adolescent behavior* (3rd ed.). Belmont, CA: Wadsworth.

Blocher, D. (1974). *Developmental counseling* (2nd ed.). New York: Ronald Press.

Brammer, L. (1988). *The helping relationship: Process and skills.* (4th ed.). Englewood Cliffs, NJ: Prentice-Hall.

Burks, H., & Stefflre, B. (1978). *Theories of counseling* (3rd ed.). New York: McGraw-Hill.

Carkhuff, R. (1987). *The art of helping* (6th ed.). Amherst, MA: HRD Press.

Christensen, O. C. (Ed.). (1983). *Adlerian family counseling.* Minneapolis, MN: Educational Media Corp.

Corey, G. (1986). *Theory and practice of counseling and psychotherapy* (3rd ed.). Monterey, CA: Brooks/Cole.

Corsini, R. (Ed.). (1984). *Current psychotherapies* (3rd ed.). Itasca, IL: Peacock.

Dinkmeyer, D., Sr., & Dinkmeyer, D., Jr. (1982). *Developing understanding of self and others.* Circle Pines, MN: American Guidance Services.

Dinkmeyer, D., Sr., & McKay, G. (1976). *Systematic training for effective parenting.* Circle Pines, MN: American Guidance Services.

Dinkmeyer, D., Sr., McKay, G., & Dinkmeyer, D., Jr. (1980). *Systematic training for effective teaching.* Circle Pines, MN: American Guidance Services.

Dinkmeyer, D. C., Sr., Pew, W. L., & Dinkmeyer, D. C., Jr. (1979). *Adlerian counseling and psychotherapy.* Monterey, CA: Brooks/Cole.

Dreikurs, R., Corsini, R., Lowe, R., & Sontegard, M. (Eds.). (1959). *Adlerian family counseling: A manual for counseling centers.* Eugene, OR: University Press.

Dreikurs, R., & Grey, L. (1968). *Logical consequences: A new approach to discipline.* New York: Hawthorn.

Dreikurs, R., & Soltz, V. (1964). *Children: The challenge.* New York: Hawthorn.

Dusay, J., & Dusay, K. (1984). Transactional analysis. In R. Corsini (Ed.), *Current psychotherapies* (3rd ed.) (pp. 392–446). Itasca, IL: Peacock.

Ellis, A. (1962). *Reason and emotion in psychotherapy.* Secaucus, NJ: Lyle Stuart.

Ellis, A. (1973). *Humanistic psychotherapy.* New York: McGraw-Hill.

Ellis, A. (1979). The theory of rational emotive therapy. In A. Ellis & J. Whiteley (Eds.), *Theoretical and empirical foundations of rational emotive therapy* (pp. 33–60). Monterey, CA: Brooks/Cole.

George, R., & Cristiani, T. (1990). *Counseling theory and practice* (3rd ed.). Englewood Cliffs, NJ: Prentice-Hall.

Gilliland, B. E., James, R. K., & Bowman, J. T. (1989). *Theories and strategies in counseling and psychotherapy* (2nd ed.). Englewood Cliffs, NJ: Prentice-Hall.

Glasser, W. (1965). *Reality therapy: A new approach to psychiatry.* New York: Harper & Row.

Glasser, W. (1969). *Schools without failure.* New York: Harper & Row.

Glasser, W. (1972). *The identity society.* New York: Harper & Row.

Glasser, W. (1984). Reality therapy. In R. Corsini (Ed.), *Current psychotherapies* (3rd ed.) (pp. 320–353). Itasca, IL: Peacock.

Glasser, W. (1986). *Control theory in the classroom.* New York: Harper & Row.

Harris, T. (1969). *I'm OK—You're OK.* New York: Harper & Row.

Krumboltz, J. D., & Krumboltz, H. B. (1972). *Changing children's behavior.* Englewood Cliffs, NJ: Prentice-Hall.

Krumboltz, J. D., & Thoreson, C. E. (1976). *Counseling methods.* New York: Holt.

Maslow, A. (1970). *Motivation and personality* (Rev. ed.). New York: Harper & Row.

Maultsby, M. C., Jr. (1984). *Rational behavior therapy.* Englewood Cliffs, NJ: Prentice-Hall.

Patterson, C. H. (1980). *Theories of counseling and psychotherapy* (3rd ed.). New York: Harper & Row.

Patterson, G. R., & Gullion, M. E. (1968). *Living with children: New methods for parents and teachers.* Champaign, IL: Research Press.

Rogers, C. R. (1942). *Counseling and psychotherapy.* Boston: Houghton Mifflin.

Rogers, C. R. (1951). *Client-centered therapy.* Boston: Houghton Mifflin.

Skinner, B. F. (1953). *Science and behavior.* New York: Macmillan.

Tosi, D. (1974). *Youth toward personal growth: A rational-emotive approach.* Columbus, OH: Charles Merrill.

Tosi, D., Leclair, S., Peters, H., & Murphy, M. (1987). *Theories and applications of counseling: Systems and techniques of counseling and psychotherapy.* Springfield, IL: Charles C. Thomas.

Watson, D. L., & Tharp, R. G. (1981). *Self-directed behavior: Self-modification for personal adjustment* (3rd ed.). Monterey, CA: Brooks/Cole.

Watson, J. B. (1930). *Behaviorism* (Rev. ed.). New York: Norton.

Woollams, S., & Brown, M. (1979). *TA: The total handbook of transactional analysis.* Englewood Cliffs, NJ: Prentice-Hall.

chapter **5**

Child Assessment

INTRODUCTION

Elementary counselors are less involved in testing now than they had been. However, this is still an area that deserves attention. Some school districts are either eliminating standardized testing or restricting its use, due to abuse over the past several decades. Testing has been used to label children, compare one school district with another, and inappropriately evaluate instruction. We do not intend to critique the past uses and misuses of testing, but to discuss its appropriate use, the counselor's role in testing, the domains or types of tests, cultural bias, considerations in organizing a testing program, and methods of presenting test data. The communication of test results is most important, since presentation and interpretation of test data to students, parents, and teachers is the meaningful result of any assessment. Testing and assessment in the present-day school setting are best left to the school psychologist, who undertakes special assessments, and to the classroom teacher, who takes on the more contemporary learning and achievement assessments demonstrated through such techniques as writing samples and portfolios.

THE USE OF TESTS IN SCHOOLS

Testing in schools has been practiced for approximately the past 40 years. The focus of testing generally has been to (1) assist teachers in planning learning activities for groups of young people; (2) enable teachers to individualize instruction more effectively; (3) determine individual or group differences in performance; (4) measure the progress of individuals or groups of young people; (5) diagnose learning or behavioral difficulties that young people are experiencing and assist in their placement in special programs; (6) verify or refute the observations of school personnel; and (7) promote greater self-understanding on the part of young people (Nelson, 1973). Although all these purposes may be valid under particular circumstances, caution must be exercised to prevent young people from becoming labeled as a result of an assessment procedure.

First, test data can help teachers devise learning activities by assessing the performance levels of children in classrooms or in entire grade levels within a school district. By determining young people's level of mastery on an achievement test, teachers can gain a better sense of those subjects needing additional emphasis.

Second, by reviewing individual performance on an achievement test, teachers can determine the needs of particular students and thereby adapt learning activities to meet those needs. Here the test is used for diagnostic purposes, focusing on levels of mastery.

The third use is to assess the differences between groups of young people. This use is known as *disaggregating* the data, or breaking them down by subgroups, such as gender, race, ethnic background, or class. This process not only provides comparisons among groups, but it also determines whether the various groups are performing at the desired level. If one group is not performing as well as others, then remedial attention is in order.

Fourth, the comparison of an individual or group performance across time is a means of determining the degree of change that has taken place. Achievement tests are aimed at assessing the amount of growth or learning that has taken place over a period of time, usually from one school year to the next. In counseling and guidance situations, the change in a personal characteristic (e.g., self-esteem) may be measured.

Fifth, diagnosis of learning or behavioral problems in young people who are being considered for special education placement is one of the most common and meaningful uses of tests in schools. This assessment will likely be undertaken by the school psychologist, with minor assistance from the counselor.

Working with young people, counselors or teachers form opinions based on information provided by others or through direct observation. A sixth valuable use of testing is to validate or refute this information.

Seventh, testing can be used to help young people increase their understanding of themselves. All types of assessment information, both formal and informal, can be used in this area. The intent is to present information to young people and use it to help them gain a more realistic view of themselves. Here, testing can be helpful when working with children who have a faulty self-view and/or need a boost to their self-assessment. Young people or their parents, who may have an unrealistic perception of certain capabilities, may gain a more realistic view through the presentation of test data.

Regardless of the particular use of a test in the school, the overall intent should be to acquire information that will enable young people to function more effectively. Therefore, effort should always be made to determine how this information will directly benefit the young people who are being assessed. If this cannot be done, the purpose for testing should be reconsidered—a task that may be difficult when testing is entrenched in the school. Most members of the school staff tend to go along with the process without considering its cost in time and dollars.

THE COUNSELOR'S ROLE IN TESTING

Your role in testing will vary with the nature of the program. You may be an administrator, interpreter, and/or consultant. As an administrator, you may be responsible for designing the program; coordinating the efforts to select the tests (which could be either a committee effort or administrative decision); ordering the tests and arranging for scoring; organizing the testing sessions (this includes providing proctors, site selection, and implementing the testing process); and arranging for the receipt and dissemination of results.

As an interpreter, you may provide information directly to students, parents, or teachers, individually or in groups. Working with individuals involves providing an interpretation to the child or a significant adult. Testing information disseminated in groups is best presented to teachers, parents, or older children—those of intermediate or middle school age—because they will have a greater likelihood of understanding the information. This understanding should not be assumed as a given, since young people and adults vary widely in their ability to comprehend test results. Group interpretation will provide general information to the group so that the individuals in attendance can make sense of the specific data on a particular child. All who are affected by the results of testing should be given an opportunity to receive, in a comprehensible manner, the information provided by the assessment.

As a consultant, your role will be somewhat instructional in nature, providing consultation regarding the meaning of the results to school staff who meet with students or parents. Staff are also given techniques for presenting the data to young people or their parents. (Note that school personnel—except special education teachers and school psychologists—do not routinely receive training on testing and data interpretation. Therefore, you would be among the three most testing-literate professionals in the school.)

TYPES OF TESTS

Tests are most commonly classified in the following categories: achievement tests, aptitude tests, intelligence tests, interest inventories, and personality tests or measures of personal characteristics (Belkin, 1981; Lewis, Hayes, & Lewis, 1986). The latter category should include informal inventories and other data collection devices. Although each of these domains of testing is discussed, we emphasize achievement tests as standardized instruments and informal inventories as devices to collect personalized information. The reason for this emphasis is that achievement tests are the most frequently used in elementary and middle schools, and informal inventories have value in adding to your volume of information about the young people you counsel.

Achievement Tests

These assess the knowledge or skills acquired as a result of systematic input, such as classroom instruction. It is not uncommon for counselors to assume responsibility for managing the achievement testing program. Most frequently the instruments used to measure achievement are general tests designed to appraise a variety of areas, such as vocabulary, math, reading, language, and social studies. Tests frequently used for this purpose are the *Iowa Test of Basic Skills,* the *SRA Achievement Series, California Achievement Tests,* and the *Metropolitan Achievement Tests.* All are classified as general achievement batteries that cover the school-grade span from kindergarten through twelfth grade (Anastasi, 1988). Other achievement tests are single-subject instruments used to measure children's performance in a particular area. These tests often are used to determine placement in an academic program and therefore are regarded as diagnostic or prognostic. An example would be an algebra screening test, used to determine if students will be admitted to algebra class in the eighth grade. Some single-subject tests are the *Orleans-Hanna Algebra Prognosis Test, Gates-McGinitie Reading Tests, Modern Language Aptitude Test* (Anastasi, 1988).

Achievement-test scores are frequently reported in terms of percentiles, with the reference point being a national sample. Local norms may also be obtained for many of these instruments. On occasion scores are reported in raw score terms (number of correct answers) or grade- or age-level scores. Each of these representational systems should be treated with care because of the confusion that may result from relating data presented in these forms. In particular, raw score data cannot be adequately interpreted because there is no reference point or comparison group. The only way to interpret raw scores is in relation to the total number of possible correct answers—which is a severe limitation. Grade-level scores are confusing because many individuals want to compare a student's performance to the grade-level number. For example, if a third-grader scores at the fourth-grade/fifth-month level on a vocabulary test, does this mean that the child has a vocabulary of a fourth-grader in the middle of the year? In reality, the third-grader is performing at the fourth grade/fifth month compared to third graders. (See "Methods of Presenting Test Data" on page 113 for more information.)

There are a number of ways in which you will employ tests in your work with young people, teachers, or parents.

1. Compare the performance of an individual over a span of time, usually from one year to the next. Through this comparison the teacher, parent, or counselor may gain some sense of the progress the young person is making in school-based knowledge. General-achievement test batteries are usually given each year. If distinct variations exist from one year to the next, further investigation should be undertaken to determine what has prompted the change in achievement levels.

2. Identify young people with learning or behavioral difficulties.

3. Provide information that may help young people better understand their strengths and weaknesses. For example: A third-grader, from all appearances a good student, thought she was "no good" at math. Upon taking an achievement test it was discovered that her highest score was in math. When this was pointed out to her she changed her self-perception and became a much better math student.

4. "Ground" either the teacher's or your own observations of young people and their academic behavior in the classroom. This is of great value when a teacher has a biased opinion of a young person.

The other uses of achievement tests that may involve you as the counselor are associated with group data. Your role in interpreting these data usually entails helping teachers, administrators, or school board members understand the relationship between the performance of a local group (e.g., classroom or school district) or subgroup (e.g., minorities or socioeconomic classes) and larger groups (districtwide, state, or national samples). This involves relating average or typical performance of the group under consideration to the larger group and explaining the differences in performance. But be advised: Achievement tests can never measure exactly the performance of a group or individual because the tests are designed to cover what is assumed to be general knowledge taught at a given grade level. What is taught might be similar to the test, but in all likelihood will only parallel the content of the test. Also, the time of year in which the test is given will influence performance because of the amount of material to which test-takers have been exposed.

In summary, achievement tests can provide meaningful information in your work with young people, teachers, and parents. But, like any source of information, achievement tests are imperfect and should always be approached with caution.

Aptitude Tests

Aptitude assessment measures both intelligence and special abilities, such as music, art, and general creativity. We will treat intelligence and aptitude separately. Aptitude is regarded as clearly defined areas of ability that can be isolated through specific appraisal techniques (Anastasi, 1988). Further, it is defined as the potential to perform in a given area or acquire learning or skill in a specific area (Gibson & Mitchell, 1990). Aptitude tests exist in two forms—general aptitude batteries and specific aptitude tests—measuring specific areas such as mechanical ability or creativity. At the elementary school level, such tests are rarely used because of the immaturity of the children. At the middle school level aptitude tests are used selectively, usually not before eighth grade.

The *Differential Aptitude Test,* used in the middle school, provides scores in eight areas: verbal reasoning, numerical ability, abstract reasoning, clerical speed and accuracy, mechanical reasoning, space relations, spelling, and language usage. This instrument has been used to help students plan their high school curriculum. (A career planning questionnaire is also available.) Both percentile and stanine scores are provided. (Stanine scores range from 1 to 9, with a mean of 5 and a standard deviation of 2.) The combination of verbal reasoning and numerical ability provides a measure of scholastic aptitude, or potential to succeed in academic subjects.

The only other area of aptitude testing relevant to the elementary and middle school is creativity assessment. The *Creativity Tests for Children* and The *Torrance Tests of Creative Thinking* are two appropriate instruments (Anastasi, 1988). The *Creativity Tests for Children* consist of five verbal and five figural tests geared to grades 4 through 6. The *Torrance Tests of Creative Thinking* consist of seven verbal tests and three pictorial tests. These tests are said to be appropriate for kindergartners through graduate students. In lower grades—K–3—the tests are administered verbally and individually. Subsequent editions added instruments called *Thinking Creatively with Sounds and Words,* administered through the used of recorded instructions; and *Thinking Creatively in Action and Movement,* designed for preschool children. Although both of these batteries are interesting and may stimulate consideration of the creative talents in a young person, the technical data—primarily validity data—appear to be lacking. Therefore, we do not clearly know *what* is being measured, and any results of testing in this area should be treated cautiously.

Although aptitude testing is meaningful with later adolescents and adults, the utility of testing aptitude in young people below high school age is questionable. At best, tests in this area may provide a basis for a discussion of abilities of children and young adolescents in particular areas.

Intelligence Tests

These instruments have been said to measure a young person's ability to successfully compete academically. They are largely verbal, and students who perform well in school ostensibly will also perform well on such tests. Tests are either group or individual, with the former most frequently used in the schools. More selective use is made of individual intelligence tests.

Group Tests.   Group measures yield a verbal, nonverbal, and total score. These scores are reported in terms of percentiles or standard scores. The three most frequently used group measures of intelligence are the *Otis-Lennon School Ability Test,* the *Cognitive Abilities Test,* and the *School and College Ability Tests.* These batteries are multilevel, covering a broad range of grade levels. Scores are usually reported in terms of a deviation IQ and some other standard system. In addition, norms are provided to compare a young person's performance with others; percentiles also are reported for this comparison.

The *Otis-Lennon School Ability Test* covers grades 1 through 12 and consists of three parts: Classification, Analogies, and Omnibus. The first two are self-explanatory. The third, Omnibus, measures the ability to follow directions, perform quantitative reasoning, and comprehend written material. This instrument is largely verbal in nature.

The *Cognitive Abilities Test* has two forms: primary (grades K–3) and multilevel (grades 3–12). The latter consists of nine subtests distributed across three batteries: verbal, quantitative, and nonverbal. The verbal and quantitative batteries best predict school performance. The nonverbal battery may not predict school achievement as well as the other two, but a comparison of all three scores can yield meaningful information for students who do not typically function well in school.

The *School and College Ability Tests* cover grades 3.5 through 12.9, and yield a verbal, quantitative, and total score. The verbal score is based on an analogies test, while the quantitative test is based on number relations and geometry. The total score is a combination of the verbal and quantitative scores.

Individual Tests.   Currently there are three basic individual measures of intelligence: the *Stanford-Binet,* the *Wechsler* scales, and the *Kaufman Assessment Battery for Children* (KABC). Virtually all intelligence tests are descendants of the Stanford-Binet. It is now in its fourth and most far-reaching revision. Items have been updated, and the verbal orientation of the earlier forms has been reduced. There is greater emphasis on quantitative, spatial, and memory activities. As with previous forms, the current edition covers a broad age spectrum, from age two to adult. The *Stanford-Binet* has been criticized for its insufficient ceiling—that is, a limited number of tests tasks for above-average-functioning older adolescents and adults. An individual's score is reported in terms of standard age scores, which are converted into deviation IQ scores with a mean of 100 and a standard deviation of 16 (*Stanford-Binet Intelligence Scale,* 1986).

In 1939 David Wechsler created his first instrument, called the *Wechsler-Bellevue Intelligence Scale*. This was an adult scale designed to clinically test mental patients. In 1949 the *Wechsler Intelligence Scale for Children* (WISC) was created as a downward extension of the initial scale. The WISC was designed to cover ages 6 to 16. This instrument was first revised in 1974. In 1991 it was again revised and retitled *WISC-III*. The *Wechsler Preschool and Primary Scale of Intelligence* (WPPSI) covers ages 4 to 6 1/2. All tests include a verbal and performance battery, each with five regular and at least one alternate test. The verbal and performance tests are alternated to balance the verbal and nonverbal skills. Scores are reported in terms of each subtest, which has a mean of 10 and a standard deviation of 2, and a verbal, performance, and full-scale score, each of which has a mean of 100 and a standard deviation of 15. Percentile scores also are available. The Wechsler scales, particularly the WISC-III, are frequently used to screen young people for placement in special education.

The most recent entry into the individual intelligence testing field is the *Kaufman Assessment Battery for Children* (KABC) (Kaufman & Kaufman, 1983). This test came about as a result of Alan Kaufman's extensive work with the Weschler scales. Kaufman's instrument yields four global scales, each of which has a mean of 100 and a standard deviation of 15. The global scales are sequential processing, simultaneous processing, mental processing (a combination of sequential and simultaneous processing scales), and achievement. There is also a nonverbal scale for hearing-impaired and speech- and language-deficient young people. There are ten subtests in the mental processing scales, and six achievement subtests. This instrument is designed for subjects between the ages of 2 1/2 and 12 1/2 years. Although KABC is a new instrument relative to its competitors, it has gained quick acceptance.

A great deal of criticism has been directed toward intelligence testing as reflecting a white, middle-class bias. Attempts have been made in various parts of the country to ban these tests. It is true that the verbal emphasis might place members of some cultures at a disadvantage. However, since most schools in the United States are largely white and middle-class in their constituency, the instruments can be helpful in determining areas of functioning that may relate to school performance. Also, if the test administrator is attentive to a student's manner of approaching the test, valuable information can be gained about that student's problem-solving skills.

Interest Measures

The measurement of interests has been stimulated by educational and career counseling (Anastasi, 1988). Here, assessment is designed to cluster the interests of a young person into convenient categories (e.g., school subjects or career families). As with aptitude testing, interest measurement is limited in the elementary and middle school years to broad categories of interests because young people at these grade levels are not experienced enough to have developed crystallized interest patterns. Therefore, this section focuses on general interest tests appropriate to the intermediate and middle school grades.

Instruments designed to measure interests rely on self-reporting, which means they elicit the young person's subjective responses to questions about such areas as academics or work activities. In either case the responses are prone to self-censoring, or what is called a socially acceptable response set: Students answer as they think they should, or in a manner that will make their overall score appear a certain way. The latter may be unintentional. In spite of this limitation, self-report inventories can yield useful information about the young person's perceptions of a particular area.

The interest inventory used in the elementary and middle school levels is the *Kuder General Interest Survey,* which is appropriate for sixth-graders. This instrument is a downward adaptation of the *Kuder Preference Record*—the original interest inventory designed by G. F. Kuder. The ten areas addressed by the *Kuder General Interest Survey* are outdoor, mechanical, computational, scientific, persuasive, artistic, literary, musical, social service, and clerical.

Several other interest surveys claim to be appropriate for middle school students, particularly eighth-graders. Unfortunately, the scores yielded by these instruments are not very stable, as the interest profiles of young people in the upper elementary and middle school grades tend to be rather flat. Students also lack strong positive or negative attitudes about the areas being assessed. This flat profile indicates a lack of exposure to a variety of aspects in the students' environment.

Measures of Personal Characteristics

Included here are personality measures that have been broadly described by Thorndike and Hagen (1977) as assessing one or more of the following elements: *temperament* (characteristic affect of the individual), *character* (traits that are valued by society), *adjustment* (intrapersonal and interpersonal adaptation to the surrounding world), *interests* (preferences for particular activities), and *attitudes* (opinions or perceptions about specific ideas, groups of individuals, or social institutions).

Although these instruments can yield some interesting and meaningful information, they should be used with caution. First, most responses are based on the subjective perception of the young person, and can be faked or otherwise skewed. Second, regardless of whether the instrument is a published and standardized measure of some aspect of personality, it still may not measure what it purports to. Third, in the case of informal measures, they may possess both low reliability—consistently measuring a characteristic in the same way—and low validity. All of these concerns should raise caution flags about relying too heavily on the results of these instruments.

Temperament.   The *Children's State-Trait Anxiety Inventory* is given to young people of about 10 to 15 years. Two 20-item scales measure a young person's tendency to become anxious, and measure anxiety as a fleeting emotional state. Since this instrument is based on a long-standing adult version, it uses longitudinal efforts to measure anxiety.

Character.   The *Behavior Rating Profile* is used with young people ages 6 1/2 to 18 1/2. This interesting instrument employs four appraisals: a child self-report form, a teacher-rating form, a parent-rating form, and a classroom sociogram. The teacher and parent forms are ratings of the child. The student form has three scales: home, school, and peer. Standard scores and percentiles are provided for the five ratings and the sociogram. Since young people are evaluated in terms of three aspects of their environment, the instrument is reasonably suited as a measure of character.

Adjustment.   The two most frequently used instruments measuring self-concept are the *Coopersmith Self-Esteem Inventory* and the *Children's Self-Concept Scale.* The school form of the *Coopersmith* is designed for ages 8 to 15. This instrument is probably the best-known and most frequently used measure of self-concept or self-esteem. The inventory provides a self-assessment of young people in terms of general self, social self and peers, school and academics, and home and parents. Normative data are available.

The *Children's Self-Concept Scale* is a global or general measure of self-concept consisting of 80 yes-or-no questions. The instrument purports to be appropriate for grades 3 through 12. In reality it should not be used much beyond the seventh grade because of the language. Although factor analytic studies have been conducted on the instrument and several separate factors have been identified, it is designed to yield a single score. Norms are provided to aid comparison of young people with their peers.

Attitudes.   Assessment here is a difficult proposition at the elementary and middle school level. One instrument that does focus on attitudes of young people from kindergarten to twelfth grade is the *School Attitude Measure.* This scores young peoples' attitudes in five areas: motivations for schooling, academic self-concept (performance based), academic self-concept (reference based), student's sense of control over performance, and student's instructional mastery (Wick & Dolan, 1989). Students are asked to respond to questions presented in a four-point likert-type format, from "never agree" to "always agree."

Another arena for assessing personal characteristics comprises nonstandard, informal inventories that cover all the personal characteristics identified by Thorndike and Hagen (1977). Techniques for collecting data in an informal manner include observation, incomplete sentences, figure drawings, journals/diaries, autobiographical techniques, and sociometric questionnaires.

Observation.   This can be very useful if a few simple guidelines are considered (Gibson & Mitchell, 1990):

1. Observe only one young person at a time to ensure that your focus is not divided or distracted.
2. Identify your purpose in observing and then specify the behavior to be observed.
3. Extend your observation over a period of time so you can collect data sufficiently broad in scope.

4. Observe the young person in a variety of settings to determine variability in the behavior under consideration.

5. Avoid tunnel vision by taking note of the surrounding environment— what are other young people doing? What is taking place that relates to the behavior under consideration?

6. Compare the observation data with other sources of data, both from instruments and other observers.

7. Observe the young person in good as well as bad times.

Broader-based data can be obtained when young people are observed in situations where they are demonstrating effective behavior. Overall, observation data can meaningfully supplement other data that have been obtained from standardized instruments and other sources.

Incomplete Sentences*.*   These are appropriate from third grade to adulthood. This simple technique uses sentences that are missing important parts, which the young person is called upon to complete (e.g., "I like school because _____ "). Take care to provide a balance between positive and negative items, and between items that are of interest and those that may be used as fillers. Further, inventories should be relatively short, not exceeding ten items. Information received from self-reports should be treated as transitory—particularly with children—because it is subject to fluctuation.

Artwork and Drawings.   These have been used in personality assessment for some time. Results are regarded as clinical information and are therefore subject to all the cautions surrounding individualized data, whose scoring criteria usually have low validity. At best, figure drawings should be treated as tentative sources of information, and only the most obvious revelations should be considered meaningful (e.g., a young boy leaves himself out of a drawing of his family and draws his baby brother larger than other siblings). A frequently used drawing test is the *Goodenough-Harris Drawing Test,* wherein a child is asked to draw a picture of a man, then a woman, and then him- or herself. The original intent of this assessment was to appraise intelligence in a nonverbal manner. Subsequently, however, efforts have been made to use drawing tests as clinical measures of personality. Use with caution.

Diaries/Journals and Autobiographical Data.   These are taken together as a collection of observations or reactions that young people make across a period of time. This technique can be most useful when young people are encouraged to describe events rather than evaluate them. If judgment is avoided, you can gain a sense of how young people view the events taking place around them, and their place in these events. This information will have the greatest meaning if young people are willing participants. If they view the activity as laborious, then the information will be skewed from the beginning and have limited value. Another limitation of this technique is timing. If there is a distinct passage of time between the occurrence and recording of an event, the information will be more subjective and blurred by memory than if it were collected immediately after the event.

Sociometric Techniques.   These were created by J. L. Moreno in the 1930s (Moreno, 1953). A questionnaire is used to collect information that describes young peoples' relationships in a group such as a classroom. This is not to say that individuals cannot be isolated in the sociogram or chart of the results. It simply means that the broad purpose of a sociogram is to provide a picture of the group based on the dimensions identified in the questions. In its most basic form a sociometric questionnaire lists several questions that all the young people in a group are asked to answer. Typically, sociometric questions ask students to identify a number of group members (usually about three) as individuals with whom they would like to work on a project or whom they like the most. On occasion young people are asked to identify individuals (usually no set number is specified) that they do not like or with whom they would not like to work on a class project. Scores on this questionnaire are most easily tabulated on a grid of the classroom. Once the information is summarized it can be plotted on a scatter diagram to describe the group as a whole. This information can be useful in examining relationships within the group. Also, some significant correlations have been found between sociometric status and self-concept (Bradley & Newhouse, 1974).

Informal techniques of collecting assessment data are just that—informal. Therefore, only limited meaning can be attached to this information. Data of this sort should be regarded as a tentative source of information, which has its greatest meaning when it seems to corroborate information received from other sources.

Summary

The material presented in this section on types of tests is not intended to provide you with a recipe for your testing program or a list of the best instruments to use in particular situations. Moreover, it is intended to provide you with a general understanding of the domains of testing and give some examples of measure used in each of these areas. The section of this chapter on organizing a testing program should prove helpful in selecting instruments. Probably the greatest caution is to limit your testing for specific purposes; keep in mind that your endeavor is to collect additional information that will help you or other adults in your ongoing work with young people. Finally, efforts should be made to avoid collecting data through several techniques that overlap with one another.

CULTURAL BIAS IN TESTING

As Cronbach (1990) has indicated, young people from different cultures or subcultures within society may not perform as well as members of the traditional white middle class in some testing situations. The unique characteristics of culture influence the way in which people function. Young people growing up in an environment that is different from the mainstream may be at a disadvantage in a testing situation or may respond in a less predictable manner. The resultant bias that is reflected in testing is a function of a number of different considerations, namely, language skill or mastery; approach to test tasks, response time; and desire to compete (Cronbach, 1990). If we consider each item separately we may be able to shed some light on broad cultural differences and how these differences affect young people's performance.

First, a knowledge of English is extremely important, because most standardized tests are highly verbal in content.

Second, one's approach or mind-set to a testing activity may be culturally influenced. Some cultures place no importance on completing a test. Also, the approach to the task may seem unconventional to the thinking of test designers from traditional Western cultures.

Third, the cultural conception of time may not be the same as that of mainstream Western culture. You are probably familiar with students who work very slowly and deliberately on test questions. They may have performed quite well on the items attempted, but because the test was timed they may not have completed it. Their score would be lower than the accuracy of their responses would have led you to believe. In this situation the test was speeded in some way. The issue of time can also be a function of a culture in that some cultural groups do not regard time as much of an issue as Western cultural groups do.

Fourth, in a competitive testing environment, some cultural groups will not respond with the same commitment as young people from traditional Western cultures. Native Americans, for example, may feel that to distinguish oneself over one's peers is disrespectful. If young people of certain cultural groups feel they are separating themselves from the group, they may deliberately misrepresent their performance.

The intent of this brief section on cultural bias is to sensitize you to the fact that young people from certain cultural groups may not perform well on some tests. This is due to cultural reasons, and not lack of ability. Hence, decisions regarding placement or grouping should be made only after a thorough investigation of the circumstance that led to the level of tested performance.

ORGANIZING A TESTING PROGRAM

Kubiszyn and Borich (1990) have enumerated five steps in organizing a testing program. We have edited and augmented this list, providing a six-step process.

1. What is the purpose of testing in this school district? The testing program begins with an analysis of how the school district can benefit from the use of tests. The likely starting point is to consider the philosophy of the district, and then the needs of the district for information that can be provided through testing. Next, the procedures used in screening and identifying young people for inclusion

in various programs need to be reviewed. Once these efforts have taken place you will have a general frame of reference for testing needs of the school district.

2. How will these purposes be fulfilled by the testing program? What kinds of information are needed to meet the district's purposes? A review of "The Use of Tests in Schools" (pp. 100–101) will be helpful in matching instruments to the purposes of the school district (e.g., if the school board is intent on measuring progress of groups of students from one year to the next, a multilevel achievement battery covering a broad range of grade levels will require consideration).

3. The total nature of the program must be envisioned, including frequency and timing of tests. After you have worked through each of the purposes of testing, you will delineate the categories of tests that need to be included. Also, to provide the scope of the program, you will need to develop a master plan for testing by grade level and time of year. Where multiple tests are used at the same grade level, the issue of timing must be considered. Similarly, the time of year when a test is administered is a function of the ultimate use of the results. This master plan should at least be in draft form before you select the instruments. Admittedly, you may need to adjust your time line based on the necessary processing time once the instruments have been administered.

4. The available tests must be evaluated, and appropriate ones selected. This important step involves the time-consuming task of scrutinizing a large number of instruments, some of which may be redundant or of questionable value. Ideally, this step should be a committee effort, involving a sample of all those affected by the testing program—teachers, school psychologists, administrators, special teachers, and parents. Although this group would vary in level of knowledge about testing, their input could be helpful, and each represents a body of others who will have a vested interest in the program.

Wherever possible, avoid unnecessary duplication of tests. It is important that testing meet the minimal requirements set forth by the purposes and needs; avoid overtesting. Finally, take care to eliminate cultural bias in testing and avoid labeling.

5. Establish a district-wide schedule for testing. This step is the natural culmination of the preceding. Purpose, balance of testing, and timely availability of the results should dictate the master schedule. A thorough review of the school calendar is necessary to fit in the tests to be administered. Also, it may be helpful to discuss with classroom teachers the testing plan to ferret out any small, easily overlooked issues that could interfere with creating the best con-ditions for administering the instruments.

6. Construct the means of disseminating the test results. Here, you and possibly the school psychologist can be most helpful to the school district because of your collective expertise in understanding test results and relating them to teachers, parents, and students. Your task becomes twofold: helping teachers understand and communicate results to parents and students, and summarizing the group data to assist the administration and school board in making meaningful use of the results. The first of these issues will be addressed in the next section. The second issue is the essential one of summarizing the comparative norms

provided by the various testing companies and highlighting particular elements of the data that seem most meaningful.

Although developing a district-wide testing program is seemingly a cut-and-dried sequential process, address each step with care to ensure that issues have been properly considered. Slow, methodical planning will surely prevent unforeseen problems.

METHODS OF PRESENTING TEST DATA

Ironically, this area—the most important part of the process—has received the least attention. The means of communicating tests results is determined by *what* data are presented, to *whom* you present information, and *how* you communicate the results.

The *what* of test interpretation is easiest to define: Communicate only what the person receiving the information wants or can handle. For example, you might ask parents, What would you like to know about your child's test results? Your aim here is to discover the level of knowledge and sophistication of those receiving the results. Once you have gained a sense of their knowledge and interest, you can shape the information to provide them with a meaningful interpretation. However, you must guard against overloading the recipients with meaningless information.

The kind and amount of information to provide will be determined by *to whom* you are providing the data. Members of the administration—building principal, district office, or school board—will have particular interests in group data and likely will want information that enables comparisons between schools, school districts, or the district and state and national norm groups. By contrast, parents may want to know how their child is performing compared to others at the same grade level or what their child's relative strengths and weaknesses are. Teachers may want to know how their class is performing in math compared to other classes in the school or district, as well as the general strengths and weaknesses of their class. Finally, teachers may want to know specifics about the performance of a particular student. The student may want to know, What do I do best? or Will I pass the fourth grade? Each of the these groups has specific needs, and you will need to tailor your information accordingly.

How you communicate test results is a function of the time you have to provide the interpretation, to whom you are providing it, and your style of interpreting. Goldman (1971) has presented four methods of interpreting test data (p. 412).

1. Involve the recipients. Ask them what they would like to know or what the results might mean to them. In this case you will disseminate the data based on the recipients' level of understanding.
2. Report only the scores. Ask the recipient to react to the information provided. In this case, both you and the recipient are sharing responsibility for the discussion of test results—you provide the parameters

of the interpretation by the score data you present, and the recipient takes over to raise issues he or she wants addressed.

3. Reduce the recipient's participation. Present the data with an emphasis on the meaning or implications of the test results. Here the recipient's role is passive because he or she is simply provided information and asked if there are any questions.

4. Make recommendations to the recipient based on your interpretation of the results. Here the recipient becomes a passive participant. This form of interpretation has similarities to some Individualized Education Plan (IEP) staffings that you might have attended, where parents are told their children's test results and precisely what will happen as a result of this testing. We do not endorse this method.

Which methods you use is entirely up to you. The first two are relatively time-consuming because they involve the recipient to a greater extent. Correspondingly, the latter two are more expeditious because you assume more control over the dialogue. Thus, there is likely a greater recipient understanding of the assessment in the first two methods and the last two are much quicker. Actually, in moving from method 1 to method 4, recipient participation and understanding of the total test results are likely reduced; also, the interpretation time is drastically reduced. The method you choose may be a function of the person to whom you are providing the interpretation or your perception of how much information people can handle and the role you see yourself taking in the interpretive process. We do not recommend the fourth method because young people are the ones most affected by the test results and, therefore, in their interest, whoever receives the results has the right to as much information as they can meaningfully use on behalf of the young person.

The interpretation of test data is much like any counseling process because it is designed to enhance decision making on the part of young people, regardless of who receives the data. Always keep in mind that the *meaningful* transmission of information is of the greatest importance.

SUMMARY

This chapter acquainted you with the field of testing as it relates to the school setting and your role in it. Although the nature of testing in the schools is changing with the advent of newer forms of assessment, you will likely continue to have some responsibility. We have endeavored to highlight your involvement as it relates to the typical educational activity. You will most frequently be involved in the organization and management of the general achievement testing program and may have responsibility for the administration and use of particular instru-ments related to career exploration and personal characteristics. We believe that your fundamental role will lie in the interpretation of test data to the various recipients of this information. Most notably, you will need to help teachers in their efforts to communicate results to parents. Similarly, you will need to develop skill in transmitting results to children, parents, teachers, and administrators. We have outlined several methods to interpret test data and have provided a basis for the use of each. Finally, we provided caveats regarding the misuse of tests and highlighted the meaningful use of these data collection devices. Most important, we emphasized the use of tests to benefit young people and to supplement their growth in the educational environment.

REVIEW

1. Differentiate between the use of tests to meet the needs of school districts, teachers, and students.
2. Identify the basic issues of cultural bias in testing.
3. What are the limitations of using interest inventories at the elementary level?
4. Describe two ways that counselors can assist teachers in the use of tests in the classroom.
5. Describe the counselor's unique role in testing.
6. Outline the pitfalls of measuring personal characteristics.
7. Identify the step that you regard as the most important in organizing a testing program. Indicate why this step is of particular importance.
8. Discuss the pros and cons of each method of presenting test data.

REFERENCES

Anastasi, A. (1988). *Psychological testing* (6th ed.). New York: Macmillan.

Belkin, G. S. (1981). *Practical counseling in the schools.* Dubuque, IA: William C. Brown.

Bradley, F. O., & Newhouse, R. C. (1974). Sociometric choice and self perception of upper elementary school children. *Psychology in the Schools, 12*(2), 219-222.

Cole, N. S., & Moss, P. A. (1989). Bias in test use. In R. L. Line (Ed.), *Educational measurement* (3rd ed.) (pp. 201-220). New York: American Council on Education & Macmillan.

Cronbach, L. J. (1990). *Essentials of psychological testing* (5th ed.). New York: Harper & Row.

Gibson, R. L., & Mitchell, M. H. (1990). *Introduction to counseling and guidance* (3rd ed.). New York: Macmillan.

Goldman, L. (1971). *Using tests in counseling* (2nd ed.). New York: Appleton-Century-Crofts.

Kaufman, A., & Kaufman, N. (1983). *KABC: Kaufman Assessment Battery for Children.* Circle Pines, MN: American Guidance Services.

Kubiszyn, T., & Borich, G. (1990). *Educational testing and measurement: Classroom application and practice* (3rd ed.). Glenview, IL: Scott, Foresman.

Lewis, M. D., Hayes, R. L., & Lewis, J. A. (1986). *An introduction to the counseling profession.* Itasca, IL: Peacock.

Moreno, J. L. (1953). *Who shall survive?—A new approach to the problems of human inner-relations* (Rev. ed.). Beacon Hill, NY: Beacon House.

Nelson, R. C. (1972). *Guidance and counseling in the elementary school.* New York: Holt.

Stanford-Binet Intelligence Scale (1986). *Guide for administration and scoring* (4th ed.). Chicago: Riverside.

Thorndike, R., & Hagen, E. P. (1977). *Measurement and evaluation in psychology and education* (4th ed.). New York: John Wiley.

Wick, J. W., & Dolan, L. J. (1989). *Comprehensive assessment program: School attitude measure.* Chicago: American Testronics.

chapter 6

Play Media in Counseling

OUTLINE

INTRODUCTION

Through the use of play as a medium of communication, you can learn a great deal about children's situations, be in a better position to understand their attitudes, and help them alter their behavior as well as understand their feelings with regard to a particular situation or problem.

The purpose of this chapter is to help you develop an understanding of what play means to a child, and how various play media can be used to counsel children. To define play media, we first define play, then media, and finally we combine the two terms.

DEFINITIONS

Play

In the context of this book, *play* is defined as an activity engaged in by children for the purpose of self-expression and communication. Since young children engage in play more frequently than older children, we have found that the use of play in counseling is more appropriate for younger children. During play, the young child is often exploring, practicing roles, developing skills and relationships, and acting out feelings (Dimick & Huff, 1970). As the child develops better verbal skills, the need to use play as a means of self-expression and communication diminishes. However, until the child has developed highly sophisticated verbal skills, this need continues in varying degrees depending upon age and maturity.

Media

For our purposes, the term *media* is defined as those materials or objects that children use in their play. Frequently these materials or objects are toys. However, a child may prefer to play with a cardboard box or a kitchen pot rather than a commercial toy. The use of various forms of media in play makes it possible for the child to show feelings effectively and communicate behaviors that otherwise might not be realized. It has been noted that adults frequently utilize some form of media in their efforts to communicate. Instead of using toys, they are more likely to use a pencil, coffee cup, eyeglasses, or some other handy object to assist them in their communication efforts. It is clear that using media in counseling with children is an effective way to help them communicate.

Play Media Defined

This is a counseling technique used to enhance and supplement talking to maximize children's self-expression and communication. It is a means to an end in the counseling process and not an end in itself.

PHILOSOPHICAL ASSUMPTIONS

Play is an integral part of a child's life. Through play children strive to explore their innermost thoughts and feelings, as well as test their skills. Using play media in counseling facilitates the child's communication and expression, and therefore assists the counselor in better understanding of and more positive interaction with the child. The following assumptions help to clarify the philosophy of the use of play media in counseling:

1. Play facilitates the child's communication and therefore promotes the expression of thoughts and feelings.
2. Play is a wholesome activity.
3. The child uses play for experimentation and growth in the area of human relationships, as well as for skill development with inanimate objects.
4. Play serves as an expression of the child's relationship to the world.
5. Adults are better able to understand the child's world by relating to the child during play.
6. Play greatly enhances the possibility of developing a meaningful and constructive child/counselor relationship.

Nelson (1966), in commenting on the philosophy of play media, states the following:

The younger elementary school child is only beginning to emerge from the stage wherein all objects are toys, all the time is for play, and work is a construct developed through role playing. While he is being indoctrinated successfully into the concept that his work is schoolwork, he remains a creature who, largely through play, develops his social relations, tests various roles and concepts, and works through his frustrations and concerns. In contrast with his older sibling who can and does verbalize frustrations, love, anger, and acceptance, the younger child acts these feelings. He crashes cars together, he hugs his Mom, he shoots the enemy, and he hands another child a toy. He tends less to talk about his feelings than to live them; he is an activist. (p. 24)

Play media, when used appropriately, can help open the door to the child's world. Keep in mind that the use of play media brings about better communication and expression of feeling on the part of young children. It is not, in and of itself, a philosophy or theory of counseling, and as such is not appropriate to every counseling situation.

THE COUNSELOR/CHILD RELATIONSHIP IN PLAY

Importance of Play

Critical to the use of play media in counseling is the establishment of a good counselor/child relationship. It is important that you be patient and not focus too quickly on specific behaviors that may have been observed previously. You will find yourself feeling many different emotions as you use play media with children. You may find yourself wanting to react to these feelings, some of which may be negative. If the relationship is to develop into a trusting and lasting one, you must practice restraint in responding to feelings that may be perfectly normal, given the situation. Of utmost importance is that you convey unconditional acceptance, and that the child be encouraged to act out and verbalize feelings. Although it may be necessary to impose some limitations, the child must feel unthreatened about expressing words, acts, and feelings during play. While most counseling theorists agree that a good relationship with the client is important, the importance of a strong relationship in the use of play media is even more apparent.

Developing the Relationship

The child's perception that a helpful relationship has been established is critical to the successful use of play media. In discussing child/counselor relationships, Muro and Dinkmeyer (1977) state:

> To work with children as a counselor, you should yourself be psycho-logically healthy, secure, and able to tolerate ambiguity, aggression, and other behaviors that may well deviate from your or your school's value system. The counselor should be young at heart and accept children; yet, you must not react to the youngster as child to child, but as a listening empathic adult who understands that the child may fear the closeness of the relationship. . . . (p. 225)

In addition to being a psychologically healthy, secure, and tolerant individual, you must demonstrate positive attitudes and actions. This is essential if the relationship is to strengthen and allow the child to communicate and express openly, honestly, and without fear. Central to developing a positive relationship is your unconditional positive regard for the child. Not only must you demonstrate this, but the child must perceive it. Otherwise, as is true in many aspects of relationship building, the child will not experience the feelings that come from knowing that he or she is truly accepted. Unconditional positive regard communicates that you care, are interested in the child as a person, and will understand if he or she says or does something that might be unacceptable in another situation. Therefore, it is imperative in the use of play media that you take the time to develop a strong relationship with the child. This can best be done by the counselor who is psychologically strong, likes children, and is able to consistently demonstrate tolerance, understanding, and effective communication.

USING PLAY MEDIA IN THE ELEMENTARY SCHOOL

When to Use Play Media

The use of play is certainly not indicated in all instances. Sometimes, beginning counselors attempt to rely on play as a means of compensating for their inadequacy in one-to-one counseling. Simply stated, play media should be used when the child has difficulty communicating verbally and the use of play will enhance this communication, or when the child has certain feelings that need to be expressed if he or she is to grow as a result of the counseling experience. As Schaefer and O'Connor (1983) point out:

> Since play is the language of the child, play provides a medium for building the essential relationship between the counselor and child. The counselor is able to enter into the child's emotional world as it is freely revealed and acted upon by the child. Play media materials thus facilitate the development of a dynamic living relationship because the child is able to act upon and experience the totality of the immediacy of his or her behavior. The child is not restricted to discussing what happened; rather he or she lives out, in play, a moment of his or her life. The child's play is current, concrete, and specific. (p. 202)

Especially with young children, you should not hesitate to use play media if the child's ability to communicate and express feelings will be inhibited without them. In the final analysis, you must make the decision as to when their use is indicated.

Landreth (1987) states that regardless of the theoretical orientation of the counselor, there are seven objectives in the use of play. However, he cautions that the primary objective of play is not to solve problems but to help the child grow. Landreth lists the initial objectives as follows:

1. To establish an atmosphere of safety for the child.
2. To understand and accept the child's world.
3. To encourage the expression of the child's emotional world.
4. To establish a feeling of permissiveness.
5. To facilitate decision making by the child.
6. To provide the child with an opportunity to assume responsibility and to develop a feeling of control.
7. To put into words what is experienced and observed in the child's behavior, words, feelings and activity. (pp. 257–258)

In addition to knowing when to use play media and having a feel for the desired objectives, you must set some limits. A brief discussion follows.

Setting Limits

The primary reason for setting limits within a play media session is to protect the child and the counselor from physical harm. A child's free expression is essential in the use of play media. However, there is a certain amount of freedom of activity within play media that, if carried on outside the counseling session, might bring criticism from administrators or others (Axline, 1947). Differences exist with regard to the extent of the freedom that should prevail. Some practitioners believe that it is essential to allow completely unrestrained activity (Slavson, 1952). Others, such as Moustakas (1959), believe that to have therapy, there must be limits. Dimick and Huff (1970) found that although there are differences in the kinds of limits employed, there are some that are widely accepted. They list three:

1. limits preventing the child from endangering his own health and safety.
2. limits preventing the child from doing injury to the therapists.
3. limits preventing the unrestrained destruction of the playroom materials and equipment. (p. 175)

Setting limits should help children understand their feelings and actions while at the same time maintaining their self-respect. However, Bixler (1949) suggests that limits be set with which the counselor is comfortable:

1. The child should not be allowed to destroy any property or facilities in the room other than play equipment.
2. The child should not be allowed to physically attack the therapist.
3. The child should not be allowed to stay beyond the time limit of the interview.
4. The child should not be allowed to remove toys from the playroom.
5. The child should not be allowed to throw toys or other material out the window. (p. 2)

Limits in the play process help children learn that there are limits in the real world; that the child has rights, as does the counselor; and that it is all right to have negative feelings if they are appropriately channeled. Following are some illustrations of limit setting by the counselor during the play media process.

1. Jerry takes the hammer and starts to strike the typewriter.
   COUNSELOR: You may type on the typewriter with your fingers; you may not hit it with the hammer.
2. Macy, with crayon in hand, starts for the wall to draw on it.
   COUNSELOR: [handing Macy a piece of construction paper] You may draw on this piece of paper, not on the wall.

3. Billy moves to hit the counselor with the boxing glove.
COUNSELOR: You may hit Butch [the inflated clown], but you may not hit me. I'm here to talk with.

When setting limits with play media, you should treat behavior as if it were something being verbalized. Stay in the here-and-now of the situation; do not attempt to project into the interpretation of the past or present.

FORMS OF USEFUL PLAY

Hundreds of examples of toys, materials, and activities could qualify as forms of play in counseling elementary school children. You must decide when the use of play media is indicated, based upon the needs of the child with whom you are working. Likewise, it is going to be up to you to select the kinds of toys and materials you will have in the playroom. As you begin to work with a child, you may advise him or her what to play with. In the final analysis, however, the child will make the final choice. Your job is to have choices available, to guide the child in the selection, and to set the parameters—including the limits—of the session. Having done this, you can then begin responding as the child goes about communicating and expressing through play.

Facilities

Play media sessions with children can be held in a variety of places, including your office, a classroom, the cafeteria, the gymnasium, or the playground. Landreth (1983) suggests that the counselor carry a tote bag. This is especially important if you have to move from place to place to engage children in play media activities. However, in most instances, a specially designed and equipped room is recommended. It should be as close to your office as possible, so that the transition from traditional counseling to play can be easily made. The room should be in a place where privacy and confidentiality can be assured. Since it is likely that occasionally considerable noise will issue from this room, it should be properly soundproofed. The room should be attractively decorated but not so elaborately furnished and arranged that it intimidates the children. If you are fortunate enough to have such a room, make sure it is equipped with storage shelves, tables, and boxes so that materials may be appropriately displayed when they are to be used, and stored out of sight when they are not. A well-equipped, attractive playroom signals that the child can be comfortable, and greatly enhances the use of play media in the counseling process.

Effective Play Media Activities and Materials

Following are some examples in the use of play that have proven to be effective in counseling with young children. We have not attempted to establish an all-inclusive list. Rather, we have tried to offer examples of toys, materials, or techniques that you might find useful as you embark upon the use of play media when counseling with children. Essentially, you are limited only by your own creativity. Whenever possible, we have included titles of articles that deal with a particular medium.

Puppetry.   There are two approaches in the use of play: structured and unstructured (Carter, 1987). Puppetry falls in the unstructured (or nondirective) category. Sometimes children will not be comfortable talking directly to you. They may not be accustomed to talking with adults, or they may have difficulties with certain feelings. For example, angry children may be afraid to talk directly about their feelings for fear of losing control. By using puppets to "talk through," the feeling can be expressed verbally or acted out without this fear. The use of puppets has also been found to be effective when working with children who are resistive to verbal counseling. There are no specific guidelines for determining which puppets to have in the playroom. However, it is probably best to have an assortment of "person" puppets as well as those representing animals. In addition, a puppet "family" is essential for the playroom. We highly recommend Carter (1987) and James and Myer (1987) for more information on the use of puppets in play media.

Art Media.   This unstructured activity involves drawing, painting, coloring, and finger painting; constructing or playing with clay, sand, and water; and using other media that may be related in any way to art.

Dinkmeyer and Caldwell (1970) note that color and line can often convey feelings and meanings more effectively than can actions and words. To utilize art in counseling, you must attempt to create an atmosphere in which the child will want to use materials willingly and freely (Rubin, 1974). Although counselors are not psychometrists or psychotherapists, it is possible, by intently listening to what children have to say about their creations, to make generalizations about feelings that may not be obvious in other situations.

Vinturella and James (1987), in writing about sand play, indicate that it has two uses. "First, it serves as a diagnostic tool, and second, it is a means of therapeutic intervention" (p. 230). Allan and Berry (1987) state that teachers often found children more relaxed and able to become involved in schoolwork after sand play. Perhaps Rubin (1988) best summarized the use of art in counseling:

> Children are drawn to art materials as spontaneously as they play with food on their plates or create monuments in backyard mud. Because making and marking are so natural and appealing to children, the use of art media is a valuable avenue for expression when counseling the young. (p. 180)

Physical Activities.   Normal, active children both need and want to be involved in physical activity. Sometimes, the restriction of movement in the classroom is a problem for children. As you work with them in physical activities, you should encourage free movement and promote the use of personal meanings (Muro & Dinkmeyer, 1977). It is through this that children are motivated to communicate their true, and sometimes unexpressed, personal feelings.

One of the most obvious physical activities is hitting or punching. Many children who are behaving aggressively need to find an acceptable way to express themselves. You can provide a punching bag or inflatable plastic punching toy that children feel free to strike while talking about their aggressive or angry feelings. During this process children can be helped to learn that it is appropriate to express hostile or angry feelings, but that this expression may be released only upon inanimate objects. Further, there are certain inanimate objects children may strike and others they may not.

Another useful tool for helping relieve anger or aggressive behavior is the pounding board. This is nothing more than a heavy board or other surface that can be struck with a hammer made of plastic or soft rubber. Again, during this process children are encouraged to express themselves verbally as they act out their feelings.

Another interesting technique involves placing an overabundance of hand lotion on the hands of both counselor and the child. They then grasp hands and pull in opposite directions, at the same time trying to hang on to each other. This is especially useful with children who are known to have difficulty in making physical contact with people. Other useful physical activities are walking, running, throwing a soft rubber ball against a wall, dancing, or riding a stationary bicycle.

Other Forms of Play Activities.   Irwin (1987) suggests that *drama* can make use of many forms of play, especially with children who have regressed or become blocked in their development. Closely related to drama is *role playing,* often used in conjunction with puppets. Role playing enhances children's communication in counseling, and assists in the projection of the child's feelings. The use of *magic* can be helpful in the counseling process. Illusions can be excellent ice breakers, and tricks can often be used to reinforce desired behaviors (Bowman, 1986). Johnson (1987) writes about the use of *computers* in counseling, and describes how computer graphics helped a child "talk about painful feelings, gain self-confidence, and become less anxious about losing his mother's emotional support" (p. 247). Other techniques, such as music, writing, toys, imagery, modeling or sculpturing, and construction, are all acceptable media if they enhance the communication and expression of children's feelings during counseling. You are limited only by your own creativity.

SUMMARY

The use of play media in elementary school counseling offers a unique opportunity for children to experience growth under favorable conditions. It is philosophically sound since it assists children in meaningfully relating to the world.

We defined play media as a technique that enhances and supplements verbal communication. We listed six philosophical assumptions based upon the premise that play is an integral part of a child's life. We pointed out that the establishment of a good relationship with the child is critical to the use of play media in counseling. Especially important is the counselor's unconditional positive regard toward the child.

The issue of when to use play in the counseling process was briefly addressed. We described the facilities that are needed, as well as forms of play including puppetry, art media, and physical activities.

The process of play can be viewed as the child's effort to communicate and gain control over feelings that result from environmental or other factors. Setting limits within the confines of the play media process assists children in learning that there are also limits in the real world.

REVIEW

1. Why is the use of play counseling more appropriate for younger children?
2. Define play media.
3. What are some philosophical assumptions of play?
4. Why is a strong relationship with the child important in the use of play?
5. When should play media in counseling be used?
6. List and discuss the reasons for limits in the use of play media.
7. How does having a tote bag assist the counselor in the use of play media?
8. Discuss some effective play media activities.
9. What are some acceptable play techniques for helping children express anger and/or aggressive behavior during counseling?
10. Make a list of toys and materials that would be helpful to have in a play media room.

REFERENCES

Allan, J., & Berry, P. (1987). Sandplay. *Elementary School Guidance and Counseling, 21*(4), 300–306.

Axline, V. M. (1947). *Play therapy.* Boston: Houghton Mifflin.

Axline, V. M. (1964). *Dibs: In search of self.* Boston: Houghton Mifflin.

Bixler, R. (1949). Limits are therapy. *Journal of Consulting Psychology, 13,* 1–11.

Bowman, R. P. (1986). The magic counselor: Using magic tricks as tools to teach children guidance lessons. *Elementary School Guidance and Counseling, 21*(2), 128–138.

Carter, S. R. (1987). Use of puppets to treat traumatic grief: A case study. *Elementary School Guidance and Counseling, 21*(3), 210–215.

Dimick, K. M., & Huff, V. E. (1970). *Child counseling.* Dubuque, IA: William C. Brown.

Dinkmeyer, D. C., & Caldwell, E. (1970). *Developmental counseling and guidance.* New York: McGraw-Hill.

Irwin, E. C. (1987). Drama: The play's the thing. *Elementary School Guidance and Counseling, 21*(4), 276-283.

James, R. K., & Myer, R. (1987). Puppets: The elementary school counselor's right or left arm. *Elementary School Guidance and Counseling, 21*(4), 292-299.

Johnson, R. G. (1987). Using computer art in counseling. *Elementary School Guidance and Counseling, 21*(4), 262-265.

Landreth, G. L. (1987). Play therapy: Facilitative use of child's play in elementary school counseling. *Elementary School Guidance and Counseling, 21*(4), 253-261.

Moustakas, C. E. (1959). *Psychotherapy with children.* New York: Harper & Row.

Muro, J. J., & Dinkmeyer, D. C. (1977). *Counseling in the elementary and middle schools: A pragmatic approach.* Dubuque, IA: William C. Brown.

Nelson, R. C. (1966). Elementary school counseling with unstructured play media. *Personal and Guidance Journal, 45,* 24-27.

Rubin, J. (1974). (Mimeo.) So you want to use art in therapy. Pittsburgh, PA: Child Guidance Center.

Rubin, J. A. (1988). Art counseling: An alternative. *Elementary School Guidance and Counseling, 22*(3), 180-185.

Schaefer, C. E., & O'Connor, K. J. (Eds.). (1983). *Handbook of play therapy.* New York: John Wiley.

Slavson, S. R. (1952). *Child psychotherapy.* New York: Columbia University Press.

Vinturella, L., & James, R. (1987). Sand play: A therapeutic medium with children. *Elementary School Guidance and Counseling, 21*(3), 229-238.

chapter 7

Classroom Guidance

OUTLINE

Review

References

INTRODUCTION

Classroom guidance is an integral part of the total elementary school guidance program. Through this activity, you can reach and developmentally assist virtually every child in the elementary school. For the program to succeed, you must plan and implement a comprehensive classroom guidance program that is focused upon the needs of students in the school setting being served. However, in setting objectives and planning activities, you must not only be concerned with meeting local needs, but flexible enough to respond to changing conditions. Flexibility and change should be distinguishing characteristics of a classroom guidance program.

Peters and Farwell (1959) were the first to outline developmental guidance and to discuss possible outcomes of such an approach. From this beginning, Peters, Shertzer, and Van Hoose (1965); Thompson and Poppen (1979); Myrick (1987); and others made valuable contributions. All seem to agree that developmental guidance is for *all* students, and that properly implemented will assist them in the learning process, as well as help them better understand themselves and the world in which they live.

Peters, Shertzer, and Van Hoose (1965), in discussing this approach, state:

> Developmental guidance is based on the regular order of progressive change in the dynamic human being. This is in contrast with guidance focused on repair work to bring an individual to a level of adequacy so that he then may proceed once again along the developmental path toward maturity and responsible adult living. Developmental guidance focuses on the characteristic behaviors considered typical for the various ages or stages of development. (p. 7)

The purpose of this chapter is to define what classroom guidance is, and how it can assist elementary and middle school students.

DEFINITION OF TERMS

Classroom or Group Guidance

Classroom guidance activities are often led by the counselor, with usually between 20 and 30 students in attendance. In a well-coordinated program, the classroom teacher is involved as well. Such groups aim to be preventive and to engender growth. The activities are designed to assist children with their growth and development and help them deal more effectively with everyday occurrences. For example, a discussion of the similarities and differences among individuals may help first-graders understand their uniqueness and to better understand why others behave in a certain way. Or, a discussion concerning appropriate ways to behave in a group may help kindergartners with socialization. Sometimes classroom guidance is provided for the purpose of passing along information: for example, an orientation for fifth-graders moving to a new building for sixth grade.

Group Counseling

Gazda, Duncan, and Meadows (1967) define group counseling as

> a dynamic, impersonal process focusing on conscious thought and behavior involving the therapy functions and permissiveness, orientation to reality, catharsis, and mutual trust, caring, understanding, acceptance, and support. (p. 306)

If students are to receive the full benefit of this counseling, group size is an important consideration. The members of a relatively small group might accept more responsibility, and feel more inclined to participate. Loeser (1957) reports that as groups increase in size, transference reactions weaken until members no longer experience meaningful relationships within the group. We believe that three to eight students is an ideal size for the elementary/middle school setting.

Student age and maturity, along with the counselor's training and experience, also determine the size of the group. For example, an inexperienced elementary school counselor would likely be more successful with a group of three or four first-graders, than with a group of seven or eight (eight being the maximum in our opinion). Group counseling is a demanding task, and should be undertaken only by qualified school counselors or other specialists with equivalent or higher training. In contrast with classroom *guidance*, it should not be attempted by the classroom teacher.

In our discussion of the terms *guidance* and *counseling*, we stressed that guidance leads students toward making appropriate choices, while counseling helps them change their behavior. These definitions are also applicable to group guidance and counseling.

The overall purposes of group counseling, as with classroom guidance, could be classified as preventive, growth engendering, and developmental. However, unlike classroom guidance, group counseling also serves a remedial function. For example, in many elementary or middle schools you will find groups organized to assist students with such issues as interpersonal relationships, divorce, drug abuse, and behavioral and attitudinal problems. As Shertzer and Stone (1971) state:

> In groups, collective judgment can be focused on common problems, critical issues can be examined, opinion and judgments can be compared, and new ideas and information not always available in individual situations can be applied. (p. 221)

Although there are limitations to group counseling (see chapter 8), overall it is an important aspect of the elementary/middle school guidance program.

Group Therapy

Group therapy serves a remedial function for the more seriously disturbed. Therefore, school counselors usually do not engage in this as a part of the school guidance program.

As Gibson and Mitchell (1990) explain,

> Therapy groups provide intense experiences for people with serious maladjustment, emotional, or developmental needs. Therapy groups are usually distinguished from counseling groups by both the length of time and the depth of the experience for those involved. (p. 183)

Group therapy is usually conducted with groups of 5 to 15 individuals. The word *therapy* indicates that a psychiatrist, clinically trained counselor, psychologist, or social worker serves as facilitator. Group therapy is also distinguished from classroom guidance or group counseling in that group members—except children in certain circumstances—are almost always self-referrals. Although this may sometimes be the case with group counseling, members frequently come from the counselor's caseload and may or may not have been self-referrals.

Table 7.1 summarizes the relationship and defining characteristics among classroom guidance, group counseling, and group therapy.

GOALS AND OBJECTIVES

As shown in Table 7.1, the purpose of classroom guidance is to assist students through the stages of development. A primary goal of classroom activities is to prevent personal problems from developing. This can be accomplished only when elementary school students have a feeling of self-worth and are accepting of others. The topic is broad; we discuss general goals and some specific objectives, and outline some appropriate activities leading toward these goals and objectives.

Classroom guidance should assist students in experiencing personal growth, learning problem-solving and decision-making skills, and acquiring better study skills and an awareness of vocational and educational opportunities (Rye & Sparks, 1991). Not all goals listed are appropriate at all levels, nor are the needs the same from school to school. Therefore, you will need to use your judgment in adopting the goals and objectives that are appropriate for your school. Keep in mind the overall mission of the school system in which you work, and ensure that the classroom guidance goals are consistent with those of the school. (See "Organizing a Classroom Guidance Program," p. 137.)

TABLE 7.1 Defining characteristics of three types of groups

Defining Characteristics	Types of Groups		
	Classroom Guidance	Group Counseling	Group Therapy
Group Purpose(s)	Preventive, Growth Engendering Developmental, Information Giving	Preventive, Growth Engendering Developmental, Remediation	Remediation
Group Size	Classroom 20–30	Grades: Number: K–2 3–5 3–5 4–6 6–8 4–8	5–15
Usual Session Length	20–40 Minutes	1 Hour	1–2 Hours
Who Facilitates	Classroom Teacher and/or Counselor	Counselor	Clinical Counselor Psychologist Psychiatrist
Level of Training Needed to Facilitate	Bachelor's through Master's Degree	Master's Degree Including Group Process	M.D., Ph.D. or Equivalent

DIFFERENCES IN GOALS AND OBJECTIVES

It is important to distinguish between goals and objectives. We view *goals* as general statements indicating what is to be accomplished overall (e.g., "To develop an awareness of the world of work"). *Objectives* tend to be more specific and indicate what is to be accomplished relative to the goal (e.g., "By the end of the school year, students will increase their knowledge of occupations by 25 percent").

In other words, goals offer a general direction; objectives provide a blueprint for action. The next step is to design classroom guidance activities that would help satisfy the objectives, which in turn would meet the goal. Of course, for most goals there will be several objectives, and you will be able to develop several classroom guidance activities accordingly.

Examples of Classroom Guidance Goals

It is difficult to develop a list of goals that is all-inclusive, yet specific enough to avoid redundancy. Keep in mind that goals are intended to offer *general* directions. Therefore, needs of a unique target group may dictate goals that are more specific than the ones offered below. However, we believe that the list covers most of the general directions that should be undertaken in a classroom guidance program. The goals are as follows:

1. to assist students in developing an understanding of self and others;
2. to assist students in developing interpersonal skills that will help them get along with others, regardless of age, personality, or culture;
3. to assist students in developing decision-making and problem-solving skills;
4. to assist students in developing knowledge about and appreciation for the educational process;
5. to assist students in developing an awareness of and appreciation for the world of work;
6. to assist students in developing study skills that will enhance their learning now and in the future; and
7. to assist students by providing them with timely personal, social, educational, and career information.

We believe that all of these goals, to some degree, are appropriate for all grade levels. The differences lie in the children's maturity and need at a particular grade level. For example, kindergartners may neither be ready for nor need a full-blown classroom guidance activity on study skills. However, they would certainly benefit from learning the importance of listening to directions from the teacher. (The rationale is that listening requires concentration, and concentration is important in developing good study skills.)

To clarify each goal in the list, we discuss them in more detail.

1. Developing an Understanding of Self.   This is of great importance if children are to feel good about themselves. They need an understanding of their strengths and weaknesses along with a knowledge of their uniqueness as individuals and similarities with others.

2. Developing Interpersonal Skills.   Increasing technological sophistication has made the world much "smaller." Consequently, it is imperative that children develop communication skills that will enhance their relationships with friends, family, and people from different cultures.

3. Developing Decision-Making and Problem-Solving Skills.   This is needed now more than ever. Children are faced with decisions that will have far-reaching effects. For example, fourth- and fifth-graders may face pressure to use illegal drugs. Strengthening decision-making and problem-solving skills will help them decide what is best for them.

4. Developing an Appreciation of the Educational Process.   Too often, children see education as important because adults tell them it is. This goal aims to increase children's understanding, knowledge, and appreciation of education through carefully designed activities.

5. Developing an Awareness of the World of Work.   This attempts to increase the student's career awareness while developing an understanding and appreciation for work in general. Too often, work is a "four-letter word." Through planned activities, counselors assist children in accepting work as a pleasant aspect of their lives. For children in the later elementary/middle school grades, this could entail career exploration based on their interests and abilities.

6. Developing Study Skills.   This is designed to assist children in becoming more successful in their learning. Depending on their grade level, students focus on time management, good study habits, and the significance of positive attitudes toward education, along with other areas relevant to becoming a successful student.

7. Providing Students with Timely Personal, Social, Educational, and Career Information.   This may overlap with other classroom guidance goals. However, such a broad approach provides an opportunity to ensure that students receive pertinent information on vital issues at any time. Topics may include sexuality, drug abuse, AIDS, career changes due to technological advancement, and changing educational opportunities.

We have identified general goals for a classroom guidance program; we continue with some objectives that may be germane to stated goals.

Examples of Classroom Guidance Objectives

Goal 1	**Develop Self-Understanding.**	
Objectives:	1.	Students will develop an awareness of different feelings.
	2.	Students will explore appropriate occasions and ways to express feelings.
	3.	Students will develop an understanding of their strengths and weaknesses.
	4.	Students will explore differences as well as common characteristics among individuals.
	5.	Students will develop an understanding of, and appreciation for, cultural differences.
Goal 2	**Develop Interpersonal Skills.**	
Objectives:	1.	Students will be able to define friendship as it relates to their lives.
	2.	Students will develop an understanding of how to make and keep friends.
	3.	Students will develop an understanding of the worth and dignity of others regardless of age, sex, or culture.

4. Students will develop positive attitudes toward the rights and privileges of others.

5. Students will develop an understanding of the importance communication plays in getting along with others.

Goal 3   **Develop Decision-Making and Problem-Solving Skills.**

Objectives: 1. Students will recognize the importance of decision making in their lives

2. Students will develop skill in identifying problems.

3. Students will develop skill in analyzing problems.

4. Students will develop an understanding of the techniques involved in making informed choices.

5. Students will develop an understanding of the consequences decision making has on their lives.

Goal 4   **Develop an Appreciation for the Educational Process.**

Objectives: 1. Students will learn how much education costs and how it is financed.

2. Students will become familiar with the organizational structure of their school.

3. Students will learn how education assists them in becoming better and more productive citizens.

4. Students will develop an understanding of the role of teachers, counselors, administrators, and others in the educational process.

5. Students will develop a positive attitude toward the educational process.

Goal 5   **Develop an Awareness of the World of Work.**

Objectives: 1. Students will explore the attainment of self-satisfaction from work.

2. Students will increase their knowledge of the occupations available in their community, state, and region.

3. Students will learn how success in education correlates with success on the job.

4. Students will become knowledgeable about the use of leisure time as it pertains to the world of work.

5. Students will learn to attach worth and value to all who work, regardless of the type or status of the work.

Goal 6   **Develop Study Skills.**

Objectives: 1. Students will become aware of productive study techniques.

2. Students will develop an understanding of the need to listen and follow directions.

3. Students will learn how to budget their time for study.

4. Students will develop skills that will assist them in taking tests.

5. Students will learn how to reduce their anxiety through relaxation techniques.

Goal 7   **Provide Students with Timely Personal, Social, Educational, and Career Information.**

Objective: 1. Students will be provided with information relevant to the next level of their education.

2. Students will be provided with information that will enhance their awareness of social issues such as drug abuse, AIDS, and dysfunctional families.

3. Students will be provided with information on how their attitude affects their academic success.

4. Students will be provided information on resources that may be important to them now or in the future.

5. Students will be provided with information about rules in school and society and the importance of cooperation.

The preceding list is not intended to be all-inclusive, but to assist you in putting together your own goals and objectives, which may be converted into a comprehensive classroom guidance program.

ORGANIZING A CLASSROOM GUIDANCE PROGRAM

President George Bush outlined six goals that America must meet by the year 2000:

1. all children ready to learn when they start school;
2. a high school graduation rate of 90 percent;
3. American students leaving grades 4, 8, and 12 with competency in English, mathematics, science, history, and geography;
4. U.S. students first in the world in science and mathematics achievement;
5. every adult American literate and able to compete in a global economy and exercise the rights and responsibilities of citizenship; and
6. every school in America free of drugs and violence while offering a disciplined environment conducive to learning.

Much of what you can do to help meet these national goals will be accomplished through classroom guidance activities. Given the current state of affairs in our country, the task will not be easy. As Myrick & Myrick (1990) point out:

One in five children live below the poverty level. America's childhood-poverty rate is two to three times higher than most other industrialized nations, which offer more generous benefits for the poor.

One in five children live with one parent, and half of these parents are poor. The number of female heads of households has doubled since 1970 and tripled since 1960. One-third of such woman live below the poverty level.

The teenage pregnancy rate in the United States is the highest of 30 developed nations and has increased 12 percent since 1973. Fifty percent of these girls fail to complete high school and earn less than half the income of those who wait to start their families.

The average public high school today loses 25 percent of its potential graduates. The range of dropouts for states is 11 percent to 44 percent.

There is a high rate of youth unemployment and a greater threat of prolonged periods of unemployment and low earnings for Black and Hispanic groups.

By the end of the 9th grade, about 30 percent of all students have experimented with illegal drugs. Before graduating from high school, 90 percent have experimented with alcohol, some use cocaine, and many have become dependent on stimulants. (p. 3)

Although counselors have no direct control over most societal problems, they can organize programs which will, in time, move our country in a more positive direction.

Organizing a Classroom Guidance Committee

No classroom guidance program can succeed without the support of the majority of the school staff. One way to increase support, while also seeing that the program is geared to students' needs, is to organize a classroom guidance committee.

Committee Size and Makeup.   To some extent, the size of the committee will depend upon the size of the school. For example: A K-6 school contains only one classroom for each grade level. This would call for representation by one teacher from the K-2 level, one from 3-4, and one representing grades 5-6. If the school has multiple classrooms per grade level, or more grades, then the committee would have a representative from each grade level. In addition to teachers being on the committee, having parents and one or two representatives of the special staff (psychologists, social workers, etc.) adds a great deal of credibility to the committee.

Committee Responsibilities.   The committee should deal with the global concerns of the program, not the day-to-day organizational issues that may arise. The committee should help answer the following questions:

1. What is the overall goal of a classroom guidance curriculum?
2. Is this goal consistent with the stated philosophy of the school?
3. What are the needs of the students? How can they be determined?
4. How can the committee best support the efforts of the classroom guidance program?

The committee will need to spend considerable time deliberating these questions. It is important that they come to a consensus about the overall goal of the program, and that this goal is consistent with the school's aims. The possibility of success is greatly enhanced under these circumstances.

Frequently, such a committee has a clear idea of students' needs. However, it should thoroughly discuss the matter and find more objective ways of determining these needs. For example, as a means of receiving input, the committee may want to prepare a questionnaire or survey to be sent to parents. They could also prepare another instrument to be administered to teachers, administrators, and others within the school. And—just as important—the committee should find a way to gain input from students as to what they believe their needs are.

Finally, the committee members need to explore ways in which they can help publicize and support the classroom guidance curriculum. Being ambassadors of the program is useful, but usually not enough. They can actively assist in the orientation of teachers, administrators, parents, and students as to the purpose of the program. At times the committee can even be active in soliciting funds for the purchase of classroom guidance materials and supplies. This will become increasingly important if education funding continues to decline at the federal and state levels.

Counselor Responsibilities

Although the committee can supply important data, make meaningful suggestions, and be supportive in a variety of ways, it is you, the counselor, who are responsible for the day-to-day organization and operation of the classroom guidance program. As an ex-officio member of the committee, you should listen carefully to committee discussions, findings, and suggestions. Taking all of this into con-sideration, you should then set about answering the following questions:

1. Based on identified needs, who is the target population?
2. What activities could be used to satisfy those needs?
3. Who should carry out these activities?
4. When should these activities be carried out?
5. What preparation is needed to carry out the activities? What materials are needed? Is a special skill required? What is the approximate cost?
6. How is the effectiveness of these activities to be evaluated?

To see how this process might work, we examine a hypothetical situation that could take place in a middle school. The classroom guidance committee has determined that eighth-graders need a better understanding of their upcoming high school education. This need clearly fits under Goal 7: *provide students with timely personal, social, educational, and career information.* To help you plan the activity, we suggest the completion of an activity planning form (see Figure 7.1). A completed form will not only ensure that you have considered the questions as outlined above but will also serve as a document that would inform committee member as to what is planned to meet the identified need.

Figure 7.2 shows a completed classroom guidance activity form. We have left Figure 7.1 blank so that you can duplicate it for use in your school.

As is evident from the example, there are no set activities for carrying out high school orientation for eighth-graders. This will be true for many of the needs

NAME OF SCHOOL _____   COUNSELOR _____

GRADE LEVEL _____   TEACHER _____

TITLE OF ACTIVITY _____

PURPOSE OF ACTIVITY _____

_____

_____

MATERIAL AND EQUIPMENT NEEDED (Books, films, videos, paper, etc.)

_____

_____

NUMBER OF SESSIONS NEEDED TO COMPLETE THE ACTIVITY (Include the approximate time needed for each session)

_____

_____

DATE(S) AND TIME(S) ACTIVITY IS TO BE CARRIED OUT

_____

_____

NAME(S) OF PERSON(S) WHO WILL CARRY OUT THE ACTIVITY

_____

EVALUATION (Process and criteria for success)

_____

_____

_____

FIGURE 7.1 Classroom guidance activity planning form

NAME OF SCHOOL Upstart Middle School   COUNSELOR Al Smart

GRADE LEVEL 8   TEACHER Pat Head

TITLE OF ACTIVITY Orientation to High School

PURPOSE OF ACTIVITY To provide information and orientation to eighth-graders that will assist them in being better prepared for the transition to high school.

MATERIALS AND EQUIPMENT NEEDED Bus and driver for the field trip to the high school on April 27.

NUMBER OF SESSIONS NEEDED TO COMPLETE THE ACTIVITY Four.

DATE(S) AND TIME(S) ACTIVITY IS TO BE CARRIED OUT Session 1, April 13, 1:00 pm; Session 2, April 20, 2:00 pm; Session 3, April 27, 10:00 am; Session 4, May 4, 3:00 pm.

NAME(S) OF PERSON(S) WHO WILL CARRY OUT THE ACTIVITY Session 1, "High School Curriculum and Expectations," Mr. Jones, HS Counselor. Session 2, "High School Life and Activities," President of Student Council. Session 3, "Tour of High School Facilities," Guides: Mr. Border, Principal; Ms. Head, MS Counselor; Mr. Jones, HS Counselor. Session 4, "Preenrollment for Ninth Grade," Ms. Jewell, HS Assistant Principal.

EVALUATION A follow-up questionnaire will be administered to student participants during the sixth week of their ninth-grade year. For each activity to be considered a success, 70 percent or more of the students will grade it with a positive response. Results of the survey will be shared with each building principal and the classroom guidance activity committee.

FIGURE 7.2 Completed classroom guidance activity planning form

that are identified within a school. Some commercial activities are available to help satisfy the goals and objectives set out earlier, but many times you will have to create these activities.

Although you have the overall responsibility for organizing and implementing the program, teachers and others can and should be frequent activity facilitators. In some schools, especially those with larger enrollments, the responsibilities are divided so that counselor and teacher alternately facilitate the group once a month. It might be more or less frequent depending upon the number of classrooms, the number of students, and their needs.

GROUP LEADERSHIP TECHNIQUES

Be Well Prepared

Nothing will reduce the effectiveness of a worthwhile classroom guidance activity quicker than poor preparation. When you go into the classroom, be well prepared so that you can avoid slip-ups. This includes having enough handouts, and ensuring that all equipment is in working order. Further, it is imperative that you clearly understand and can communicate the objectives of the activity.

State the Objective or Purpose of the Activity to the Students

The objective should be made clear to the students at the very beginning. If you just walk into the room and begin the activity, students may see it as a "fun and games" session. Tell students the purpose of the session; they will then have a feel for what they are to learn, and consequently will be more apt to do so. Also, they will more likely view classroom guidance as part of the regular school curriculum.

Use Good Communication Techniques

Most activities will require some group discussion, either during or after the presentation. Facilitating this discussion in a meaningful way requires that you use good basic counseling skills along with classroom teaching techniques.

Listening.   Listen carefully and respond to all contributors. Usually, in classroom guidance, there are no right or wrong answers. The important thing is that students feel free to express themselves without fear of being admonished.

Eye Contact.   This is imperative if students are to feel comfortable and accepted. It is a sign that you are being attentive to what they are saying.

Responses.   Be careful not to use too many value-laden words, such as *good, excellent, wonderful,* and so on. By using such words, you send a message that you are looking for a certain answer. Before long the students will be offering the responses they think you want to hear. A simple response, such as "thank you" or "Mary says . . . ," will increase the probability of honest, free expression.

Student Contributions.   If possible, during a discussion, be sure every student gets a change to contribute. Sometimes this is very difficult since some will volunteer often and others only once or twice a session. Again, regardless of the discussion offered, acknowledge the student's contribution. This will encourage all to participate.

Practice Sound Classroom Management Techniques

Involve students in setting guidelines for discussion. Focus on positive expectations and be sure everyone understands them. During discussions, and sometimes during presentations, be kinetic. Students will stay involved and interested when they see you moving about, looking at them, and being enthusiastic about what they are doing. Use your seat only when appropriate (e.g., coloring a figure at your desk to help kindergartners remember a concept).

Closure

Taken care to end each session in a positive way. If you were well prepared, used good communication techniques, showed enthusiasm, and provided meaningful activities, students will leave feeling good about what has taken place. It is important to close the session by reviewing the objectives of the activity. Preparing and offering a purposeful summary is imperative to concluding a classroom guidance activity. This leaves the students with a feeling of accomplishment.

CLASSROOM GUIDANCE RESOURCES

There are times when you will have to come up with creative and appropriate classroom guidance activities. There are also excellent kits, books, videotapes, films, filmstrips, and audiotapes to assist you. Many of the following publishers offer materials suitable for elementary and middle school students. We suggest you write or call them, and ask to be placed on their mailing list. Most publishers have catalogs that describe the purpose of an activity, and offer other information, such as grade level and the amount of time needed for the activity.

PUBLISHERS WHO OFFER CLASSROOM GUIDANCE ACTIVITIES

AAA
7 Travelers Trail
Burnsville, MN   55337
Phone: (612) 890-2500
Films, videos

Accelerated Development Publishers, Inc.
3400 Kilgore Avenue
Muncie, IN 47304-4896
Phone: (317) 284-7511
Books, audio- and videotapes, workbooks

American Counseling Association
5999 Stevenson Avenue
Alexandria, VA 22304
Phone: (800) 347-6647
Books, audio- and videotapes, brochures, public relation kits

American Guidance Service
4201 Woodland Road, Suite 1134
Circle Pines, MN 55014-1796
Phone: (800) 328-2560
Books, videos, self-concept kits, puppets, posters

American School Counselors Association
5999 Stevenson Avenue
Alexandria, VA 22304
Phone: (703) 823-9800
Books, curriculum guides, brochures

Churchill Films
12210 Nebraska Avenue
Los Angeles, CA 90025-9816
Phone: (800) 334-7830
Films, videos

Films for the Humanities and Sciences
P.O. Box 2053
Princeton, NJ 08543-2053
Phone: (800) 257-5126
Films, videos

Good Apple, Inc.
Box 299
Carthage, IL 62321
Phone: (800) 435-7234
Activity books, posters, teacher resources

Guidance Associates
Communications Park, Box 3000
Mount Kisco, NY 10549
Phone (800) 431-1242
Books, filmstrips, videos

Hazelden Educational Materials
Pleasant Valley Road
P.O. Box 176
Center City, MN 55012-0176
Phone: (800) 328-9000
Films, videos, books, complete programs

Health Edco
P.O. Box 21207
Waco, TX 76701-1207
Phone: (800) 433-2677
Computer programs, filmstrips, games, videos

Human Relations Media
175 Tompkins Avenue
Pleasantville, NY 10570-9973
Phone: (800) 431-2050
Filmstrips, videos

Human Services Institute
P.O. Box 14610
Bradenton, Florida 34280

Phone: (813) 746-7088
Books, videos, workshop materials

Kidsrights
3700 Progress Boulevard
Mount Dora, FL 32757
Phone: (800) 892-KIDS
Books, games, resource materials, videos

MAC Publishing
A division of CLAUDJA, Inc.
5005 East 39th Avenue
Denver, CO 80207
Phone: (303) 331-0148
Books, games, videos

Pops Foundation
4325 Dick Pond Road
Myrtle Beach, SC 29575
Phone: (800) 521-2741
Books, kits, videos

Research Press
Dept. C
2612 North Mattis Avenue
Champaign, IL 61821
Phone: (217) 352-3273
Coloring and activity books, audio- and videotapes

Rosen Publishing Group
29 East 21st Street
New York, NY 10010
Phone: (800) 237-9932
Books, videos

Sunburst Communications
39 Washington Avenue
P.O. Box 40
Pleansantville, NY 10570-3498
Phone: (800) 431-1934
Board games, curriculum modules, videos

Timberline Press, Inc.
P.O. Box 70071
Eugene, OR 97401
Activity sheets, audiotapes, kits, storybooks

William Gladden Foundation
79 Carley Avenue
Huntington, NY 11743
Phone: (516) 673-4584
Audio- and videotapes, activity books, software

SUMMARY

In this chapter we discussed the defining characteristics of classroom guidance groups, group counseling, and group therapy. The general purpose of a classroom guidance program is to assist students through their stages of development; a primary goal of the activities provided is to prevent personal problems from developing. We listed seven examples of classroom guidance goals, and offered five objectives that might be used as a guide for satisfying a particular goal.

We stressed the importance of organizing the classroom guidance program around the school's mission and the students' needs. We discussed the important part a classroom guidance committee plays in organizing a program, and offered suggestions on how to establish such a committee, decide on it size, and delegate responsibilities. We also discussed the counselor's responsibilities as they pertain to organizing a classroom guidance program, and offered a form to assist in planning classroom guidance activities. Suggestions on how to facilitate a classroom guidance activity were made. These covered planning, classroom management, and the importance of utilizing sound communication techniques. Finally, we listed a number of publishers offering commercially developed classroom guidance materials.

REVIEW

1. Why is it important that classroom guidance activities be developmental in nature?
2. What is the difference between a goal and an objective?
3. Discuss the part a classroom guidance committee plays in organizing a classroom guidance program.
4. How does one distinguish between classroom guidance, group counseling, and group therapy? In what ways, if any, are they similar?
5. Write five objectives for the goal "To assist students in developing a positive self-concept."
6. Prepare a classroom guidance activity for each of the objectives in number 5.
7. Outline some techniques that could be used to ensure a successful classroom guidance activity.
8. Write a sample letter to publishers requesting information on their materials.
9. Complete a classroom guidance activity planning form for each of the activities in number 6 above.

REFERENCES

Gazda, G. M., Duncan, J. A., & Meadows, M. E. (1967). Group counseling and group procedure—Report of a survey. *Counselor Education and Supervision, 6,* 305-310.

Gibson, R. L., & Mitchell, M. H. (1990). *Introduction to counseling and guidance.* New York: Macmillan.

Loeser, L. H. (1957). Some aspects of group dynamics. *International Journal of Group Psychotherapy, 7,* 5-19.

Myrick, R. D. (1987). *Developmental guidance and counseling: A practical approach.* Minneapolis, MN: Educational Media Corporation.

Myrick, R. D., & Myrick, L. S. (1990). *The teacher advisor program: An innovative approach to school guidance.* Ann Arbor, MI: ERIC Counseling and Personnel Services Clearing House.

Ohlsen, M. M. (1970). *Group counseling.* New York: Holt.

Peters, H., & Farwell, G. (1959). *Guidance: A developmental approach.* Chicago: Rand McNally.

Peters, H., Shertzer, B., & Van Hoose, W. (1965). *Guidance in elementary schools.* Chicago: Rand McNally.

Rye, D. R., & Sparks, R. (1991). *Strengthening K-12 school counseling programs.* Muncie, IN: Accelerated Development.

Shertzer, E. F., & Stone, S.C. (1971). *Fundamentals of guidance.* Boston: Houghton Mifflin.

Thompson, C. L., & Poppen, W. A. (1979). *Guidance activities for counselors and teachers.* Monterey, CA: Brooks/Cole.

chapter 8

Group Counseling

OUTLINE

INTRODUCTION

Why work with young people in groups? This chapter addresses the question by presenting material related to the establishment of counseling groups, indicating what behavior to expect from group participants, providing means of appraising your own leadership style, suggesting a way to consider the process of group counseling, and presenting some ideas about how to evaluate the effectiveness of your efforts. It is not our purpose to present a comprehensive view of counseling in groups. We focus selectively on some important elements of designing and conducting group counseling. Through this selective approach, you will gain a better notion of whether you want to learn more about groups and experience them as a participant and leader.

The primary reason to work in groups is that we are social beings who live in a group-oriented society. Virtually all daily activity involves other people and takes place in a group setting. Therefore, counseling through the group medium provides young people with a natural setting for working through adjustment difficulties. Yalom (1985) points out that relatively unstructured groups develop into a social microcosm of the participants, and as such the longer young people participate in a group the more they have the opportunity to work realistically through the issues they face.

Dinkmeyer and Muro (1971) state, "group counseling is an interpersonal process led by a professionally trained counselor and conducted with individuals who are coping with typical developmental problems. Group counseling focuses on thoughts, feelings, attitudes, values, purposes, behavior, and goals of the individual and the total group" (pp. 1-2). Further, Gazda (1989) regards counseling in groups as both preventive and remedial: preventive in that participants are assisted in adjusting to tasks they face at each stage of life, and remedial for those young people who may be engaging in self-defeating behavior (see Table 7.1, page 133).

Counseling is a process of assisting young people to make changes in their behavior, and group counseling is a process of initiating change in the behavior of young people through the medium of groups. These changes may be either intrapersonal or interpersonal. Counseling groups may focus on issues young people face in their adjustment to school, with peers or adults, or on broader issues such as family difficulties and other problems beyond the youngsters' control. In the main, it is our contention that counseling groups, like all groups, are problem-solving settings. People come together in a group setting with a collective and/or individual purpose in mind—to find solutions to the issues they face.

Advantages of Groups

1. An important advantage of groups is economy of time: You can work with more individuals in the same time period. This becomes obvious when you are assigned upward of 500 students, who may be located in more than one attendance center.

2. Groups provide a convenient place to work with young people who share similar difficulties. Some counselors regard this as a disadvantage because they feel young people with similar adjustment difficulties tend to reinforce each other in their frustrations. Despite this potential disadvantage, we feel that placing young people with similar difficulties together provides a common ground to address the issues, and each young person can feel that she or he is not alone.

3. Groups can provide a strong basis for support among the members. As people work together over time, they become more sensitive to each other, which in turn can translate into a supportive attitude.

4. Because young people tend to be more comfortable with their age-mates, groups can aid them in becoming more open. Particularly between fourth grade and the end of middle school, when young people are most sensitive to the opinions of their peers, they may not share much of themselves with an adult, although they will do so with their friends.

5. Groups composed of age-mates can be good places to try out new behaviors because this setting approximates a "real world" situations. As young people express their thoughts and feelings in front of their peers, they can receive input from those whose opinions they regard highly.

6. Troubled young people can find their place in the group. For individuals who may feel alienated, the group can provide a sense of belonging.

7. Groups are highly adaptable to a variety of settings. Age is not a limiting factor in conducting groups because the group accommodates varied maturity levels. Also, groups are flexible and can address a wide variety of problems.

Disadvantages of Groups

1. Confidentiality is an ever-present difficulty in groups because of the number of participants. Therefore, maintaining complete privacy for each member is impossible. This issue is of considerable significance

when you work with younger children, who are spontaneous and if asked will reveal practically anything.

2. Since you are working with a number of people, each young person will receive less individual attention. This limitation is offset by the supportive nature of the group and the bond between members that seems to develop over time.

3. Groups impose natural pressure on each member to conform to a set of perceived, although not necessarily stated, standards of behavior. This might grow more serious when you attempt to protect the individuality of each member. When you address socially accepted behaviors that are considered necessary for comfortable living in our society (e.g., getting along with one's peers), you will need to treat the issue of conformity with great care.

4. Groups often scapegoat members, either to ventilate collective frustrations or to avoid working through issues surrounding the group's own development. This comes to light when the group works together over a period of time, usually beyond six or seven weeks.

5. The complexity of group counseling compared with individual counseling is underlined by the number of young people involved. This situational variable is a disadvantage because there is more dialogue, behavior, and interaction for you to monitor. Therefore, counseling in groups requires training and experience beyond that which you will receive in your training. The ASGW ethical standards and training guidelines (ASGW, 1989) clearly spell out the issues germane to group counseling and the training necessary to enable you to more effectively counsel in groups.

6. Counseling in groups, by its nature, is less structured than individual counseling, and you may not have control over what a young person may say or do. If this is troublesome to you, then groups may not be the best professional medium for your counseling work.

7. Counseling groups are not for everyone. You need to screen out individuals who seem to be experiencing difficulties that extend beyond the limits of the group.

As Ruten and Groves (1989) indicate, groups can be assets or liabilities, depending upon a number of variables (e.g., member composition, size, goals, or purposes, maturity or age of members, and your leadership). The advantages and disadvantages may be moderated or enhanced, depending on the overall complexion of the group and your approach to working in this setting.

ORGANIZING COUNSELING GROUPS

The success of your group counseling effort is strongly influenced by how well you organize the group prior to the first session. In this section we present a brief series of steps that will help to set the proper tone for your group, while at the same time enabling you to consider ethical issues.

Purposes, Goals, and Objectives

The first consideration is the overall purpose, companion goals, and subsequent objectives for your group. The purpose of group counseling is prevention and possibly moderate remediation. Within this lies a more specific purpose based on your reason for forming the group (e.g., divorce adjustment, developing peer relations, or improving attitudes). In counseling groups, goals are tailored to the needs of each member. Your goal may be for the members to improve their awareness, understanding, or behavior in an area the group will address. From goals spring objectives, which are more specific. (See chapter 7 for a more detailed differentiation of the two.)

Member Selection

Your initial encounter will occur when you select members for your counseling group. Unlike classroom guidance groups, where members frequently come from the class at large, members of counseling groups are either referred for a particular reason or are volunteers. Prospective members may be referred by a teacher, parent, administrator, or another helping professional in the school. Most experts in the group field believe that the self-referred members are the most committed. Voluntary participation provides a better chance for successful participation (Dinkmeyer & Muro, 1971). However, you may not enjoy the luxury of having self-referred participants in your groups (Corey, 1990; Dinkmeyer & Muro, 1971; Gazda, 1989; Yalom, 1985). Ethically, nonvolunteers must be given the right to leave the group at any time (ASGW, 1989). Similarly, referrals should be treated somewhat like unwilling participants.

Your selection of a young person for possible inclusion in a group should be based on the bifold considerations of benefitting from the group and contributing to it. It is best if you give both these considerations equal weight.

Once you have addressed the issue of member identification, you must turn to screening potential group members. Screening is a process wherein young people have the opportunity to consider whether they really want to participate. (You may have difficulty enlisting extensive involvement of younger individuals in this process.) The issue of screening has been clearly addressed in the ASGW ethical standards (ASGW, 1989). Four screening methods have been identified in the standards: individual interview, group interview, interview as a part of a staffing, and completion of a written questionnaire (ASGW, 1989). We prefer the personal interview. It enables you not only to address the purpose, goals, and objectives of the group but also to discuss participation with the young person. As well, you have the opportunity to address the young person's feelings about referred or nonvoluntary participation—which does not automatically mean that he or she will be an unwilling participant. Finally, through the personal interview you can most effectively address the young person's expectations, confidentiality, the right to leave the group, and, as needed, informed consent to participate. Gregory and McConnell (1986) state that informed consent should be discussed to ensure understanding on the part of the young person; it definitely should be used with anyone age seven and over.

Structural Features

Included here are group composition, size, meeting site, length of session, number of sessions, and frequency of meetings. Most of these issues can be addressed quite simply and directly before the first session.

Group Composition.   Decide on the best combination of members to accomplish your purpose, goals, and objectives. According to Gazda (1989), there is no research to indicate the ideal composition for a counseling group. We believe that your best guideline will be your members' level of development. In other words, use your own judgment about the maturity level of each candidate.

Size.   This was addressed in the previous chapter, and we include only a footnote here. With the youngest grades, K–2, between three and five members is optimal. Fewer do not make a group and more are harder to manage. With grades 3–5, generally four to six is a good number. With grades 6 through 8 you can increase the size to the upper limit of eight. This limit remains constant even with high schoolers. You should know how many you can effectively handle, given your purpose and experience.

Meeting Place.   Gazda (1989) states that the setting should be natural to the group members and should suit the activity level of the group. The primary concern is privacy, since privacy enhances confidentiality and presents a more serious or professional environment.

Length and Number of Sessions.   How often you should meet and for how long are also dependent on age. Younger individuals in grades K–3 will have difficulty maintaining concentration or focus for longer than 30 minutes. The intermediate (4–6) and mid-level (7 and 8) grade levels may meet for upward of any hour, equivalent to a class period. The number of sessions will likely be determined by the purpose and goals of the group. You should determine a set number of sessions and inform your group members at the outset how many sessions have been planned. The finite number gives participants a boundary for what needs to be done in the time available. If necessary, you can extend the life of the group.

Frequency of sessions may be determined by group members' availability. Typically, counseling groups meet once a week (Gazda, 1989). If your group needs more time, consider seeking outside support or referring these individuals to someone who can work with them more frequently. An additional issue is conflict with classes. If you meet during the school day, vary the meeting time so that students do not always miss the same material. Some teachers will not release students from their class. To get around this, you will need to schedule meetings before school; during lunch hours; after school; or in rotation, meeting at a different time and day each week. (Counselors have been able to conduct effective groups over lunch in a private room. If teachers resist, be inventive and hope they will soften in time.)

Session Planning

Consider how you would like to conduct each session. The degree of structure can vary considerably, depending on the purpose and age level of the group. Both these considerations will determine the extent to which you will direct the discussion. The two most important sessions to plan are the first and last. The first session should establish the commitment to continued attendance and participation; the final meeting will review previous sessions and reinforce the learning experiences that have taken place.

During the last session you should receive feedback regarding the success of the group. There are three approaches to evaluation:

1. provide feedback to the group members on your perception of what they have gained from the group experience;
2. members provide their own assessment of the effectiveness of the group, either through their recollections or by providing feedback to each other; or
3. you *and* the group provide the feedback.

Each method has its merits.

The first approach allows you to highlight your observations from a less biased perspective. The shortfall of this approach is that the members do not contribute.

The second method has as its strength the individual perceptions of the group members, which add up to represent their collective perspective. This method takes longer for the members to provide their assessment because of the number of members and because they have to work hard at drawing forth the meaningful experiences. Also, group members tend to be myopic, seeing only what is closest to them.

The third method draws on the best features of the other two: It embraces your judgment as a detached observer, as well as the unique perceptions of each member who chooses to contribute to the process. Use the third method whenever possible. If you must employ either of the first two approaches, please recognize their inherent limitations.

LEADERSHIP APPROACHES

The most important ingredient in the success of your group counseling is you—the leader. Schmuck and Schmuck (1992) define classroom leadership as "behavior which influences others in the classroom group to follow" (p. 111). Although this definition is broad, it captures the essence of what a leader does. Under this definition are numerous conceptual approaches to leadership, including personality trait, situational, individual style, functional, and integrated approach.

Trait Approach

The personality trait approach is the oldest and least supported today. It attempts to identify traits necessary for effective leadership. This approach subscribes to the notion that leaders are born and not made. The strength in the approach lies in its systematic attempt to identify the qualities of a leader. Its limitation is its fatalism: Either you have the necessary traits, or you don't.

Situational Approach

This approach is more eclectic. It subscribes to the idea that to be an effective leader, you must adapt to your situation (Hersey, 1984; Hersey & Blanchard, 1972). Its strength lies in its in-depth attempt to review various group situations in terms of leader behavior. However, it can lead you to believe that you can be effective in any situation as long as you appropriately vary your approach. This is misleading, as it implies that you can be all things to all people.

Individual Style Approach

This approach asks you to consider what leadership style fits you. To some extent this approach is a typology, because its advocates endeavor to identify types of leaders. Lewin (1944), Hersey and Blanchard (1972), and Merill and Reid (1983) describe leadership style. Lewin uses the three-part linear model, which considers leadership as either leader-centered, leader-group shared, or group-centered. The others describe four leadership types:

1. high task and low relationship;
2. low relationship and low task;
3. high relationship and low task; and
4. high task and high relationship.

Functional Approach

Here, functions are the means through which the leader facilitates the group in its activities or processes. Gibb and Gibb (1955) outline the following functions necessary for a group to be successful:

initiating, getting the group started or keeping things moving;
regulating, influencing the direction or pace of the group activity;
informing, providing the group or individual members with information;
supporting, creating an atmosphere of acceptance for all members; and
evaluating, helping the group appraise its progress, goal accomplishments, or decisions.

Integrated Approach

Napier and Gershenfeld (1993) note that "today, it is generally acknowledged that leadership qualities are intimately linked to our personalities—which in turn are products of our upbringing plus our inherited traits" (p. 241). Trotzer (1977) further states, "leader personality is the core of leader style" (p. 73). Earlier, we posited that you possess a theory that is in line with your personality. The same holds true with leadership. Your task is to discover what you believe about leadership, and from that deduce your leadership style. The fit between your personality and your approach will determine the development of your own leadership pattern and will greatly influence your effectiveness as a group counselor.

GROUP MEMBERS

Since the group medium has as its unique characteristic the therapeutic quality of members working together, you need to give careful consideration to the nature of each group member. Unlike individual counseling, the group brings into one setting a collection of unique individuals who endeavor to help one another. Therefore, the key factor in membership is the personality of the individual.

As members possess unique personality characteristics, they also display patterns of personal behavior. These patterns will be of particular importance to you in directing the interaction of your group. Your members bring unique qualities to the group; they also bring particular needs. Trotzer (1977) points out that group members share common needs that motivate behavior.

These young people are experiencing pain or frustration, and all have a need to ventilate the pressure they feel. Since they are facing difficulties, they hope to find support and acceptance within the group. Invariably, young people who enter group counseling have a need to improve their social relationships; their problems usually interfere with healthy social interaction.

They will probably share some ambivalence toward being in the group. Trotzer (1977) likens this to approach-avoidance conflict, wherein all want help but fear that their weaknesses will be exposed, and they will not be accepted. Most important, the relative strength of each of these needs will influence the behavior of each group member.

Member Roles

There are a number of approaches to describing or categorizing the roles of participants in group activities (Bales, 1951; Benne & Sheats, 1948; Ohlsen, 1977; and Yalom, 1985). Bales divided role behaviors into two classes: task or instrumental behaviors and expressive or social-emotional behaviors. Benne and Sheats subdivided roles into three groups: task behaviors, building and maintenance (relationship) behaviors, and individual roles. These two systems are similar in that both emphasize getting the job done (task behaviors) and getting along together (interpersonal behaviors). Individual roles serve the self-interest of the member; these are generally disruptive to the group. Because the behavior of elementary and middle school young people is less stylized than that of adults—the groups for whom these schemes are designed—we do not discuss further these conceptual approaches to member behavior.

Trotzer (1977) identifies four roles: "the client, the helper, the model, and the reality check" (p. 145). The *client* role is obvious; it represents the reason why participants attend the group—to receive help with the difficulties they face. The *helper* provides assistance by acting as a sounding board, sharing with others, providing feedback, confronting, supporting, or participating in the activities of the group. The role of *model* results when members provide an example of appropriate behavior for others to follow. Since all members usually do not experience identical difficulties or function at the same level, they can serve as credible and appropriate models for one another. The role that from time to time provides a *reality check* to group members is an important one. It helps members gain a sense of how things are outside the group. In this role, group members serve as members of society beyond the group. It is through this role that members assess how others outside the group will react to them, and consider alternative behaviors. Trotzer (1977) considers this role as representing the group as a social microcosm.

Members will demonstrate these roles by varying degrees and at varied times. Do not expect everyone to display all four role behaviors at the same time. Most important, look for the members who naturally display certain behaviors and make use of their contribution to help others in the group. If you cannot identify members who can fulfill these roles, as needed, it will be up to you to provide the needed role.

Member Behavior

Member roles relate to the assistance provided to participants. Member behavior is more individualized and serves the purposes of each member. Trotzer (1977) has organized member behavior in four categories: "resisting behaviors, manipulating behaviors, helping behaviors and emotional behaviors" (p. 146).

Resisting Behaviors.   Most resistance is within the member, and not a result of your poor leadership. Usually members are more resistive in the early stages of the group. As Dinkmeyer and Muro (1971) indicate, early resistance typically surrounds personal exploration and is largely a product of the lack of trust and cohesiveness among the group members. These mild initial forms of resistance usual disappear once the members have spent some time together and have developed some rapport.

A truer form of resistance may appear later in the group, when members are called upon to directly address their adjustment issues. Then you must carefully monitor the resistive actions and directly address the behavior when it impedes progress in counseling. Ohlsen (1977) proposes two methods of handling resistance: to interpret the nature of the resistance to the member, and to confront it. Both approaches need to be handled delicately, because there are side effects. Interpretation may invite defensive rationalization or intellectualization; and confrontation may initiate a stronger reaction to being placed on the spot. Nonetheless, at times you will need to take action, and how you handle the situation will depend on your best judgment about how to help the particular individual.

The second form of resisting behaviors is dominating or monopolizing behaviors. Some members will fall into this behavior mode because they want attention from you and/or other members of the group. These individuals tend to be verbally active and can consume large chunks of the group's time with their antics. Not only can they be troublesome to you, but they can also invoke negative feelings in the other group members, who will likely resent having one person dominate the conversation. You cannot assume that these young people are aware of what they are doing. Although the behavior is relatively easy to spot, you must approach the dominator with care—possibly outside the group setting. The earlier you act, the better your chance of correcting the behavior without meeting intensified resistance.

The third form of resisting behavior is hostility. Although this behavior does not frequently occur among children, if their participation in the group is forced or they view their involvement as punishment, they may react strongly to any request made of them. Hostile children have a tendency to intimidate and create unease among the other participants (Trotzer, 1977). Overcoming hostile resistance is a slow and delicate process. Trotzer (1977) recommends that you demonstrate a firm but compassionate attitude. We suggest that you address this behavior outside the group.

Silence is the fourth form of resistance. Although we support the right to silence, there are times when this behavior is disruptive. Silent members eventually wear on the group because their reluctance to participate gives other members mixed messages. Your first consideration is to determine the reason for the silence. Sometimes members are silent because they have nothing to say. This is an acceptable reason, but when this behavior persists over time it likely represents fear—of self-disclosure, censorship, or rejection. Silence can also be influenced by culture. Some Asians and Native Americans view silence as an expression of respect, not resistance.

We recommend that you invite the silent members to participate but respect their right to refuse. If the behavior persists, then you may need to privately discuss the matter with the individual and offer the option of leaving the group.

Clowning is a behavior that you may face with young people in fourth grade and above. They use humor as a means of gaining attention and diverting the group from its purpose. This is a difficult role to manage. Clowns often have the support of the group because their behavior is more enjoyable than much of the other content focus of the group.

Probably the best way to handle this behavior is to recognize the value of humor and comment on the possible meaning of the behavior: "When we make jokes it provides us with a way of not having to feel bad about the things that happen to us."

Intellectualization is the last behavior we will address. Trotzer (1977) indicates that those who intellectualize tend to talk in terms of "there and then" or "if and when" instead of "here and now" (p. 152). These individuals do not talk about themselves—their problems, feelings, or behaviors—but focus on issues external to them. To manage this, you may initially ignore the behavior, hoping that the intellectualizer will feel more comfortable with the group and be able to address pertinent issues. If this does not work, speak with the individual privately, outside of the group, and try to interpret the meaning of the behavior.

Manipulating Behaviors.   Trotzer (1977) points out that "the primary difference between resisting behaviors and manipulating behaviors is that the former are used as direct protection of self, and the latter are used to control others" (p. 154).

Socializing.   In one of the more subtle forms of manipulation, the individual distracts the group from its purpose by overemphasizing the relationships between members. Compared to resisting behaviors, socializing is a relatively minor distraction. Nevertheless, this social interaction is at the expense of the topic or purpose of the group. Socializers are pleasant, well-liked group members who are seemingly harmless. To handle this behavior, first remind the member of the purposes of the group; then use individuals with good social skills as positive role models who can help those who do not possess such skills.

Scapegoating.   This involves setting up one member for attack by the group. Usually this situation is arranged by one other member. This behavior focuses attention on the scapegoat, diverting attention from the attacker. This is a difficult situation to remedy. First, you must protect the scapegoat by directly intervening and denouncing the inappropriateness of such behavior in the group. Second, you will need to address the behavior of the instigators. You can talk with them privately and raise questions regarding their feelings about the scapegoated individual and how their actions may have affected this individual.

Dependency.   Dependency appears to be a position of weakness—deceptively so. In fact, it is a manipulative behavior wherein individuals have others assume responsibility for them. You are vulnerable to these individuals: After all, your job is to help people. Also, you may be flattered by the way dependent people defer to your expertise and wisdom. To manage this situation, refuse to take responsibility for these "victims" and try and teach them independent behavior. The latter will occur only if you move in small steps, supporting each effort toward independence.

Counselor Behavior.   The behaviors presented here represent actions the counselor uses to model facilitative behaviors for the group members. Group members may vicariously adopt these behaviors or they can be taught directly to assume them. The purpose of these behaviors is to promote a therapeutic atmosphere in the group.

Helping Behaviors.   This is a group of behaviors that in their natural state have largely a positive effect on the group and are developed through your modeling. Helping behaviors in groups are similar to those in individual counseling, but do possess some differences because you work with a number of young people simultaneously.

Effective Listening.   Adopt an attentive posture toward the speaker. By modeling good listening skills, you provide the group with the tools to act in kind. Listening has both physical and psychological components. Physically, you present yourself in a manner that shows others you are interested in what they are saying. Psychologically, your attentiveness is demonstrated through your verbal interaction with the speaker. The congruence between what the young person has said and your response indicates how attentively you are listening.

Self-disclosure.   We do not suggest that you spend a lot of time telling the group about yourself. Rather, self-disclosure here is a matter of letting the group know how you feel about something that has been said or has happened in the group. This is a modeling behavior, because you are helping the members understand how they may self-disclose. At the same time, you are setting a tone for members to disclose their thoughts and feelings about the activities of the group. Appropriately used, self-disclosure can help develop an atmosphere of trust when you, as a leader, reveal your thoughts or feelings.

Feedback.   Feedback, built on self-disclosure, involves letting others know your thoughts or feelings about them. It may focus either on the actions of the group or the behavior of a particular member, and cannot be effective until a level of trust has been achieved. This behavior is vital to the growth of group members. However, it is difficult to develop because most of us are threatened by comments on our behavior.

To be effective, feedback—unlike other helping behaviors—should conform to specific guidelines. Hansen, Warner, and Smith (1980) have enumerated eight criteria for effective feedback, drawn from the National Training Laboratory guidelines. We list several that are crucial to the success of any feedback effort.

1. Always ask yourself, How will what I am about to say be helpful to the other person? If you cannot answer, do not proceed with your feedback statement.
2. Describe the behavior observed; do not evaluate the person or group.
3. Be specific.

4. Give feedback about behavior the recipient can do something about.

5. Give feedback in close proximity to the behavioral occurrence.

Leveling.   Trotzer (1977) refers to leveling as a process wherein you are genuine in your self-expression and open to allowing other people know your true thoughts and feelings—a combination of self-disclosure and feedback. Trotzer likens leveling to Carl Rogers's concept of congruence. This is a higher-order behavior because it is usually effective only when group members have been working together for some time and have come to trust one another. Leveling is particularly helpful when plateaus are reached and members appear to with-hold from the group. As Trotzer (1977) points out, "leveling is both a remediating group behavior and a developmental one" (p. 161). This means that leveling behaviors can help a group clear the air of unresolved issues among members, and can help members move forward by providing them with new information about them-selves and their relationships with others.

Although the roles and behaviors presented in this section appear more relevant to adolescent and adult group counseling, they do begin to appear in the later elementary school grades. Since most group counseling at the elementary level does not begin until fourth grade, we chose to include this material on member behavior because you will devote significant time to intermediate and middle school students.

THE GROUP COUNSELING PROCESS

As Ohlsen (1977) has indicated, to be effective in group counseling you must be able to determine your group's level of functioning and facilitate the members to move to a more effective level of group interaction (p. 60). There are numerous models of group development (Hansen, Warner, & Smith, 1980; Jones, 1973; Peterson & Nisenholz, 1991; Trotzer, 1977; Tuckman, 1965; Yalom, 1985). These models are similar, usually having four or five steps essentially involving orientation, conflict, harmony and productive activity, and closure or termination.

Our approach is based on the work of Jones (1973), Peterson and Nizenholz (1991), and Trotzer (1977). From Jones we have taken the concept that groups vary in their development, both in task completion and in interpersonal relations. The task mode involves getting the job done; and the interpersonal mode represents the way in which group members work together to accomplish that task.

Peterson and Nisenholz (1991) contribute the premise that the behaviors of group member and leaders vary at each stage. This separates the behavior of the two group components, enables us to highlight how you can understand or predict the behavior of your group, and provides us with a basis for identifying your corresponding behavior.

Finally, we have used Trotzer's approach to linking the stage-level constructs to the psychological orientation of the group. Trotzer (1977) depicts the group counseling process as one of growth and development, which "entails the interaction between our needs and our relationships, resulting in the nature of our personal identity" (p. 43). Because of the developmental focus of elementary and middle school counseling, we believe that an enhanced sense of personal identity is the substance of group counseling for young people.

In counseling, the group member experiences two forms of development: intrapersonal and interpersonal. *Intrapersonal* development relates to individual need fulfillment, and *interpersonal* development is the acquisition of social interaction skills. These two areas are not mutually exclusive, and students focus upon each in a blended and simultaneous manner. From this perspective, effective groups enable students to increase their self-acceptance and to be more effective in their group interaction. Trotzer's approach is a meaningful way to draw together the foci of Jones (1973) and Peterson and Nizenholz (1991).

Orientation

At this stage, the group is getting started. The student participants are unsure of themselves and their situation, particularly at the fourth-grade level and above. Correspondingly, there is a sense of dependency on you as the leader. Group members are highly sensitive to how others act and react toward them. Much of the initial interaction, particularly with older children and participants of middle school age, is superficial and surrounded by observation of the reactions of others—to determine the acceptance level. Because of the tentativeness and related lack of trust among group members, they rely on structure to find their security. They want to know what the rules are, what they are to do, and what is to happen. This reliance on structure naturally leads to a dependence on you, which has both positive and negative aspects. On the one hand, dependency provides you with the opportunity for control; on the other, it might skew the students' interaction toward doing the "right thing."

In sum, group members are inclined to be dependent, and you are inclined to assume more responsibility for group interaction. The group is clearly task-oriented during this stage, seeking structure to provide a sense of security and direction. They are watchful and polite with one another, spending much of their time sizing up both you and other members. Virtually everything your students do in this early phase will be to maintain their sense of security. In time, your group members will become familiar with one another. The differences that exist among them will become apparent, bringing forth the struggles of the second stage.

Conflict/Acceptance

Since groups, by their nature, involve a heavy emphasis on interaction, conflict is inevitable. As Yalom (1985) has noted, much of the conflict is focused around the issues of dominance and control. This conflict occurs among members and between group and leader. The intragroup conflict surrounds members' finding a meaningful role in the group. The conflict with you, the leader, is a rebellion over such issues as dependency, group rules, agenda, and activities. You are targeted because if the students feel they can disagree with you and not experience a humiliating confrontation, they can disagree with one another without fear of rejection. As members work through their differences, your role is to remain nonthreatening and accept their challenges as a natural part of growth.

Since conflict is the theme at this stage, the interpersonal dimension predominates over the task dimension. Group members are preoccupied with their differences and with finding a place in the group. Conflict creates uncertainty and discomfort. As a hedge against these disquieting feelings, the group places its task emphasis on organization—the rationale being, if we spend our time on the details of organizing our group's activities, we will not have to face the issues of conflict. The initial efforts to resolve conflicts, therefore, are tentative and gradual. Once you can assist the group in working through some of the early conflicts, members will become more skilled and confident about handling subsequent ones. During this phase, you assume somewhat of a teaching role. You might teach by setting an example as you respond to challenges. Or you might guide members through their own conflicts, teaching them how to disagree and still come out with their integrity intact.

With the development of skill in conflict resolution, the group is ready to move to the next stage. Conflicts will occur in the future, but they likely will be resolved more quickly and effectively. Most important, they can move to a higher level of functioning because the members are more comfortable with themselves and others in the group.

Productive Activity

Gibson and Mitchell (1986) regard this stage as one of stability, wherein members establish commitment to the group and its purposes. Although there is strong interpersonal involvement by the members, the task dimension stands out. Jones (1973) regards this phase as one in which there is a data flow in the task dimension: If the group is working on a project, things just seem to get done; and with personal issues, there is considerable sharing without fear of censorship. In the interpersonal dimension this is a time of cohesion, because group members support each other and develop a bond. They share more freely, exploring the personal issues and receiving support from others. You will also find increased responsibility among group members, both for themselves and for the group. The group can now become an effective agent of change (Peterson & Nizenholz, 1991). Members increase their self-understanding and can move forward to resolve their problems. Your role is largely to facilitate the interaction, orchestrating the group to achieve the purposes for which it was formed. To move the group forward, you might need to alternately support the members and confront them. You can now draw upon the resources of the members to assist their peers in the problem-solving process.

Not every group reaches this stage. Some cannot come to grips with the conflict in stage two. But, if they do, you can see your group come of age, and will delight in the progress they make both as individuals and as a group.

Closure and Termination

Counseling groups come to an end either because you have predetermined the number of sessions or because the group has reached its goals. (If you are unsure of the duration, it is best to establish a shorter period of time than you believe necessary. If you need additional time you can always renegotiate the number of sessions.) Because counseling groups are oriented toward developing close interpersonal relations, most participants might not be ready for the sessions to end. Your role is to remind them of the time limit, to prepare them for closure, and then to terminate the sessions.

Closure. This is the act of helping the group collectively consider what has transpired during its existence—with emphasis on the life skills that members have learned. Closure is a time to review past sessions and to emphasize the higher level of functioning that each member has gained through the group experience.

Termination. This is either the natural conclusion of the group, having accomplished its mission, or of some individuals within the group who can no longer benefit because they are either unwilling to participate or are disruptive. These situations are the sole responsibility of the leader. Usually, the most effective way to release an individual member is through a private interview. Point out that the individual does not appear to find the group enjoyable or helpful, and therefore you believe it would be best for all if he or she would drop out or seek individual counseling.

In sum, we regard this developmental schema to be a road map of the life of your group. The sequence of stages enables you both to diagnose the level of your groups' functioning and to facilitate movement toward the goals and objectives for which you have created the group. Note that groups do not always progress smoothly through these stages of development. In fact, many become stuck in the first or second stage. Nonetheless, this stagewise schema will prove to be a valuable tool with which to assess the progress of your group.

EVALUATION

Generally, helping professionals who conduct counseling or other forms of group activity do not routinely evaluate the effectiveness of their efforts. It is not known whether they are opposed to evaluation, do not see its value, or lack the skills or procedures to evaluate.

There are two forms of evaluation: outcome evaluation and process evaluation. According to Trotzer (1977), *process* evaluation "refers to what goes on in the group and has three basic components: the leader, the members, and the group interaction" (p. 194). *Outcome* evaluation is "what happens in a group member's life as a result of experience in group counseling" (p. 196). We briefly review each of these.

Process Evaluation

Through process evaluation, you can appraise what is happening in your group and improve your effectiveness as a leader. As Trotzer (1977) notes, process evaluation focuses on group dynamics, such as your methods as a leader, the behavior of the group members, and the nature of the group interaction.

There are several ways to undertake process evaluation. First, you can solicit outside observation—long-term or single-visit—from colleagues experienced in group counseling, who will be able to provide an unbiased opinion.

The most frequent method of process evaluation is to solicit reactions from the members themselves. Ask for their input at regular intervals or when you feel an impasse has been reached—and hope that they are fully candid with you. You can also ask them to submit a written evaluation form. Give members a blank sheet of paper or note card and ask them to react to how the group has been getting along. You can write out questions about areas that especially concern you, and solicit an anonymous reaction. You might also ask the members to complete a check sheet or likert-type scale about various aspects of the group's activities.

Another method of evaluation involves member reaction and leader analysis. Here, group members are asked to write in journals or diaries their reaction to each session. You then analyze these records to rate the functioning of the group. To make the most of this method, solicit the journal entry immediately at the close of a session, when thoughts and reactions are fresh in members' minds.

Process evaluation is informal and subjective, because is relies on the perceptions of individual members. Such methods of evaluation cannot guarantee members' anonymity, and therefore may not reflect the true feelings or observations of the group. Regardless of the possible lack of objectivity, this evaluation can provide a wealth of information about the functioning of your group if used with caution.

Process evaluation will present problems with elementary school students. They have limited verbal skills, and below fourth grade have difficulty with cause-and-effect relationships. Also, younger children do not have a strong grasp of events over time. Therefore, you will be limited in the depth of process evaluation.

Outcome Evaluation

The purpose of outcome evaluation is to determine how the group has made a difference in the lives of its members. You might not have access to clear methods of judging the degree to which individual members have met the goals of the group. In spite of such difficulties you must attempt to assess the outcomes for each member. To begin, you can help members establish their own goals. This can be done through individual screening interviews or a pregroup meeting.

Outcome evaluation should take place at the last session or shortly afterward, at which time you will attempt to determine the extent to which members have met their goals. Outcome evaluation can coincide with closure and termination.

During the final session, you should solicit input from each member. The typical means of acquiring this input at closure is through "public testimony," which entails asking each member to report what has transpired for him or her in the group. Members trace their experiences and comment on how far they think they have progressed. Another approach is to have each group member comment on the changes every other member has made as a result of the group. This method is usually carried out in something of a "fish bowl" design, where each member, in turn, is the focus of comments by all others. Other closure techniques include soliciting information through a written report, where specific questions are addressed.

The outcome evaluation might be made by an observer. In that case, he or she should be in a position to detect behavior change. Those most likely to fill this criteria are teachers or parents. Either at the end of the group or within a reasonable time thereafter, ask these individuals to respond about each group member, either in an open-ended fashion or through a specific instrument of the type mentioned above. Your evaluation will be more meaningful if you can be specific in identifying the evaluation items so that they can be easily measured. The most difficult criteria to assess are affective—changes in feelings or attitudes. You should not be discouraged by such difficulties. Any information you collect may provide you with a sense of how the young people in your group have been influenced by their experiences.

The most meaningful evaluation data you can collect will come through a follow-up assessment. The only way you can know whether members have been affected by the group experience is to conduct your evaluation some time after the close of the group. How much time is necessary or desirable is determined by the individual goals of the members. In all likelihood, the immediate positive effect of the group will have worn off within a month to six weeks, so you can see if the changes are taking place.

Regardless of how you approach evaluation, we strongly urge you to routinely evaluate your counseling methods. Without an assessment you will have to rely on your intuitive feelings about the success of your group—and we have found that leaders are usually the least effective evaluators of their own efforts.

SUMMARY

Group counseling is a meaningful approach to direct intervention because it provides a real-world setting in which to help young people work through adjustment difficulties. It also promotes an atmosphere in which they can receive input and support from others. With group counseling, you can economize the use of your time. You can work with as many as six or seven young people simultaneously. Since they may be experiencing different adjustment difficulties, each can be a valuable resource for the other.

This chapter discussed practical considerations for forming and conducting counseling groups. Particular emphasis was placed on your role as a leader. We hope that this material will stimulate you to consider and further explore your own leadership style. We recognize that the development of leadership skills is a task that might evolve over your lifetime.

Other material included understanding your group members and the process that takes place over the life of the group. We encourage you to use the material contained here as a departure point to a more comprehensive consideration of group counseling. For more detailed discussions of the topics presented, see the reference materials at the end of the chapter.

REVIEW

1. Identify two advantages of counseling groups compared to counseling individuals.
2. Select several disadvantages of groups and suggest possible remedies.
3. Construct a hypothethical group and construct a purpose statement, goals, and objectives for its members.
4. Discuss the screening of members, addressing ethical considerations.
5. Think of someone you regard as an effective leader. Discuss this individual's character and compare his or her leadership qualities to yours.
6. Identify the member behaviors that occur frequently in groups. Discuss with several others how these behaviors can be most effectively handled.
7. Pose two methods for handling the conflict stage in a group. Construct dialogue statements that might be used to initiate group discussion of a conflict situation.
8. Develop a brief process evaluation questionnaire that could be used by group members to consider their interpersonal relationships.
9. Identify three things that you like or dislike about groups and consider the basis for your feelings. Translate these attitudes into a statement about your interest in working as group leader.

REFERENCES

Association for Specialists in Group Work (1989). *Ethical guidelines for group counselors and professional standards for the training of group workers.* Alexandria, VA: AACD.

Bales, R. F. (1951). *Interaction process analysis.* Cambridge, MA: Addison-Wesley.

Benne, K. D., and Sheats, P. (1948). Functional roles of group members. *Journal of Social Issues, 4* (2).

Corey, G. (1990). *Theory and practice of group counseling* (3rd ed.). Pacific Grove, CA: Brooks/Cole.

Dinkmeyer, D. C., & Muro, J. (1971). *Group counseling: Theory and practice.* Itasca, IL: Peacock.

Gazda, G. M. (1989). *Group counseling: A developmental approach* (4th ed.). Boston: Allyn & Bacon.

Gibb, J., & Gibb, L. (1955). *Applied group dynamics.* Bethel, ME: National Training Laboratories.

Gibson, R. L., & Mitchell, M. H. (1986). *Introduction to counseling and guidance* (2nd ed.). New York: Macmillan.

Gregory, J. C., & McConnell, S. C. (1986). Ethical issues with psychotherapy in group contexts. *Psychology in Private Practice, 4*(1), 51-62.

Hansen, J. C., Warner, R. W., & Smith, E. M. (1980). *Group counseling: Theory and process* (2nd ed.). Chicago: Rand McNally.

Hersey, P. (1984). *The situational leader.* New York: Warner.

Hersey, P., & Blanchard, K. (1972). *Management and organizational behavior: Utilizing human resources* (2nd ed.). Englewood Cliffs, NJ: Prentice-Hall.

Jones, J. (1973). A model of group development. *The 1973 annual handbook for group facilitators.* Iowa City, IA: University Associates.

Lewin, K. (1944). The dynamics of group action. *Educational Leadership, 1,* 195-200.

Merill, D. W., & Reid, R. H. (1983). *Personal styles and effective performance: Making your style work.* Radnor, PA: Chilton.

Napier, R. W., & Gershenfeld, M. K. (1993). *Groups: Theory and experience* (5th ed.). Boston: Houghton Mifflin.

Ohlsen, M. M. (1977). *Group counseling* (2nd ed.). New York: Holt.

Peterson, J. V., & Nisenholz, B. (1991). *Orientation to counseling* (2nd ed.). Boston: Allyn & Bacon.

Ruten, J. S., & Groves, J. E. (1989). Making society's groups more therapeutic. *International Journal of Group Psychotherapy, 39,* 3-16.

Schmuck, R. A., & Schmuck, P. A. (1992). *Group processes in the classroom* (6th ed.). Dubuque, IA: William C. Brown.

Trotzer, J. (1977). *The counselor and the group: Integrating theory, training and practice.* Monterey, CA: Brooks/Cole.

Tuckman, B. (1965). Developmental sequence in small groups. *Psychological Bulletin, 63*(6), 384-399.

Yalom, L. D. (1985). *The theory and practice of group psychotherapy* (3rd ed.). New York: Basic Books.

chapter 9

The Teacher's Role in Guidance

OUTLINE

INTRODUCTION

Because elementary school guidance programs are relatively new, it is important that the role of the teacher in guidance be clearly understood. In fact, the success of the guidance program may very well be determined by the clarity with which teachers, counselors, administrators, and other staff articulate their roles.

The teacher is one of the most significant adults in the life of the elementary school child. Next to the parents, the teacher manifests more influence than anyone else. According to Myrick (1987), surveys show that elementary students first turn to their parents and then their teachers. Traditionally, elementary school teachers have shown considerable interest in their students, and have recognized the limitations of subject-centered teaching. This underlines the positive role teachers can play in elementary school guidance.

CLASSROOM CLIMATE

Helping children develop requires a team effort among the teacher, counselor, administrator, and other specialists. One of the most meaningful things the teacher can do is provide a classroom climate that not only promotes academic achievement but helps students feel comfortable in their surroundings. Children should be helped to study and to understand that they are unique personalities who are growing, changing, and developing in response to the demands of society. Self-understanding assists students in being able not only to adjust to themselves but to their peers as well. One way the teacher can develop a pleasant and productive climate is to adopt a guidance orientation in the day-to-day operation of the classroom.

The Guidance Point of View

In chapter 2 we discussed the counselor's deep commitment to individuals and to the fulfillment of human potential. Teachers who wish to have a classroom where the guidance point of view prevails will find that this commitment is necessary for them, too. The best way to define this point of view in the classroom is to discuss some of its important characteristics.

The Teacher's Beliefs and Characteristics.   Guidance-oriented teachers not only give lip service to the idea that children are people but treat children as people. Unfortunately, you need only look as far as the elementary school in your own community to find teachers who do not treat children humanely. In the guidance-oriented classroom, children are treated with dignity and respect. Many teachers understand this principle and operate their classrooms accordingly.

Another essential teacher characteristic is a belief in the uniqueness of people, especially children. Guidance-oriented teachers do not make comparisons but realize that children—even those growing up in the same house—can be unique in their interests, abilities, and personalities. The teacher's role is to help children develop to their greatest potential regardless of their strengths and weaknesses.

To operate a guidance-oriented classroom, the teacher needs to look inward to understand the behavior that he or she might exhibit in the day-to-day interactions with children. It is no longer acceptable for teachers to practice behavior based upon how they feel at a given moment. Rather, the more successful teachers will have systematically explored their own personalities and needs structure. Based upon that self-understanding, they will enhance learning by responding to children in appropriate ways.

The extent to which children will become more independent in their thinking and behavior can be a direct result of teachers who believe in, and practice, classroom discipline based upon democratic principles (Stone & Peer, 1970). Therefore, an important teacher characteristic is the belief that a classroom should function where order and freedom prevail. This atmosphere will encourage children to think for themselves and become more responsible.

The guidance-oriented teacher recognizes the importance of knowing children as individuals. A positive teacher-child relationship is inherent to this understanding. Such a relationship—developed through conferences, observation, and sociometric and other techniques—will show the teacher how students relate to their classmates and others. Teachers who take the time to get to know their students not only will have more positive relationships with them but will also find them more willing and able to learn.

Guidance-oriented teachers emphasize individual learning whenever possible, and attempt to help children learn at a pace consistent with their abilities. As difficult as this may seem, teachers who practice individualization report progress both in academics and personality development.

The use of encouragement may well be the most important characteristic of the guidance-oriented classroom teacher. Encouragement results in children acknowledging their self-worth. Dinkmeyer, Dinkmeyer, and Sperry (1987) state: "If someone feels discouraged and inadequate, the lack of self-esteem produces dysfunctional behavior and failure to become involved in the tasks of life" (p. 124).

Teachers spend a significant amount of time with their students. The opportunities for encouragement, as well as discouragement, are many and varied. Dinkmeyer and Dreikurs (1963) state that the teacher who encourages

1. places value on the child as he is;
2. shows faith in the child that enables the child to have faith in himself;
3. has faith in the child's ability; wins the child's confidence while building his self-respect;
4. recognizes a job well done. Gives recognition for effort;
5. utilizes the group to facilitate and enhance the development of the child;
6. integrates the group so that the child can be sure of his place in it;

7. assists in the development of skills sequentially and psychologically paced to permit success;
8. recognizes and focuses on strengths and assets;
9. utilizes the interests of the child to energize instruction. (p. 50)

Teachers who are truly interested in the wholistic development of the child are well advised to use encouragement as often as possible.

An integral part of the teacher's role in the guidance program is to develop and maintain a classroom climate conducive to learning and to a positive view of the learning process. The guidance orientation and the teacher's beliefs and personal characteristics are two critical elements in a positive classroom climate.

THE TEACHER'S ROLE IN PROMOTING THE GUIDANCE PROGRAM

Cooperation with the counselor is the most important way in which the classroom teacher can assist with the promotion of the guidance program. Without teacher cooperation and supports the program's chances for success are limited. We discuss how the teacher can promote the guidance program through orientation activities and through cooperation with you, the counselor.

Promotion through Orientation

At the beginning of each school year, teachers should set aside some time to talk with students about the guidance program. They should note the counselor's name, location of his or her office, how to make an appointment, and when it might be a good idea to talk with the counselor, along with the overall goals and objectives of the guidance program. During this orientation the teachers can arrange a tour of the building, including your area. The student can then be introduced (or reintroduced) to you. Talking with students about the counselor and program not only orients the students but indicates that the teacher is supportive of the program.

After the teacher has provided an initial orientation, you should be invited to visit the classroom. You can go into more detail about the guidance program and answer the children's questions. Frequently, younger children are curious about this person who professes such an interest in their well-being, and will want to test it by making an appointment right away. Try to accommodate as many of these students as possible. Even though curiosity might be the only reason for coming in, this gives you an opportunity to get to know the children, let them see what counseling is, and begin developing a relationship that could have far-reaching effects.

The teacher can also promote the guidance program by including you in classroom events such as birthdays, Valentine's Day parties, and the like. This will mean a lot to the students and help persuade them of your interest. The teacher can also assist the program by inviting you to stop by when parents are present.

To further promote the program, you should be available as a guest speaker at school and community functions. Teachers can help by recommending you to group leaders as a possible presenter. Not all counselors can meet such demands. Some have produced videotapes that outline the goals of the guidance program and offer examples of program activities. Counselors who are visible in the community and are willing to give freely of their time will experience the greatest success in their efforts to provide a meaningful guidance program.

Promotion through Cooperation

The classroom teacher's cooperation is essential if individual or small-group counseling is to take place. This cooperation includes making referrals, allowing students to miss part of an academic exercise and entering into counselor consultation with regard to student needs and progress. Also imperative is teacher involvement in guidance program committees and councils. Teachers can provide valuable input by serving on the guidance program advisory council. It will probably meet only two or three times per semester, but through this group you can find out how the program is being accepted.

Teachers can also serve on other committees organized to conduct needs assessment, to review and make recommendations with regard to testing, or to organize a parent education program. As we pointed out in chapter 7, it is essential that teachers serve on the committee to organize the classroom guidance curriculum. Teachers who willingly and conscientiously serve on counselor-organized councils and committees will make a valuable contribution toward the promotion of the guidance program, and should be given recognition for their help.

During the course of the year you will conduct orientation sessions for students, teachers, parents, and the community. Teachers can show support for the program by participating in these sessions whenever possible, as well as encouraging others to attend.

THE TEACHER'S ROLE IN CLASSROOM GUIDANCE

Classroom guidance is an essential part of the elementary school guidance program. Activities assist elementary school students in better understanding themselves, feeling better about themselves, and being able to make positive and far-reaching decisions. The interrelation of classroom guidance and curriculum is an integral part of the developmental approach to guidance (Peters, Shertzer, and Van Hoose, 1965). Classroom teachers have the best opportunity to help students develop positive feelings about themselves and to develop attitudes and habits that will determine future learning success. It is imperative, therefore, that classroom teachers be actively involved in classroom guidance.

The Teacher's Role in Assessing Needs

The classroom teacher, more than anyone else in the elementary or middle school, has the best *feel* for the needs of students. However, there are times when even the teacher may not be fully cognizant of their extent. Therefore, a more formal assessment of student needs must be carried out. You must accept the primary responsibility for carrying this out, but the teachers should be involved as well.

The teacher can join a needs assessment committee. There, teachers will share those needs that are known to be present, and help determine those less evident. By this means the teacher can help devise questionnaires and other instruments that might be administered to students, parents, and on occasion other members of the school or community. Once such an instrument has been developed, the teacher plays an important role in field testing to see that it solicits appropriate information and is understandable to those who will be completing it. The teacher can then help with the administration, scoring, and analysis of the data.

The Teacher's Role in Organizing

Once the needs of a particular group, classroom, or grade level have been determined, the next step is to organize a program directed at meeting those needs. The classroom teacher can again make a tremendous contribution by agreeing to serve on the organization committee. This committee is headed by the counselor but includes teacher and sometimes student and/or parent representation. (Not all teachers need to serve on all committees. For example, if there are more than two classrooms at the same grade level, one teacher might serve on the needs assessment committee, another on the organization committee, and so on. The important thing is that teachers who have basic understandings of the growth and development of the students at a particular grade level be present.)

Based upon the determined needs, the organization committee begins to set goals for how and at what level the needs are to be met. Once the goals are in place, the next step is to identify or develop materials that will help students satisfy the goals. At this point it would be a good idea for the committee to use the classroom guidance activity planning form (Figure 7.2), which outlines how to convert needs into well-planned activities.

The Teacher's Role in Implementing

Up to now, teachers have served on committees and assisted in developing and carrying out needs surveys, in setting goals, and in finding ways to meet these goals. Now the program must go into action. The teacher, in cooperating with the counselor, must determine when, how, and by whom the activities are to be carried out. This includes deciding how, many sessions will be needed, how long each session will be, what dates and times will be optimal, and who will be responsible for carrying out each session. Usually, it works out best if you lead the first session. This way, the teacher can observe your techniques and gain a better understanding of what is to be accomplished. The teacher then follows up to be sure that the students have understood the concepts, and to integrate what has been learned into the normal curricula whenever possible. (In a multi-session activity, you can conduct the first session and have the teacher accept responsibility for subsequent sessions.)

The Teacher's Role in Evaluation

The last section of the classroom guidance activity planning form calls for an evaluation. In evaluating the classroom guidance program, the evaluation committee might want to summarize from all of these procedures, or they may devise another means of rating the program. Specifically, the teacher's role here is as follows:

1. To serve on the evaluation committee during the development of the evaluation process and the establishment of the criteria for success.
2. To assist the counselor in the development of pretest surveys to determine "where the students are" prior to being exposed to the guidance activity.
3. To assist in the development and administration of the posttest to determine the extent to which the activity satisfied the stated purpose of the activity or the program as a whole.
4. To assist in analyzing the data generated by the pre- and posttests, and with preparing documentation to show the results.
5. To work with the counselor and the classroom guidance committee in making program changes based upon results of the evaluation findings.

The role of the classroom teacher in needs assessment, organizing, implementing, and evaluation is extremely important. As Gysbers and Henderson (1988) point out: "Staff members are important members of the guidance team, and as such their competencies and their contributions to the program need to be identified" (p. 99). Those schools that involve teachers in classroom guidance and that recognize teacher competencies and contributions will, in the end, have programs that will meet their students' needs.

THE TEACHER'S ROLE IN COUNSELING

Teachers are not professional counselors, nor should they necessarily conduct counseling sessions (Muro & Dinkmeyer, 1977). In most cases, they have neither the training nor the time to counsel in the classroom. However, since they spend a tremendous amount of time with students—sometimes even more than parents—the teachers, more than any other professional in the school, can get to know the students best. Teachers have an opportunity to establish a relationship with students based upon mutual trust and respect, and will frequently be called upon to serve in a listening-advising capacity (Gibson & Mitchell, 1990). Thus, even though teachers might not "counsel" according to the traditional definition, they can serve as the initial counseling contact in the school.

The Teacher's Role in Student Referrals

When to Make Referrals.   The following list, although not extensive, can help teachers judge when a referral to the counselor may be appropriate:

1. any student who requests to see the counselor;
2. when students exhibit learning difficulties;
3. when students are having difficulties with peer relationships;
4. when students exhibit classroom behavior problems (These students should understand that they are not being *sent* to the counselor to have their behavior *corrected*, but that the teacher feels the counselor can help them in a nonthreatening way);
5. when students are not accepted by their peers;
6. when students are frequently late to school or have difficulty getting their schoolwork done on time (Again, the purpose here is not to send the student to the counselor, but to offer the counselor as a way of obtaining help with planning, etc.);
7. when students are excessively absent;
8. when students exhibit a sudden change in their behavior;
9. when students abuse drugs or are being sexually or physically abused (Teachers should be aware of school policy and state law with regard to their responsibility, especially in the case of sexual or physical abuse);
10. when students have recently experienced a death or a divorce in their family;
11. when students are new to the school;
12. when students exhibit excessive aggression;
13. when students exhibit daydreaming and/or withdrawal behavior; and
14. when students are facing a move to a new community.

Before making a referral, the teacher must carefully appraise the severity of the situation and the student's behavior. For example, not all students will be affected in the same way by the death of a family member. The referral should be made only when there is evidence that the student is having difficulty dealing with the situation.

How to Make Referrals.   Most school counselors know that simply being available does not mean that students will beat a path to their door. How many students come to you on a voluntary basis will depend largely upon the orientation to counseling they have received from their teacher and the counselor. In the elementary school, and to a lesser degree the middle school, you may encounter students who have little perception of what a counselor is or does. It is imperative, therefore, that teachers and counselors work together to orient students to the counseling process.

A guideline for teacher referrals should be established by the guidance program advisory committee. This should include possible reasons for making referrals (such as the list we provided earlier) and show teachers how to proceed once they have determined that a student needs to see you.

Every effort should be made to turn a teacher referral into a self-referral. Elementary and middle school students will refer themselves for counseling if they have a clear understanding of who you are and what you do. The teacher might guide a student toward self-referral by scheduling a conference. A hypothetical dialogue from such a conference follows:

TEACHER: Lacey, I've noticed that ever since your grandmother died you seem to spend quite a bit of time looking out the window, sort of distracted from your schoolwork. I'll bet you miss your grandma a lot, don't you?

LACEY [a second-grader]: Yes. I miss her. She was my very best friend in the whole world, and I want her to come back. Why did she have to die, anyway?

TEACHER: Do you remember when we talked about when students might want to see the counselor, and our counselor came in and talked with our class about it?

LACEY [nodding her head]: Uh-huh.

TEACHER: Well, I think that going to see the counselor might help you with some of the feelings you have about your grandmother's death. Have you ever thought about seeing her?

LACEY: Yes, I've thought about it but I wasn't quite sure how to do it.

TEACHER: If you like, I'd be glad to help you make an appointment.

LACEY: OK.

This is a case of teacher referral turning into self-referral. Lacey now knows it's OK to see the counselor, how to do it, and what they will talk about. In a teacher referral, students may not be fully aware of their reason for seeing the counselor, and may feel as if they have been sent against their will. In the self-referral, the student is more in control of the situation and more likely to share openly with you. Self-referral can be encouraged by other adults who have contact with the children (e.g., parents, coaches, or music teachers). The classroom teacher and counselor should recognize the importance of such adults and discuss when and how to encourage self-referrals.

If it is not possible to turn a teacher referral into a self-referral, the teacher can follow a predetermined procedure. Figure 9.1 is an example of a referral form to be used in conjunction with a teacher-counselor conference. In fact, some teachers prefer to fill out the form as they talk to you. (It was our experience, when working as elementary/middle school counselors, that teachers are apt to

Please complete this form for each student whom you wish to refer for counseling. Please place an X or check mark in the appropriate column.

TEACHER'S NAME _____ TODAY'S DATE _____

STUDENT'S NAME _____ GRADE _____ AGE _____ ROOM NO. _____

Suggested date(s) and time(s) for student to see counselor:

Date(s) _____ Time(s) _____

	YES	NO
1. Usually gets along with peers.		
2. Usually gets along with adults.		
3. Is shy, timid, or withdrawn.		
4. Is aggressive.		
5. Can sit still for a reasonable amount of time.		
6. Could probably do better schoolwork.		
7. Is cooperative.		
8. Seems to be OK physically.		
9. Daydreams frequently.		
10. Is achieving up to apparent capacity.		
11. Gets emotionally upset easily and inappropriately.		
12. Has had a sudden change in behavior.		

COMMENTS: (Summarize the reason for the referral. Use back if necessary.)

FIGURE 9.1   Classroom teacher's counseling referral form

make referrals when they see the counselor. This might be in the hall, on the playground, or in the lunchroom. It was not uncommon to receive three or four referrals while making a trip across the playground during recess.) The conference helps teachers to better think through why they believe the referral is necessary and what they think the outcome of the counseling should be. The conference also assists counselors by giving them an opportunity to ask the teacher about the needs of the student. The items on the referral form are general in nature. This is by design, so that the form itself will not become the only communication between you and the teacher. However, the form contains enough specific information to remind you what the referral was about.

Receiving a referral form either during the informal conference or soon afterward will assist you in remembering and responding to the referral.

Following Up on Referrals.   Once a teacher referral has been made, and you have had at least one session with the student, a teacher-counselor consultation should be held. You probably will not be able to discuss the content of the counseling session. However, the follow-up session will assure the teacher that you did indeed see the student. Although you should initiate this session, it is imperative that the teacher cooperate by being available and by understanding the confidentiality required between counselor and student. You may, even after one session, have a recommendation that will assist the teacher with a particular student. Also, if you let the teacher know what behaviors to observe, he or she can serve as a professional observer (Blum, 1986).

The teacher's role in referral cannot be stressed too strongly. Without the teacher's knowledge and cooperation, many students might not receive your help.

The Teacher's Role in Parent Referrals

As teachers frequently are the first to hear of students' needs, so they may be the first to be consulted by parents regarding a variety of domestic situations. In many cases teachers have neither the time nor the expertise to deal with these problems and will refer the parent to you. As with student referrals, the teacher can turn a parent referral into a parent self-referral, encouraging a parent to seek your help. This can best be accomplished by explaining how to make an appointment to see you, and what the parent may reasonably expect from the consultation.

SUMMARY

We discussed the important role of teachers in the organization and ongoing success of an elementary/middle school guidance program. We pointed out that an integral part of this role is to develop and maintain a classroom climate that promotes both learning and well-being. An important aspect of the teacher's role is to promote the guidance program through orientation and by cooperating with the counselor in various organizational activities.

Teachers should be involved in the assessment of student needs and in organizing, implementing, and assisting in the evaluation of the classroom guidance program. They should also be available to serve on committees.

We offered suggestions as to how the teacher can best participate in the counseling aspect of the guidance program. We discussed the teacher's role in student referrals—when and how to make them and how to follow up. We also discussed referral of parents who may need help with their children.

Teachers play a critical role in the success or failure of an elementary/middle school guidance program. Their interest, enthusiasm, and cooperation in the organization and implementation of such a program are vital if the needs of the students are to be met.

REVIEW

1. Why is the teacher's role in the guidance program so crucial to its success?
2. Briefly discuss what is meant by teachers' assessing their own personalities and determining their needs as they pertain to classroom instruction and interaction with students.

3. Prepare an outline for presenting a guidance program orientation session to students at various grade levels.

4. Discuss the teacher's role in needs assessment, organization, implementation, and evaluation of a classroom guidance program.

5. List several student behaviors possibly indicating that a referral is necessary.

6. Using role play with another adult, show how you would turn a potential teacher referral into a self-referral.

7. Discuss some reasons why teachers should use a referral form when making student referrals.

8. What should teachers reasonably expect from a follow-up session with the counselor?

REFERENCES

Blum, L. (1986). Building constructive counselor-teacher relationships. *Elementary School Guidance and Counseling, 20,* 236–239.

Dinkmeyer, D. C., Dinkmeyer, D. C., Jr., & Sperry, L. (1987). *Adlerian counseling and psychotherapy.* Columbus, OH: Merrill.

Dinkmeyer, D. C., & Dreikurs, R. (1963). *Encouraging children to learn.* Englewood Cliffs, NJ: Prentice-Hall.

Gibson, R. L., & Mitchell, M. H. (1990). *Introduction to counseling and guidance* (3rd ed.). New York: Macmillan.

Gysbers, N. C., & Henderson, P. (1988). *Developing and managing your school guidance program.* Alexandria, VA: AACD.

Muro, J. J., & Dinkmeyer, D. C. (1977). *Counseling in the elementary school: A pragmatic approach.* Dubuque, IA: William C. Brown.

Myrick, R. D. (1987). *Developmental guidance and counseling: A practical approach.* Minneapolis, MN: Educational Media Corporation.

Peters, H. J., Shertzer, B., and Van Hoose, W. (1965). *Guidance in the elementary schools.* Chicago: Rand McNally.

Stone, L. A., & Peer, G. G. (1970). *Implementing a functional elementary school guidance program.* Topeka, KS: State Department of Education.

chapter **10**

Parent Education and Consultation

OUTLINE

INTRODUCTION

According to Dodson and Kurpius, the family "is a unit of people who live together and share life's basic day-to-day functions (1989 p. 3), whose purpose "is to create a vessel or an environment for the development of mature, fully-functioning individuals" (p. 3). At the head of the family have been the parents, or perhaps more appropriately today, the parent. Regardless of any societal changes, rearing children is still considered a parental responsibility.

Parenting is one of the few tasks in life for which there is little or no organized training (Bradley & Stone, 1992). Although the concept of parent education has been around since the 1920s, only recently has it been used to include experiences that will assist parents to be more effective in their roles (Hammer & Turner, 1990). LeMasters and DeFrain (1989) state:

> It is usually assumed in our society that people have to be trained for difficult roles: Most business firms would not consider turning a sales-clerk loose on the customers without some formal training; the armed forces would scarcely send a raw recruit into combat without extensive and intensive training; most states now require a course in driver education before high school students can acquire a driver's license. Even dog owners often go to school to learn how to handle their pet properly. (pp. 80–81)

Given the complexity of being a parent, you must be on the cutting edge of parent education and consultation, and must devote a substantial amount of time to parents. Many parents are unsure about their roles and their relationships with their children. Parent education and consultation, organized by the counselor, can go a long way toward alleviating such confusion.

This chapter addresses the importance of parent education and consultation as well as your role therein. In addition, we review some contemporary parent education programs, and offer suggestions on how you might go about choosing one for your school. Finally, we discuss your role as a consultant to parents.

THE NEED FOR PARENT EDUCATION AND CONSULTATION

Parents face increasing difficulty in dealing with the behavior of their children. This is evidenced by the increasing number of dropouts and at-risk students. The growth in the divorce rate, dual-career families, and the large number of single-parent families—in a society whose complexity continues to spiral—helps build a good case for parent education (Kottman & Wilborn, 1992).

Traditional methods of parenting are not as effective as they once were. This adds to parents' confusion and frustration, sometimes with tragic consequences. Dinkmeyer, Dinkmeyer, and Sperry (1987) state:

> Parent education is badly needed. Its essential goal is to improve the relationship between parent and child by making more alternatives available and by promoting greater understanding and acceptance. Parent education brings an openness to new ideas and techniques that can be crucially important in resolving present problems and avoiding new ones. (p. 319)

It is ironic that we educate people to raise and fatten cattle and to keep the dairy cow contented so that she will give more and sweeter milk. Yet, anyone may become a parent who is biologically able and psychologically willing (Bradley & Stone, 1992). As a result, teachers and counselors are faced with student problems that might have been avoided had the parents been prepared for their difficult task.

A Brief History of Parenting

Given the lack of training, where did parents learn what they do know? The only consistent answer is that the parent was at one time a child and parenting techniques were handed down.

Then, where did our parents learn, and their parents, and so on? Looking back two or three centuries reveals that modern child-rearing practices had their origins in Europe.

Europe was for centuries an autocratic society, governed by rulers who thought themselves chosen by God. People did what they were told, on pain of death. Within this hierarchy existed a chain of command, ranging from nobles to slaves. The family reflected this chain of command. The husband was superior to the wife, who in most cases was superior to the children. (We say "most cases" because an elder son was considered by society to have more value then his mother.) Children had to do what their parents said. If they didn't, the local authorities could be engaged to make the child behave.

Generally, wives and children were beaten into submission. This method of discipline was passed down from generation to generation, and while we are beginning to see some change, it is still largely practiced today. Although this autocratic approach (Bradley & Stone, 1992) seems to have lost much of its effectiveness, many parents do not understand its failings or how they might need to change their techniques.

The explanation for the failure of the autocratic approach has political overtones. Over the past 150 years this country has experienced a series of democratic revolutions. This includes the demise of slavery, followed by women's suffrage, workers' rights, and so on. We have, to some extent, recognized racial and sexual equality. However, the group of people for whom social justice has been slowest to arrive are our children. Their struggle, while quieter and more subtle than other social movements, has been taking place for many years. It is only in the last 25 to 50 years that self-determination on the part of our children has caused child-rearing methods, learned from our parents, to be less effective.

The Concept of Equality

Many people, when first confronted with the idea that children see themselves as equal to adults, deny this and talk about how things "ought to be." Usually this is the result of not understanding what the concept of equality really means. It does not mean, as often interpreted by parents, that children see themselves literally the same as adults. Dreikurs and Soltz (1987) defined equality in terms of worth as a person: equality in terms of dignity, and perhaps more important, in terms of the right to respect. Once children realized this, the autocratic approach was doomed.

Your role as counselor is to help parents understand not only why their present techniques might be failing but how they can appropriately deal with their children's behavior. This is the primary goal of parent *education.* Parent *consultation* is recommended for parents who experience problems after receiving special training, or whose children are experiencing such extreme difficulties that outside help is indicated.

Outcomes of Parent Education and Consultation

The need for parent education and consultation, as provided by the counselor, may be best understood by considering some of the expected outcomes of these processes.

Improved Behavior at Home and at School.   The results of parental participation in education groups include positive changes in their attitudes toward children, positive changes in children's behavior, and improvement in the family atmosphere (Campbell & Sutton, 1983; McKay & Hillman, 1979). Kottman & Wilborn (1992) found that

> Parents who have attended parent study groups led by either counselors or counselor-trained parents differ significantly in general attitudes toward their children from parents who have not attended such groups. (p. 13)

Improved Parent/Child Relationships.   An essential goal of parent education is to improve relationships between parents and children. As parents become more understanding and accepting, children are less likely to misbehave, and the relationship between them improves.

Improved Acceptance of Responsibility.   In working with parents, both in parent study groups and in consultation, we found time after time that children who began to feel better about their parents were more willing to accept responsibilities. For example, Marvin, a nine-year-old, had been locked in an intense power struggle with his mother over getting up in the morning. After repeated attempts to rouse the boy, his mother finally would scream at him and pull the covers off. Marvin would then grudgingly get out of bed and begin getting ready for school. During our consultation we were able to ascertain that Marvin heard his mother each time she called, but resented being told what to do.

Through consultation we taught Marvin's mother how to let Marvin accept the responsibility for getting *himself* up in the morning. We explained that Marvin really didn't mind getting up. What he resented was being robbed of the opportunity to get himself up, and that staying in bed was his way of protesting. Once Marvin realized that his mother was no longer going to be responsible for getting him up in the morning, he accepted the responsibility himself. He felt good about being responsible, and his mother felt good about regaining her composure in the morning.

More Involvement of Parents with the School.   Parents who have positive relationships with their children, and whose children are more apt to accept responsibility, are more likely to become involved with the school. This would account for the number of well-adjusted parents participating in school programs. But what about those who aren't experiencing complete success with their children? Parents' involvement with the school will often begin with parent education. As their attitude toward their children and the school improves, so will their level of involvement with the school.

Improvement in the Student's School Achievement.   When students' behavior has improved, when they are more likely to accept responsibility, when they have a better relationship with their parents, and when their parents become more involved with the school, their schoolwork will improve. Students' feelings about their relationship with family members are an extremely important aspect of motivation.

To the inquiring counselor, the need for parent education and consultation will become obvious in virtually every elementary or middle school across the country. It is not a matter of whether to offer parent education and consultation, but rather *where* and *when* it should be provided. When counselors deal only with students, they neglect to consider the influence that parents share with educators (Dinkmeyer, Dinkmeyer, & Sperry, 1987). The counselor, through parent education, can assist many more parents in a shorter amount of time than can more traditional school-based programs.

PARENT EDUCATION

Parents are hungry to learn new techniques. Education groups provide an opportunity to effectively reach many parents in a relatively short time. For years, parents have been bombarded with conflicting methodologies. One magazine article might recommend that they become more autocratic; a later edition might recommend a laissez-faire approach. Between these two extremes lies a variety of "how to" suggestions, often without informing the parent of the philosophical bases for these suggestions.

As parents have been bombarded with conflicting information, so has the school counselor regarding parent education. You must sort through the ever-growing list of parent education programs and materials to offer parents a visible, workable program.

In selecting a parent education model, we suggest that you take the time to ensure that the model will impart appropriate information to parents, and that it provides a philosophical base in keeping with these needs.

Models of Parenting and Parent Education

Parenting Models.   We present a brief review of the parenting models. Understanding them should assist you in selecting a parent education program. We examine three societal, family, and parenting models.

The Autocratic Model.   This model, discussed earlier in this chapter, is characterized by order without freedom. It seems to work on a short-term basis; but usually about age 12 to 14, and sometimes sooner, the child rebels. In the early days, the primary method of discipline, under the autocratic model, was punishment. Later, reward was utilized along with punishment because it added an element of humanity that punishment alone did not have. Punishment and reward—nowadays called negative or positive reinforcers—are still used for discipline. Corporal punishment is seldom recommended, but is often practiced by many well-intentioned parents.

In the autocratic model, children do not learn to think for themselves and frequently have difficulty making decisions. In addition, they seldom accept responsibility without being told to do so.

The Anarchic Model.   This is the exact opposite of the autocratic model, characterized by freedom without order: Children should be able to do whatever they want to do, whenever they want to do it. Here, as with the previous model, children do not learn to think for themselves. Why should they, when they are free to do as they please? As they are expected to care only about themselves, the same can be said for responsibility. As a social model, anarchy has not been successful, and fared no better with parenting.

The Democratic Model.   It is ironic that the United States, which touts its democratic system, has been so slow to switch to this model. It stands to reason that children growing up in a democratic society should be reared, educated, and disciplined using this model, characterized by order with freedom. Where the autocratic model lacks freedom, and the anarchic model order, this one contains both. It is based upon the idea of mutual respect; parents are guides or facilitators of their children's behavior and learning, and children are treated with respect and dignity. Based upon their capabilities and stage of development, children are encouraged to make decisions for themselves. From this they learn to think about what is best for a given situation. They will, of course, make the occasional mistake. From this they learn to be more careful and accept responsibility for the outcomes of their decision.

The primary goal of parenting is to rear children in such a way that they will become thinking, responsible adults. The democratic model comes closest to producing this kind of adult. Several researchers, including Kottman and Wilborn (1992), Lauver and Schramski (1983), and McKay and McKay (1983), provide evidence that parents who participate in parent education groups founded on democratic principles are more likely to learn effective strategies for understanding and dealing with their children's behavior.

Parent Education Models.   Several parent education programs are now in existence. We review primarily those models developed after 1980, with a couple of exceptions. Models are presenting in no particular order. (Fine, 1980, offers a creditable summary of many parent education programs developed prior to that year.)

Active Parenting.   Developer: Michael Popkin. Publisher: Active Parenting. Length: six sessions of 2 hours each. Includes 95 minutes of videotape, a parent handbook and action guide, leader's guide, promotional brochures, announcements, and a 12-minute video demonstration. The philosophical approach is primarily democratic, using the ideas of Alfred Adler, Rudolph Dreikurs, Carl Rogers, and others. No special training needed, other than familiarity with the leader's guide. Uses brief video scenes with group discussion following. Parents are also assigned structured reading and writing exercises, along with real-life practice of concepts learned. Leader's guide gives direction to the leader in terms of discussion guides and course activities (Popkin, 1983).

Teaching Involved Parenting—A Total Workshop.   Developers: Bill Wagonseller and Richard McDowell. Publisher: Research Press. Length: five sessions of 90 minutes each. Includes leader's guide, 100 transparency masters, and other materials for parents. The philosophical approach is behavioral and is based primarily on the book *You and Your Child.* No special training needed. Teaches basic concepts in behavioral technology, including behavior management principles designed to help shape observable behavior. The first three sessions deal with parental responsibility, expectations, and effective communications. The final two focus on behavior management principles and how to set up and use a behavior management program (Wagonseller & McDowell, 1982).

Parent Effectiveness Training (PET).   Developer: Thomas Gordon. Publisher: Effectiveness Training Associates. Length: eight sessions of three hours each. Uses the work of Carl Rogers as its philosophical base, stressing the need for sensitivity in responding to children's needs and the honest expression of parents' feelings. Includes audiotapes and Instructor's Guide. Prospective group leaders are strongly advised to enroll in a PET course, complete a week-long instructor training workshop, co-teach with an experienced instructor, and then practice by teaching a course offered primarily to neighbors. The course focuses most heavily on the concrete experiences from the daily lives of the participants. The emphasis of the training also focuses on learning human relations strategies of active listening, sending "I" messages, and the "no-lose" method of resolving conflicts through negotiation (Gordon, 1975).

Responsive Parenting.   Developer: Saf Lerman. Publisher: American Guidance Service. Length: 9 sessions, with provision for as many as 13 follow-up sessions. Emphasizes a positive approach to family discipline through straightforward communication. Includes participant's packets, set of illustrated booklets, leader's manual, charts, audiocassettes, and carrying case. No formal training needed; leader's manual provides step-by-step instructions. Approach offers flexibility to parents who seek specific information; sessions are designed to invite participation, warmth, humor, and support (Lerman, 1984).

Systematic Training for Effective Parenting (STEP).   Developers: Donald Dinkmeyer and Gary McKay. Publisher: American Guidance Service. Length: nine sessions of 90–120 minutes. Based on the democratic principles of Rudolph Dreikurs. The materials, also available in Spanish, include a leader's manual, parent's handbook, cassettes, charts, discussion guide cards, and posters. No special training needed. Anyone in the helping professions or who enjoys working with adults and can lead group discussions can be an effective STEP leader. Encourages the development of parenting skills that foster mutual respect, cooperation, responsibility, and self-reliance. By working together in small groups of 6 to 12 members, participants become actively involved in recognizing that their problems are not unique. By sharing common experiences, and by identifying both effective and ineffective ways of responding to children, alternative approaches are found that can lead to more satisfying relationships between parents and children (Dinkmeyer & McKay, 1976).

Parenting Skills.   Developer: Richard R. Abidin. Publisher: Human Sciences Press. Length: 19 sessions of 90–120 minutes are recommended. "Short" courses of 7, 8, or 10 sessions are also outlined. Based primarily on behavior modification principles. However, the approach assumes no predetermined set of values, ideas, or skills. Materials needed are the trainer's manual and the parent's workbook. No formal training required, but leaders should have democratic group leadership skills combined with a genuine capacity to communicate acceptance and respect for parents. Early sessions deal with building parent-child relationships, the middle sessions with managing children's behavior, and the final segment with managing feelings in parent-child interactions (Abidin, 1976).

Children: The Challenge.   Utilizes the book *Children: The Challenge* by Rudolph Dreikurs and Vicki Soltz, along with the *Study Group Leader's Manual* by Vicki Soltz. Publisher: Hawthorn Books. Length: ten sessions of 90–120 minutes. Philosophical basis is Adlerian, with the overall goal to educate the whole community toward more effective social living. No formal training needed, but leader should be familiar with the text and the leader's manual. This approach, based upon democratic principles, assists participants in identifying the four mistaken goals of behavior and how to deal with their results (Dreikurs & Soltz, 1987; Soltz, 1967).

Parenting without Hassles: Parents and Children as Partners.   Developers: Fred O. Bradley and Lloyd A. Stone. The book *Parenting without Hassles: Parents and Children as Partners* and the accompanying discussion guide are available from Sheffield Publishing Company. Length: five sessions of two hours each, or ten sessions of one hour each. Usually, parents are asked for their preference.

Based on Adlerian principles with a heavy Dreikurian influence, which makes for a democratic approach. No special training needed, other than familiarity with the text and the discussion guide. No other materials except the text and the discussion guide are needed. Parents are helped to understand the reason for their current difficulty in parenting, what to expect from their children, and how to identify and deal with behavior more effectively (Bradley & Stone, 1992; Stone & Bradley, 1992).

With this brief review, we hope to assist you in selecting the most appropriate program for parents in your school. You should select programs based upon the needs of the parents you serve. Consider such elements as parental reading level, education, and interest. In making your selection, evaluate the program's philosophical approach, along with its length and complexity. Other factors such as cost, special training of the leaders, and availability of the materials should also be considered.

Organizing a Parent Education Program

Committee on Parent Education. The first step in organizing a parent education program is to appoint a committee of teachers and parents. The primary goal of the committee is to decide what parent education model best fits its school. In a large school district with more than one elementary/middle school and several counselors, the committee should represent the entire school district. In other words, unless there are unique needs within the district, the same model should be used in all buildings. In selecting the model, the following are to be considered:

1. Needs. What gives parents the most difficulty in rearing their children? What behavioral problems are showing up at school that could be improved through helping parents? Is there a particular target group of parents—should the focus be on parents of a particular age group, or should the parent education groups comprise parents regardless of age? By addressing the needs of the community through these and other questions, the committee will gain direct knowledge that will assist in the selection of a model.

2. Education Level and Language of Parents. This may vary among school districts and even among attendance centers within a district. The committee might decide that the democratic model best fits the needs of all parents; it might also find that different programs are needed due to education level, language, or other differences within the district. Reviewing the various programs during the selection process will aid in this decision.

3. Cost of Program. The cost of running an initial study group for 16 parents ranged from $10 per parent to $30 per parent. These figures do not take into account any special training the leader might require, extra pay for the leader, facility cost, refreshments costs, and the like. The cost of the program should always be considered when making the selection for a school or district.

4. When and Where to Hold Sessions. Sometimes the most difficult task in organizing parent education groups is deciding the time and place of the sessions. Although you will have the final say in this matter, it is highly recommended that the committee make suggestions. Deciding early in the organizational process when and where the meetings will be held will help save time later. (Unfortunately, program times cannot satisfy everyone; therefore, deciding on a time that will meet the needs of the majority will obviate lengthy discussions later.)

Implementing a Parent Education Program

Once the model has been chosen, the program selected, and the time and place of the meeting decided, the implementation process begins.

1. Promotion. No parent education program can succeed unless parents and others in the community are aware of it. Creating this awareness is primarily your responsibility; however, the parent education committee, teachers, and administration can all play an important role. If a newsletter is an ongoing part of the guidance program—or of the school—run some articles, pictures, and reminders. Give the students special announcements that they can carry home. Place posters and flyers in the windows of businesses within the school community. Carefully using the media in conjunction with these ideas practically guarantees a successful turnout for the organizational meeting. Prepare news releases that can be placed in local newspapers or read over the radio, and be available to local television stations; the media are anxious to promote worthwhile school-related projects.

2. Organizational Meeting. The next step is to invite the public to an organizational meeting. The purpose of this meeting is to further inform parents and others of the parent education program, give them a preview, allow them time to ask questions, and present an opportunity to sign up for the program. Inviting a well-informed guest speaker will not only better educate the parents but likely get more parents involved. (A question-and-answer period is recommended following the speaker's presentation.)

3. Meeting Times and Dates. At this juncture you must determine the number of groups that will participate. Initially, you should not organize more than two groups. The times, locations, and duration of the meetings need to be decided, and the parents informed. (We have found that most parents prefer a five-session program of no more than two hours per session.)

4. Materials. These should be available for the first group meeting. Check them immediately to ensure that a sufficient amount of the right materials has arrived.

5. Starting the Sessions. Initially, you should lead the groups, with the aim of identifying potential group leaders among the parents who are attending. You might pick out two or three parents or sets of parents who, with some training, would be willing to lead a group.

6. Program Evaluation. The last session requires time set aside for evaluation. This can be simple, consisting of parents' written comments about the program. Or, if you prefer a more scientific approach, you may prepare a pre/post instrument and administer it at the first and last sessions. Some counselors use a combination of the two methods.

7. Orientation of Future Group Leaders. Potential leaders should be invited to attend a short orientation meeting, where they review the leader's manual and ask questions about any aspect of the program. They should be given direction on how to organize their group (with your help), where and when to pick up materials, and other pertinent details.

8. Organizing Groups Under Parent Leadership. You are instrumental in helping to organize this second round of study groups. Arrange to drop in for a few minutes each time a group is in session. During this visit we recommend that you unobtrusively observe the discussions, noting the effectiveness of each leader.

In summary: With the assistance of a committee you have

selected an approach;

promoted the program;

had an organizational meeting;

ordered materials;

been the leader of at least two groups;

evaluated the effectiveness of the experience;

identified two or three potential leaders from each group;

held an orientation meeting for them; and

using them as leaders have organized more groups.

You are now ready for parent consultation.

PARENT CONSULTATION

The counselor can effectively consult with parents on various occasions. Many of these occasions would focus on promoting parent understanding of pupil characteristics and their relationships to pupil behavior. Consultation can assist parents in coping with or modifying pupil behaviors, improving interpersonal relationship skills, and adjusting attitudes. Parents may also consult with the school counselor in regard to their children's academic planning, progress, or problems. (Gibson & Mitchell, 1990, p. 367)

We believe that parent consultation is a natural outgrowth of parent education. What better time for parents to seek consultation than while they are experiencing parent education? The method we discuss here is the "open-centered" counseling approach (Christensen & Marchant, 1983), based upon Adlerian principles. Christensen, Marchant, and others have refined this approach so that it complements parent education. Open-centered consultation provides parents with information through an education model. (Compare this with the medical model, which posits that parents are sick and in need of therapy in order to deal more effectively with their children.)

The open-centered approach, carried out before an audience,

> . . . functions as a dynamic educational experience. The merit of the direct counseling experience for the family-in-focus is apparent, in that families are being provided with information explicitly related to their needs and concerns. Furthermore, members of the audience can be viewed as active participants in a realistic sense, since vicarious learning is available to them during the counseling sessions. In many instances it is as valid a learning experiences as is direct intervention itself. For many parents it is an extremely valuable activity to sit in an audience and view another family in the process of problems resolution. The stress of participation is reduced by the fact that they are not directly involved. However, exposure is highly relevant since the concerns of one family are not that different from those of another. Expression of concerns may vary in form from family to family, but the dynamics involved are more often extremely similar. (Christensen & Marchant, 1983, p. 31)

Bacon and Dougherty (1992) discuss three other approaches to consultation in the schools: education-training model (Dougherty, 1990; Gallessich, 1982), the advocacy model (Kurpius & Lewis, 1988), and the collaborative model (Brown, Pryzwansky, & Schulte, 1987). Although these models are oriented toward preschool settings, we believe they are also effective at all levels of the elementary and middle school.

Regardless of approach, consultation with parents is an integral part of your role. If your graduate education has not adequately addressed this, we highly recommend that you take postgraduate courses and workshops to prepare for this important task.

SUMMARY

The provision of parent education and consultation are essential aspects of the elementary/middle school counselor's work. There are several parent education models from which you can choose. We enumerated eight. The importance of organizing and implementing a parent education program based on the needs of students and parents was discussed. A step-by-step process for the organization and implementation of the program was offered.

Through a discussion of the history of parenting, we traced the evolution of parenting traditions being practiced today. We defined the concept of equality and discussed its effect on parenting. Expected outcomes of parent education and consultation were listed and discussed. The autocratic, anarchic, and democratic models for parenting were presented, and we pointed out that traditional parenting has its roots in the autocratic approach.

Finally, we discussed the importance of the counselor's role in parent consultation, and offered some suggestions with regard to models and approaches that could be used to consult effectively with parents.

REVIEW

1. What societal factors might indicate the difficulty experienced by today's parents?

2. Trace the history of parenting and briefly discuss any drawbacks that might pertain currently.

3. What is meant by the concept of equality?

4. What are some outcomes that can be expected as a result of parent education and/or parent consultation?

5. What is the essential goal of parent education?

6. Discuss your understanding of the autocratic, anarchic, and democratic models of parenting.

7. Discuss the primary factors that need to be considered in selecting a parent education program.

8. What are the major activities needed for best results in implementing a parent education program?

9. Discuss parent consultation and why it is such an important aspect of the counselor's work.

REFERENCES

Abidin, R. (1976). *Parenting skills.* New York: Human Sciences Press.

Bacon, E. H., & Dougherty, A. M. (1992). Consultation and coordination services for prekindergarten children. *Elementary School Guidance and Counseling, 27,* 24-32.

Bradley, F., & Stone, L. (1992). *Parenting without hassles: Parents and children as partners.* Salem, WI: Sheffield.

Brown, D., Pryzwansky, W. G., & Schulte, A. C. (1987). *Psychological consultation: Introduction to theory and practice.* Boston: Allyn & Bacon.

Campbell, N., & Sutton, J. (1983). Impact of parent education groups on family atmosphere. *Journal of Specialists in Group Work, 8,* 125-132.

Christensen, O. C., & Marchant, W. C. (1983). The family counseling process. In O. C. Christensen & T. G. Schramski (Eds.), *Adlerian family counseling* (pp. 29-55). Minneapolis, MN: Educational Media.

Cooney, J. (1981). Parent education: A focus on the issues. *The School Counselor, 29,* 97-102.

Dinkmeyer, D. C., Dinkmeyer, D. C., Jr., & Sperry, L. (1987). *Adlerian counseling and psychotherapy.* Columbus, OH: Merrill.

Dinkmeyer, D., & McKay, G. (1976). *Systematic training for effective parenting.* Circle Pines, MN: American Guidance Service.

Dodson, L. S., & Kurpius, D. J. (1989). *Family counseling: A systems approach.* Muncie, IN: Accelerated Development.

Dougherty, A. M. (1990). *Consultation: Practice and perspectives.* Pacific Grove, CA: Brooks/Cole.

Dreikurs, R., & Soltz, V. (1987). *Children: The challenge.* New York: Hawthorn.

Fine, M. (Ed.). (1980). *Handbook on parent education.* New York: Academic Press.

Gallessich, J. (1982). *The profession and practice of consultation.* San Francisco: Jossey-Bass.

Gibson, R. L., & Mitchell, M. H. (1990). *Introduction to counseling and guidance* (3rd ed.). New York: Macmillan.

Gordon, T. (1975). *Parent effectiveness training.* New York: Academic Press.

Hammer, T. J., & Turner, P. H. (1990). *Parenting in contemporary society.* Englewood Cliffs, NJ: Prentice-Hall.

Kottman, T., & Wilborn, B. L. (1992). Parents helping parents: Multiplying the counselor's effectiveness. *The School Counselor, 40,* 10–14.

Kurpius, D. J., & Lewis, J. E. (1988). Introduction to consultation: An intervention for advocacy and outreach. In D. J. Kurpius & D. Brown (Eds.), *Handbook of consultation: An intervention of advocacy and research* (pp. 1–4). Alexandria, VA: American Counseling Association.

Lauver, P., & Schramski, T. (1983). Research and evaluation in Adlerian family counseling. In O. C. Christensen & T. G. Schramski (Eds.), *Adlerian family counseling* (pp. 367–390). Minneapolis, MN: Educational Media.

LeMasters, E. E., & Defrain, J. (1989). *Parents in contemporary America.* Belmont, CA: Wadsworth.

Lerman, S. (1984). *Responsive parenting.* Circle Pines, MN: American Guidance Service.

McKay, G., Hillman, B. (1979). An Adlerian multimedia approach to parent education. *Elementary School Guidance and Counseling, 14,* 18–35.

McKay, G., & McKay, J. (1983). Parent study groups. In O. C. Christensen & T. G. Schramski (Eds.), *Adlerian family counseling* (pp. 346–349). Minneapolis, MN: Educational Media.

Popkin, M. (1983). *Active parenting.* Atlanta, GA: Active Parenting.

Soltz, V. (1967). *Study group leader's manual.* Chicago: Alfred Adler Institute.

Stone, L., & Bradley, F. (1992). *Discussion guide for using* Parenting without Hassles: Parents and Children as Partners. Salem, WI: Sheffield.

Strother, J., & Jacobs, E. (1986). Parent consultation: A practical approach. *The School Counselor, 33,* 292–296.

Toffler, A. (1970). *Future shock.* New York: Random House.

Wagonseller, B., & McDowell, R. (1979). *You and your child.* Champaign, IL: Research Press.

chapter 11

The Counselor as a Consultant

OUTLINE

INTRODUCTION

Background

Consultation originated with nineteenth-century medical practices. Clinical consultation is a three-part process: (1) diagnosis of the problem; (2) treatment prescription; and (3) withdrawal by the consultant, leaving the consultee to carry out the plan (Brown, Pryzwansky, & Schulte, 1991). Consultation had been in decline because many questioned the relationship between diagnosis and treatment; the medical/clinical model emphasizes abnormal behavior, and diagnosis invites labeling; and the relationship between consultant and consultee is that of expert and neophyte, rather than equals.

Renewed interest in consultation is a result of several movements, including the rise of behaviorism, the advent of community psychology, the increase in professional specialization in psychology, and the rise in technology (Brown, Pryzwansky, & Schulte, 1991). Behaviorism emphasizes consultant-client interaction. Community psychology represents a departure from clinical, inpatient treatment of mental difficulties. And the simultaneous increase in technology and development of professional specialization have influenced the consultation movement.

Concepts of Consultation

All definitions should begin with Caplan (1970), regarded as the father of consultation. He defines consultation as a voluntary, nonhierarchical relationship between two professionals, who are often from different professional groups. The process is initiated by the consultee. The goals are twofold: to improve consultees' functioning with clients and develop consultees' skills so they can cope with similar problems independently in the future. In the school setting, the *consultee* usually is either a teacher or parent and the *client* is typically a child.

Some have regarded Caplan's definition as too restrictive because of the external locus of the consultant, and because the consultee is called upon to implement solutions that have been generated in the consultative process (Brown, Pryzwansky, & Schulte, 1991; Hansen, Himes, & Meier, 1990). Medway (1979) characterized consultation as a shared problem-solving process between the consultant and the recipient of the service. This definition begins to bring into focus the purpose of consultation in the schools.

Consulting is distinguished from counseling in that as a consultant you focus on relationships among people; the structure is triadic—consultant, consultee, and client/client system. Consultation is designed to have *indirect* impact on the client. By contrast, the purpose of *counseling* is to alter the behavior of the individual with whom you are working. It is *direct*, focusing intensely on the personal dynamics of the persons involved in the interaction.

In elementary school counseling, according to Umansky and Holloway (1984), "a consultant provides an indirect service to students through direct service to teachers, parents, or the entire school" (p.330). Gerler (1992 has characterized consultation as existing "both to resolve client concerns and to prevent potential problems" (p. 162). Thus, the goals of consultation are "to enhance services to third parties, and to improve the ability of consultees to function in areas of concern to them" (Brown, Pryzwansky, & Schulte, 1991, p. 8). Consultation involves the service of an outside professional—in this case, you as the counselor; an indirect service to the client—the child; and a problem-solving process implemented by the consultee—generally a teacher or parent. Your role as a consultant is to work with the significant adults in the lives of the children in the schools you serve.

THE PURPOSE OF CONSULTATION
IN SCHOOL COUNSELING

As early as 1966, consultation—along with counseling and coordination—was identified as basic to elementary school guidance (Dinkmeyer, 1968). It is an ongoing function that occupies a portion of your time each day. As Dustin and Ehly (1992) indicate, the school counselor is faced with ever-increasing job complexity. Further, they note that schools are under increased scrutiny, and there is a push for educational reform. The result of these changes is expanded responsibility and demand on the school to assume a role in the social development of children.

Consultation may be the saving grace that sees you through the coming decade. It is inescapable. You will have to spend more time working with those who directly and indirectly affect our elementary and middle school children. The question no longer is *should you* or *will you,* but *how will you* carry out this task.

Dustin and Ehly (1992) highlight four themes in the literature on education reform: "at-risk children, reintegration of special students, school-community integration of services, and restructuring of schools" (p. 172). Each theme will necessarily involve you. But don't panic—the extent of your involvement will vary.

Where, then, do you fit in? At-risk children are everyone's concern and responsibility. Along with the school psychologist, you can provide teachers and parents with meaningful information about the behavior dynamics of these young people. And, working with the significant adults in the lives of these children, you can address the negative self-thoughts that beset most at-risk youngsters.

The reintegration of special-education students aims for the participation of these young people in the regular classroom. (In some parts of the country this is called *inclusion.*) The special-education teacher and school psychologist might be more inclined to take the lead in this area, but you will prove helpful to teachers who are frequently bewildered by the challenge these children pose.

Integrating the services of the school and community may seem somewhat removed from the present scene, but with the upward-spiraling cost of social services, greater collaboration might be desirable. What form this effort will take is difficult to foretell. Without question, most schools and community agencies have not worked together harmoniously. All too often, counselors will refer a student to a community agency, and that is the last they hear of the situation unless the agency wants something. To circumvent this lack of cooperation and coordination, you might initiate regular meetings or forums to discuss the issues that affect youth in your community. Eventually you may step back and serve as a member of the team, endeavoring to keep lines of communication open in both directions.

Restructuring the schools is a massive undertaking that will likely be initiated and coordinated by the central administration. But as an advocate of the child, you can represent the emotional and social perspectives of education, and in so doing, speak to the ways teachers and administrators can integrate social skill development into all aspects of learning.

Again, we do not imply that your involvement in these areas constitutes the whole of your consultative function. In fact, your most important consultative role will be anchored in direct service to the significant adults who live and work with children.

CONSULTATION MODELS

Hansen, Himes, and Meier (1990) have appropriately indicated that consultation is still philosophically and theoretically immature. Therefore, we refer to the major approaches as models of consultation, and discuss only those that pertain to the school setting.

Mental Health Consultation

Caplan (1978) identifies four foci of consultant activity: client-centered case consultation, consultee-centered case consultation, program-centered administrative consultation, and consultee-centered administrative consultation. The first two foci will have particular meaning to you as an elementary school counselor, since they center on the client and consultee.

As you work with teachers and parents, a considerable amount of time will be spent with client-centered case consultation. You may be called upon to help teachers and parents manage the inclusion of special-education students into the regular classroom, and you could serve teachers and other school personnel when restructuring efforts begin.

The latter two of Caplan's foci center on the program and administrator, and will demand the attention of only a small number of elementary school counselors.

Behavioral Consultation

The early formulation of the behavioral approach to consultation is associated with Bergan (1977). Recent developments in the model involve the application of behavioral and social learning theory principles to the problems of school-age youngsters (Bergan & Kratochwill, 1990; Kratochwill & Bergan, 1990). The consultation emphasizes the child; the consultee is typically the teacher. Hansen,

Himes, and Meier (1990) point out that this model assumes that problems are a result of situational factors in the school setting, such as the teacher's methods or the environment of the classroom (p. 12). Because of these two mitigating factors the focus of the intervention can be on the system (classroom structure) or teacher-child interaction (teacher technique). In either case, this approach has some appeal to educators because it is directed toward improving the situation for both teacher and child. A meaningful and attractive aspect of the behavioral approach is the procedure that is used. Umansky and Holloway (1984) outline a five-step process with a reduced emphasis on behavioral terminology, closely approximating a general problem-solving sequence: "(a) defining the problem in observable terms, (b) collecting baseline data, (c) developing an intervention plan, (d) implementing the intervention, and (e) evaluating the intervention by continuing data collection" (pp. 331–332). This sequence provides a generic process for consultation, regardless of the model. Should you choose to use other models you would need to vary the specificity of definition and data collection.

Logically, this model is well suited for work with teachers, parents, and other school personnel who work directly with children. It would be appropriate for at-risk children and special-education students, and could have implications for restructuring the schools. Regardless, the most valuable aspect of the model is the process of consultation, which, as already stated, can be adapted to any approach you choose.

Adlerian Consultation

The Adlerian approach focuses on the role of parents and teachers in the discipline and motivation of young people (Dinkmeyer, 1971; Dinkmeyer & Carlson, 1973; Dinkmeyer & Dinkmeyer, 1984; Dreikurs et al., 1959). It can be used with individuals or groups. One form of this approach provides the consultative input to parents through a forum where a family is the recipient of the consultant's intervention (Christensen, 1972; Dreikurs et al., 1959). Regardless of the delivery, the intent is the same: Adlerian consultation is intended to help parents and teachers develop more effective techniques of discipline, and to help children understand maladaptive behavior (Christensen, 1972). Although Umansky and Holloway (1984) refer to Adlerian consultation as psychological education, we think it is closer to parent counseling as presented in chapter 10.

The Education and Training Model

In the education model consultants deliver their training to a group, often the entire faculty of a school. Hansen, Himes, and Meier (1990) identify the primary intent of this form of consultation as providing information and education more akin to in-service training or a staff development workshop. Typically, counselors do not participate frequently as consultants in this model. However, counselors have a great deal to offer through this form of consultation: an understanding of human behavior, and communication and problem-solving skills that can benefit teachers and other school personnel. For example, you might schedule an in-service session on how to more effectively conduct parent conferences. You could focus on communication skills and provide teachers with information regarding the parents' concerns (e.g., helping teachers provide feedback to parents about their child's performance).

THE CONSULTATION PROCESS

Consultation follows a process that varies slightly from model to model, with each model sequencing the consultant's involvement in roughly the same manner. Caplan (1970) poses a five-step process that is appropriate for the varied focus of his model:

1. Build a relationship with the consultees' organization (e.g., the administration);
2. Establish a relationship with the consultees. Caplan believes this second step is crucial because it is both a learning process for you and serves to help the consultee to develop a sense of ownership;
3. Perform an assessment, or data collection. Collect all the information available regarding the situation at hand, both from consultees and others;
4. Intervene: Here you provide your recommendations for action the consultee should take to remedy the presenting problem; and
5. Evaluate and follow up. Caplan believes that consultants should make an effort to evaluate their impact, although this is difficult because the responsibility for all action lies with the consultee.

The behavioral model of consultation is represented through four steps: problem identification, problem analysis, plan implementation, and problem evaluation (Bergan, 1977). *Problem identification* involves establishing objectives for the consultation, including identifying the client problem in measurable outcomes. *Problem analysis* is the process of working with the consultee to clearly identify the role of both consultee and client in the problem situation. As a result of this process the consultant is now in a position to formulate a plan for problem resolution. *Plan implementation* involves the consultant monitoring the efforts of the consultee to carry out the action plans devised by the former. *Problem evaluation* calls for an assessment of the extent to which outcomes conform to objectives.

The Adlerian model (Christensen, 1972; Dreikurs et al., 1959) addresses elements of both the mental health and behavioral models, but the steps are somewhat different. In this model, consultants establish the relationship and collect diagnostic data through an interview with the parents. Subsequently they interview the children to further collect data and verify their analysis. They then meet with the parents again to provide their intervention plan and secure commitment from the parents. Evaluation comes about through a follow-up interview several weeks after the initial consultation.

A process approach to education and training has not been clearly specified. Hansen, Himes, and Meier (1990) allude to a process sequence but do not specifically outline it. In this form of consultation the consultant typically is invited to provide his or her expertise to the agency. The consultant may be someone within or outside the setting. This distinction will vary the emphasis on the following steps we identify.

1. The initial contact between the consultant and agency administrators: At this first meeting, the situation is analyzed and the needs of the agency determined. If the consultant is from outside the agency, the collection of initial data will be more time-consuming.
2. Planning: This stage could include additional data collection from others in the agency or may simply involve planning the training program. If the consultant is from within the setting, time should be devoted to establishing credibility with the staff of the agency.
3. Delivery of training or education to the recipient body.
4. Evaluating the effectiveness of the education or training: Usually a formal, anonymous, instrumented evaluation is the best means of soliciting input about the effectiveness of the training session. On a number of occasions it will be desirable to conduct a follow-up evaluation to determine whether the education has produced any meaningful changes in the behavior of the recipients.

From the consultation processes outlined above we have formulated a generic five-step approach, which we use in our discussions of consultation with various populations. Our approach is similar to the one Umansky and Holloway (1984) associated with the behavioral model (the exception lies in our elimination of the behavioral language):

1. delineation of the problem to be addressed and the establishment of rapport between consultant and consultee;
2. data collection, wherein consultants use whatever means are available to thoroughly critique the situation;
3. assessment, which determines a preliminary course of action;
4. meeting with the consultee and initiating a plan of action; and
5. the systematic collection of evaluation data, to determine the effectiveness of both the consultant and the consultation plan.

CONSULTATION WITH TEACHERS

The majority of your consultative activities with teachers will involve assisting them to better manage their classroom, work with individual children, cope with parents, or work more effectively with colleagues. Classroom management is the one area where teachers are more likely to want your help. Your consultation may also address the issues of at-risk children and the reintegration of special-education students into the regular classroom. To a lesser extent, teachers may desire your assistance in their work with parents or other significant adults.

Regardless of the focus of the consultation—child, parent, or other significant adult—you begin the process by interviewing the teacher. This interview will serve to initiate rapport and gather information about the problem. It is very important that you address the teacher in a manner that does not question his or her competence or ability to work with children. This can be difficult if you are clearly aware that the situation could be handled more effectively. However, building rapport and creating a collaborative atmosphere are just as important as the information you will collect about the client.

Once you have initiated the process you need to thoroughly examine the presenting problem through ongoing contact with the teacher and others who may possess useful information. In teacher consultation, where the issue surrounds a child as the client, you may consider interviewing the child to gather additional information and gain the child's perspective. If your consultation focuses on the teacher's relationship with other adults—parents, administrators, or colleagues— your involvement with the other adult will be necessarily limited, and you likely will need to piece together the situation from the teacher's point of view. (You could be described as a mediator with access to only one party.) In this type of consultation the emphasis may well be on communication skill and conflict resolution, where your efforts will be to assist the teacher in addressing the issues with the other adult.

Once you have gathered information regarding the problem, you meet with the teacher and either provide your prescription for the situation or collaboratively work out an approach for the teacher/consultee to pursue. To complete the process, schedule a follow-up session to review the situation and evaluate the progress that has been made by the teacher. Sometimes the follow-up session renews the consultative interaction, in that you work through the situation once again to select a different course of action. On some occasions, where the situation has reached a stalemate, you may assume the true role of mediator, meeting with all parties involved.

CONSULTATION WITH PARENTS

Consulting with parents is similar to consulting with teachers. The similarities lie in the focus either on the behavior of the child or on the relationship with someone in the school who works with the child. Should a parent seek consultation regarding a personal problem, you will be venturing into the gray area between consultation and counseling. Generally, time demands do not permit you to take on parents as counseling clients. Typically, parents approach you out of concern for their child or about someone in the school setting, such as a teacher or administrator. It is usually after the initial meeting that you discover the parent might benefit from counseling. We recommend that you briefly consult with parents when they are experiencing personal difficulties, refer them to counseling outside the school to deal with the personal problems, and continue your consultation with the parent.

The parents of at-risk children and of special-education students who are being reintegrated are likely to seek consultation. These parents often feel helpless over their children's difficulties. Further, they probably feel uneasy in the school, and may hesitate to approach school personnel. Most notably, parents almost always feel that their children's problems are their fault. This feeling is often belied by their outward reaction, which may be one of anger and accusation.

In such cases, you may be called upon to initiate a contact to assist the school staff in developing a working relationship with the parents. Parents are particularly confused about special-education placement, especially when the diagnosis is made once the child has entered school. Also, in staffing meetings for special education, parents generally do not have an advocate who ensures that their questions are clearly answered. Meet with the parents to gather information about the situation and their perceptions of it. Then, either with the parents or on their behalf, present to school personnel the parents' concerns. Following the development of a plan of action to address the child's difficulty, you will likely have several follow-up meetings with the parents and teachers to establish a line of communication between them, and to ensure that all understand their respective roles. This latter contact, involving both parents and teachers, is vital since this partnership is valuable to the progress of the child. Considerable emphasis is now being placed on school-home partnerships and parent involvement in the school, and this form of consultation can well serve this effort.

When parents initiate contact with you, the pattern of involvement will be similar to that of teacher consultation. Conduct an interview to establish rapport and collect data. You may wish to meet with the child to obtain additional information and corroborate or refute the parents' view. Then, assess the situation, formulating a plan of action. The next meeting can take two forms: You can present your plan from the perspective of the expert; or collectively you and the parents can develop an approach to addressing the situation. Follow up the situation within a reasonable period of time to determine the progress that has been made and to engage in any additional planning that may be necessary.

An alternative approach to consulting with parents focuses on their concerns about child-rearing practices. This approach follows the Adlerian model and is very much like the parent education model presented in chapter 10. It involves interviews with parents and children, either with individual families or in an open forum where groups of parents are gathered. As a result of the interviews, a diagnosis is made and some prescription for change is provided.

CONSULTATION WITH OTHER SCHOOL PERSONNEL

The individuals who are most inclined to receive your consultation are administrators, special support personnel, and other groups such as food service staff and bus drivers. Your consultative activity with them usually falls into one of two categories: providing support in their ancillary role to those who work directly with the child, or in school-community integration and school restructuring.

Administrators may seek consultation once they develop an understanding of your role and skills. We recommend that you hold regular meetings, possibly biweekly, to inform them of your activities and accomplishments. These informational sessions can give administrators a greater appreciation of your value to the school and can set the stage for them to solicit your input about broader matters related to the operation of the school. It is quite likely that by creating this level of understanding you will be able to address some of the issues inherent in integration and restructuring.

Consultation can be provided to administrators regarding the behavior of children, relating to such areas as child abuse, violence in youth, domestic violence, alcohol and drug abuse, emerging sexuality, and other current concerns. (see chapter 14). In some cases, these issues will be best addressed through joint consultation between you and the school psychologist and/or social workers.

Administrators might also request consulting input regarding broader-based faculty concerns, such as morale, communication between staff and administration, and group problem-solving efforts. This consultation might best take the form of education and training, or through small-group meetings with those most directly affected by the situation.

Others within the school setting that may benefit from your consultation are members of the clerical, food service, and custodial staff; and bus drivers. Each group works closely with children. Unless individual problems exist, your consultation might best be delivered as in-service or staff development sessions on behavior management. Individual problem-solving sessions with these staff members might arise out of a referral by an administrator, in which case you would conduct your consultation in the manner outlined under teacher consultation. If the consultation is initiated by a referral, you will need time to build rapport and thereby reduce the threat that comes when one assumes that one's competence is being questioned.

Consultation in the school typically has been associated with teachers and parents. However, you can do meaningful work with administrators and other personnel if preparation is made to demonstrate your value to broader school criteria and if your skills are clearly understood by the school staff.

EDUCATION AND TRAINING

The education and training function of consultation has been little used by counselors. Either we have not demonstrated our worth or have felt this is not our province. Regardless, this is an area where we must come to the forefront and broaden our base to include the school as a system. If we regard the school as a system, then all the parts interlock and each impacts on the others. From this point of view, we can influence the entire system if we intervene with only one element. This line of thinking strengthens the need for counselor consultation on a broad range of issues that can be addressed through education and training.

Three issues must be addressed in education and training:

1. the consultant's role as insider or outsider;
2. the organizational plan of the education program; and
3. techniques for providing training.

Sometimes the problems will have been presented to you by the individual who has made the initial contact for the school. If this is the case, you need to be sure the identified problem is in fact shared by others in the school. This lack of familiarity is a time-consuming obstacle to an outside consultant.

More likely you will be a member of the staff, in which case the obstacle might be staff receptivity to your input. On the one hand, you are familiar with the situation; on the other, you are faced with bias that may result from your role as a staff member. In other words, you must demonstrate your worth. At times this is not easy because staff have preconceived notions about your expertise and sensitivity to their concerns. In either case, getting started involves addressing issues about your role as consultant and the nature of the environment in which you will be consulting.

Once you have addressed your role and the immediate environment, you are ready to move on to the broader organizational issues. First, consider your goals and objectives for the workshop. Obviously, these must grow directly from the presenting problem and should be realistic, in that you can accomplish them in the time allowed. Second, consider structural features. Where will the workshop be held, and what limits are imposed by the physical setting? How much time has been allotted, and when will the program take place? As you well know, the staff of any school are sensitive to demands on their time. If they are compelled to give their own time to your staff development workshop, resistance will likely be present at the outset. Finally, who will be in attendance, and is this voluntary? Although administrators are inclined to "require" attendance, we encourage that this be moderated to excuse those who resist attending.

After you have considered the goals, objectives, and structural features, you are now ready to consider the content of your training program. (You should not consider content until these other issues have been addressed.) Always plan for a little bit more than the time allows—but prepare a contingency plan for how you will reshape your program if time runs short. Never deliver a program based on the clock. People simply do not operate that way, and if you want them to take away something useful, gear your material to their ability to assimilate what is presented. In planning content, consider both your role and that of the participants—what will be the extent of their active involvement? As a rule, if participants are more actively involved they will gain more, but the time needed to cover material is increased by this interactivity. We cannot tell you how to accurately judge the balance of your involvement versus theirs; you will need to experiment. But, since closure and evaluation are very important, allow ample time at the end to draw together loose ends and integrate what has been learned. (See chapter 8, the section titled Evaluation.) Overall, the plan for organizing a staff development workshop consists of

1. considering your role and the environment;
2. planning goals and objectives;
3. addressing the structural elements of the environment and staff;
4. developing the content of the workshop; and
5. designing closure and evaluation efforts.

Addressing each of these elements will increase the likelihood of a successful staff development program.

Although each staff program you design will be unique, there are general issues that should be addressed.

1. Have you clearly informed the participants of the goals and objectives of the workshop, as well as what you will be doing during the training program? It is extremely important that people know what will happen to, for, and with them during training.
2. Have you considered the manner and level of your communication? Does your audience understand what you are presenting, and are they engaged by the content?
3. Have you allowed time for the participants to get involved in the workshop, either through activities or question-and-answer periods?
4. Have you provided adequate time to provide for closure?

These issues comprise the most pertinent aspects of conducting a workshop, and should be carefully considered.

Staff training is gaining increasing importance in light of the changes taking place in education. This is a prime opportunity for counselors to become more involved in the overall function of the school. As we look to the future, the team approach in education will continue to grow, and we feel that counselors can make a significant contribution to the team approach through education and training.

Table 11.1 illustrates consultant activity in the school. This graphic may provide you with a sense of with whom you work, who is affected, the content of the consultations, and a sample activity.

SUMMARY

Consultation is defined as a process wherein the counselor provides assistance to one or more persons significantly involved in the lives of children. In a school setting, this takes place primarily with teachers and parents, and secondarily with administrators and other support personnel. Beyond consultation with these key

TABLE 11.1 Consultant activity in the schools

Consultee	Focus	Target	Sample Activity
Teachers	Parents	Parent conferences	Process for bilateral conferences
Parents	Middle school child	Parent/child interaction	Communication skills
Administrators	Faculty	Teacher empowerment	Collaborative problem solving
School support personnel (e.g., bus drivers)	Children	Behavior on the bus	Joint design of a points system
Education and training	School	Faculty, administrators, and/or support personnel	In-service on crisis intervention

people in the child's life, there is increased need for consultation on matters regarding the school as a system. This often focuses on the staff and is delivered in the form of education and training.

Parents and teachers are important recipients of your consultation efforts, because they are the two most important influences in the lives of children. This importance is further dramatized when you consider that children, because of their limited maturity and autonomy, are under the control of these two groups of significant adults, who define children and prescribe the limits of their lives. Teacher and parent consultation usually follows a conventional pattern of establishing rapport, conducting data collection interviews, assessing the situation, meeting to determine a course of action, and subsequently meeting to review the situation.

Consultation with administrators and others in the school takes on a different form. One area where you can provide meaningful assistance is in the realm of current issues facing society, such as alcohol and drug abuse. Another way you can assist administrators is to open lines of communication between the faculty and administration. Finally, counselor consultation can be of help to other school personnel through staff development activities that will improve their function with children.

Education and training will be the consultation of the future for counselors. Because of coming education reform, schools will likely experience a greater emphasis on collaborative efforts in the education of our youth. There will also be more concern with the social and emotional development of young people. Both of these emphases will bring the counselor into greater involvement with staff development activities.

Whether the needs of the school are expressed by teachers, parents, administrators, other staff, or the system itself, counselors play an important consultative role. Your training and skills will prove invaluable to the school districts as they change and as society continues to place demands on the schools to provide for the social and emotional development of children. We encourage you to carefully consider your role in the school team and the ways in which you can contribute to your role as a consultant.

REVIEW

1. Contrast the mental health and behavioral models of consultation, identifying points of convergence and divergence.
2. Consider how you would function in a consultative relationship and identify whether you would best operate from expert power or collaborative base.
3. Identify two issues that you believe teachers most frequently face with children in the classroom. Describe how you would assist a teacher in addressing these issues.
4. Select a typical problem parents may face with their middle-schooler. Outline a process for assisting this parent to manage the situation.
5. Using a hypothetical situation, identify three key issues in reintegrating special-education students into the regular classroom.
6. Explain why counselors should engage in consultation with administrators.
7. Describe two situations where you can make a meaningful impact on the education or training of teachers.

REFERENCES

Bergan, J. R. (1977). *Behavioral consultation.* Columbus, OH: Merrill.

Bergan, J. R., & Kratochwill, T. R. (1990). *Behavioral consultation and therapy.* New York: Plenum Press.

Brown, D., Pryzwansky, W., & Schulte, A. (1991). *Psychological consultation: Introduction to theory and practice.* Boston: Allyn & Bacon.

Bundy, M. L., & Poppen, W. A. (1986). School counselors' effectiveness as consultants: A research review. *Elementary School Guidance and Counseling, 20*(3), 215-222.

Caplan, G. (1970). *The theory and practice of mental health consultation.* New York: Basic Books.

Christensen, O. (1972). Family education: A model for consultation. *Elementary School Guidance and Counseling, 7*(2), 121-129.

Dinkmeyer, D. (Ed.). (1968). *Guidance and counseling in the elementary school.* New York: Holt.

Dinkmeyer, D. (1971). The "C" group: Integrating knowledge and experience to change behavior: An Adlerian approach to consultation. *The Counseling Psychologist, 3,* 63-72.

Dinkmeyer, D., & Carlson, J. (1973). *Consulting: Facilitating human potential and change processes.* New York: Merrill.

Dinkmeyer, D., Jr., & Dinkmeyer, D., Sr. (1984). School counselors as consultants in primary prevention programs. *The Personnel and Guidance Journal, 62*(8), 464-466.

Dreikurs, R., Corsini, R., Lowe, R., & Sonstegard, M. (Eds.). (1959). *Adlerian family counseling: A manual for counseling centers.* Eugene, OR: The University Press.

Dustin, D., & Ehly, S. (1992). School consultation in the 1990s. *Elementary School Guidance and Counseling, 26*(3), 165-175.

Gerler, E. R. (1992). Consultation and school counseling. *Elementary School Guidance and Counseling, 26*(3), 162.

Hansen, J. C., Himes, B. S., & Meier, S. (1990). *Consultation: Concepts and practices.* Englewood Cliffs, NJ: Prentice-Hall.

Kratochwill, T. R., & Bergan, J. R. (1990). *Behavioral consultation in applied settings: An individual guide.* New York: Plenum Press.

Medway, F. (1979). How effective is school consultation? A review of recent research. *The Journal of School Psychology, 17,* 275-282.

Umansky, D. L., & Holloway, E. L. (1984). The counselor as consultant: From model to practice. *The School Counselor, 34*(4), 329-338.

chapter 12

Organization, Management, and Evaluation

OUTLINE

INTRODUCTION

The importance of careful and comprehensive organization of the elementary/ middle school guidance program cannot be stressed too strongly. As Gysbers (1990) points out:

> Both experience and research suggest that a laissez faire or unsystematic approach to the organization of guidance services can blunt the inherent impact of effectiveness of school guidance and counseling. When school guidance and counseling is organized to meet specific goals and objectives and careful attention is directed towards "who will accomplish what," the evidence suggests that both the deliverers (counselors and school faculty) and students and parents are more satisfied. (p. vii)

In chapter 2 we pointed out that your role can best be delineated by looking at the groups of people with whom you work: students, teachers, parents, administrators, and other school personnel. In our discussion of the guidance program for each of these groups, we listed specific activities in which the counselor engages, and pointed out that no matter with whom you are working, all the help ultimately goes back to the student. Our rationale is based on the idea that the guidance program should permeate the entire educational process. It should not be set apart from the goals and objectives of the school system, but rather enhance what the school as a whole is attempting to accomplish. The guidance program needs to be organized in concert with the prevailing philosophy of the school system and the local community. The task of organizing, managing, and evaluating this program results in the consideration of the following.

1. Guidance program committee. A committee of faculty and staff, parents, and others from the community willing to contribute their time and talents toward the organization of the program. In some situations, particularly at the middle school level, having student representation on the committee is a good idea.

2. Faculty, staff, student, and community orientation. If the guidance program is to succeed, there is a strong need to provide these persons with at least a general understanding of a guidance program in the elementary/middle school. This will be the first step toward a comprehensive public relations program.

3. Needs assessment. A comprehensive needs assessment should collect information that can be used to describe the student population, identify target groups, and summarize the needs of the students in a particular school or system.

4. School/district philosophy. The philosophy and objectives of the school or district must be understood and considered by those organizing the program. The program must then be carefully developed to support this philosophy, while at the same time being consistent with general guidance objectives.

5. Evaluation. Early in the organizational process, attention must be given to program evaluation. Although guidance program evaluation is an ongoing process, there is a need to outline a system that will provide a summary evaluation at the end of the school year. Provision should be made to periodically provide program evaluation feedback to the faculty and administration as well as others.

You should be aware of the importance of sound program organization, management, and evaluation if you are to satisfy your program goals. In addition, leadership ability, characteristics, and style will play an important part in how well you carry this out. This chapter provides an introduction to the organization, management, and evaluation of the guidance program, and aims to provide valuable background information that will assist you in your future studies.

PROGRAM NEEDS

The first step in organizing—or revising—a guidance program is to determine the needs that exist in the school and community (Hollis & Hollis, 1965). Once these needs have been identified, they can be categorized under the various counselor activities listed in chapter 2. The cataloging of needs not only indicates what needs to be done, and with whom, but sets the stage for determining expected outcomes that will greatly assist in the evaluation of the program.

What Are Needs?

For our purposes, *needs* are the basic physical, social, and psychological requirements essential to students' complete education, and which enable them to function normally in society. Maslow (1954) believes these can be placed in a hierarchy, from the most basic physiological needs to the highest psychological development of the individual. The Maslow hierarchy is listed by Coleman (1960) as follows:

body needs

safety needs

needs from love and belonging

needs for adequacy, security, self-esteem, self-enhancement and competencies

needs for self-fulfillment and broader understanding (p. 136)

The activities provided by the guidance program are primarily directed toward the last four needs. Although schools are accepting greater responsibility for feeding, clothing, and sheltering their students, this area is still perceived as being the responsibility of the parents and of society. The same could be said for safety needs. However, with the increasing incidence of crime and violence in schools, student safety has become by necessity a responsibility of many schools, especially at the middle and high school level.

To define needs, Monette (1977) places them in four categories:

1. basic human needs;
2. felt and expressed needs;
3. normative needs; and
4. comparative needs.

Collison (1982) states, "[The] major focus of guidance program responses should be on the felt or expressed needs" (p. 115). We concur. Basic needs are primarily the responsibility of those outside the school, and normative and comparative needs are more commonly associated with the academic curricula within the school. You, then, need to find effective ways of determining the felt and expressed needs within a given school population.

Techniques for Determining Needs

In chapter 2 we discussed the various groups of people that are served by the guidance program. In keeping with our philosophy that your job is to help people, we stress that care must be taken to assure that we aren't assessing the needs of the school or community at the expense of the students.

You can use a variety of techniques to identify the needs of individuals and/ or groups. We list and briefly discuss some of them.

1. Analysis of records. Whether you are organizing a new guidance program or revising an existing one, an early step should be a careful analysis of the objective records that have been accumulated by the school. This could include such pertinent information as students' ability levels, socioeconomic status, career aspirations, achievement records and grades, self-concept inventory results, attendance history, current curricula along with reasons for recent changes, follow-up information, and anything else that might shed light on the students' needs.

2. Personal interviews. A great deal of information can be gleaned by interviewing students, teachers, administrators, and other school personnel, along with parents and businesspersons from the community. The perceptions of these groups may vary widely. For example, teachers may say that until parents begin to take more interest in the education of their children, positive results are not possible. However, parents might counter that lack of teacher dedication is the primary cause of students' passive attitude toward learning. These different perceptions are a clear indication of the need to enhance understanding between teachers and parents. This should be converted into a program that addresses this need in a timely fashion.

3. Questionnaires and inventories. With the assistance of clerical staff and the guidance committee, you may prepare questionnaires and inventories that can be administered to various classes and groups. A questionnaire administered to teachers, for example, may reveal that erratic attendance by middle school students poses the greatest threat to learning. If additional investigation into school records tends to support this, a clear mandate for organizing guidance or counselor activities geared toward improving attendance should be implemented.

4. Counseling statistics. Careful record keeping of the kinds of problems being presented by students, the number of students being served, and the most problematic grade level or levels will reveal student needs. Sometimes you will have to treat these data statistically to determine if the need being verbalized by students is significant enough to warrant program changes or new activities. Another factor that may come to light as a result of personal counseling is a particular target group in need of information or help. For example, if a significant number of seventh-graders seems to lack information pertaining to study skills, you should convert this need into program activities that will help this group.

5. Classroom visits. Too often, we overlook the group of people with the best ideas about what is needed: the children. At least twice a year, schedule 20 to 30 minutes in each classroom to talk with the students about how school is going, how it could be improved, and related topics. Although locally constructed questionnaires and commercially prepared inventories can be administered to students, and will likely reveal expressed needs, the classroom visit will enhance this expression and probably reveal some felt needs not visible elsewhere.

6. Use of outside consultants. Sometimes bringing in outside specialists to assist with the identification of school needs is warranted. These experts can look at the guidance program more objectively and, either through a systematic review or a less formalized evaluation, identify needs that may have been over-looked or are not being satisfied through present program activities.

7. Systematic evaluation of the guidance program. Program evaluation should be an ongoing process. You can prepare and conduct surveys that will reveal whether program goals and objectives are being met. In some cases finding that a goal has been met may indicate a need to discontinue a particular activity, or to reduce the amount of emphasis being placed upon it. Other findings may indicate that certain activities are not satisfying student needs, and therefore need to be altered accordingly.

Converting Needs into a Program

Once students' needs have been identified, the next step is to assure that these are met through program activities. The following example should assist you in understanding this process. Let us assume that the administration of a self-concept inventory reveals that students in our K–6 school need to develop a more positive self-concept. Already we know that the *target group* is the students in grades K–6, and we know that the *need* is to assist these students in feeling better about themselves. Our next step is to share this information with the guidance program committee. The committee then brainstorms ideas about how this need could best be met, and formalizes the goals and objectives for satisfying the need. The overall goal might simply be *to help students develop a more positive self-concept.* The next step is to determine the management objectives. These help to set the timetable for the activities to be carried out, and offer a general delineation of those activities. A representative sample is listed below.

Management Objectives
1. By September 30 the counselor will have conducted one teacher discussion session in order to share ideas on how to increase students' positive feelings about themselves. This will be evidenced by a summary of the discussion, which will be on file in the counselor's office.
2. By November 1 the counselor, with the assistance of the teachers, will have begun a series of classroom guidance activities geared toward assisting students in developing a more positive self-concept. This will be evidenced by the classroom guidance activity planning forms, which will be on file in the counselor's office.
3. By May 1, the classroom guidance activities—offered on a biweekly basis—will have been completed, and a posttest self-concept inventory will have been administered. Evidence of this completion will be on file in the counselor's office

Not only do the management objectives include what is to be done and by when, but also evidence that the activity was carried out.

Our next step is to determine and state the evaluation criteria that will be used to determine the success of the objective. We have offered a sample statement below.

Evaluation Criteria
1. By May 1, students in the target group will show a 5 percent gain in self-concept as determined by the administration or a pre- and post-test self-concept inventory.

The final step prior to implementing fully the activities for meeting this need is to prepare a classroom guidance activity planning form for each grade level (see Figure 7.1).

To help simplify the process, we have prepared an outline (see Figure 12.1).

COUNSELOR RELATIONSHIPS

If the organization, management, and evaluation of a guidance program is to succeed, others beside the counselor must be involved and committed to the program (Gibson & Mitchell, 1990; Gysbers, 1990; Hollis & Hollis, 1965). By "others" we are referring to the administration (primarily the principal), teachers, parents, and other school support personnel. Positive relationships with these

NAME OF SCHOOL _____ COUNSELOR _____

TARGET GROUP _____

DETERMINED NEED _____
_____
_____

GOAL _____
_____
_____

MANAGEMENT OBJECTIVES: (List below) _____
_____
_____
_____
_____

EVALUATION CRITERIA _____
_____
_____

CLASSROOM GUIDANCE ACTIVITIES: (Complete form found in Figure 7.1)

FIGURE 12.1   Converting needs into goals, objectives, and activities

individuals are essential. Below we discuss the importance of these relationships and offer some suggestions as to how you can promote them.

The Counselor-Administrator Relationship

Without administration support and involvement, the program will fail to meet students' needs. Although a positive relationship with the administration at all levels is important, here we are primarily addressing the association between the counselor and the building principal. The basis for this relationship will be greatly enhanced if each has a clear understanding of the other's role. The principal is legally responsible for all programs and activities in the school. This includes the guidance program and all functions of the counselor. Because of this responsibility, you should make a practice of keeping the principal informed of your activities. Involve him or her in guidance program decisions whenever possible. Display a professional attitude by being more than a spectator in school curricular and program matters. On their part, principals need to understand fully the nature of your job. During the employment interview, offer clear statements regarding your role and functions. Be specific—don't make yourself available for *any* task. It is best to determine at this juncture whether the principal is supportive of this role.

The Counselor-Teacher Relationship

The relationship of teachers to their students is significant in terms of the latter's success. As positive teacher-student relationships are important to learning, so are positive counselor-teacher relationships important to the guidance program. Without the teacher's active participation in the program, your efforts will continually meet barriers. The ideal teacher-counselor partnership is a personal one in which the rigid formality of job titles and school-system authority concepts are sublimated. This atmosphere creates the type of humanness necessary for two professionals to meet students' needs (Stone & Peer, 1970). The relationship is characterized by an understanding of each other's role and by confidence in the ability of each to function as a professional. It is developed not only through this understanding and confidence, but through countless exchanges that may take place in the hall, lunchroom, classroom, and counselor's office; at faculty meetings; or in the lounge.

The Counselor-Parent Relationship

Parents who understand the goals of the school and the counselor are more likely to be supportive of the educational process, and become active participants in the educational lives of their children. Counselor-parent relationships are more likely to be initiated by the counselor than by the parent. It would be nice, even desirable, for you to initiate these relationships on a one-to-one basis through such activities as individual appointments or home visits. Unfortunately, most elementary/middle school counselors have such a high student/counselor ratio that this is not possible. Therefore, you must find ways to initiate and develop positive relationships with parents through other means. Some techniques:

> host a get-acquainted coffee hour;
> visit neighborhood functions where several parents will be in attendance;
> attend school functions and programs;
> participate in classroom activities where parents will be in attendance;
> invite groups of parents to the school for orientation sessions; and
> discuss school and guidance program goals.

Parents have a great deal to offer to the education of all students within the school. They can get involved in guidance activities that disseminate information on the world of work, leisure-time activities, and other topics relevant to the elementary/middle school student. In addition, they can observe the student's behavior at home, their relationship with siblings and friends, and their health, and provide other information that will help the school understand the student as a unique individual.

The Counselor's Relationship with Support Personnel

For any school to succeed there must be support personnel in a variety of areas. Support personnel include school psychologists, nurses, social workers, speech therapists, homebound teachers, librarians, secretaries, paraprofessionals, and counselors as well as building engineers, bus drivers, cooks, and others. They play an important role in the educational process. Your knowledge of student body characteristics as well as the needs of individual students can be of considerable assistance to professional personnel. Secretaries, custodians, bus drivers, and lunchroom personnel are privy to information concerning students and student needs that other staff in the school may not have. If you develop a cooperative relationship with support personnel, you will not only better meet students' needs through the guidance program, but also help the support staff. These relationships take time to develop, and you need to begin working toward developing them immediately upon arrival at a facility.

The extent of your success in developing positive relationships with others in the school may well reflect the degree of your success in meeting students' needs. Your role is complex and multidimensional. It requires a constant alertness to the contributions others may make to the educational process of students, as well as a conscious effort to contribute to the efforts of others.

DEVELOPING A JOB DESCRIPTION

Over the years we have received numerous inquiries, mostly from school administrators, regarding job descriptions for school counselors at all levels. Frequently, when a school district expresses interest in a guidance program, administrators want a job description to take to the board of education. This is especially true at the elementary level, since many schools have not heretofore had the services of an elementary school counselor. No single description applies to all situations, and it is incumbent upon the school to develop one that will best fit its situation. There are, however, common factors that go into the development of a job description. We briefly focus on these.

School and Program Philosophy

Examine the school's philosophy toward education. Next, present a philosophy for the guidance program. If this has already been developed, examine the statements to ensure that the guidance philosophy and school philosophy are compatible. These philosophical statements will indicate the overall direction of the guidance program. For example, if the guidance program is to be developmental in nature, this will be reflected in the philosophy statements. Rye and Sparks (1991) state:

> Certain philosophical viewpoints are commonly held among educators within a democratic society. Additional philosophical views are generally accepted among counseling professionals. The counseling program has a value base for assisting students with issues, pressures, decisions, celebrations, and conflicts related to the normal process of human development—all individuals have an inherent right to ample opportunity for the development of their fullest potential. Therefore, the school/community has an obligation to assist individuals in that development. (p. 23)

To formulate a clear statement consistent with the school philosophy and the basic philosophy of guidance, its developers must explore the wide range of needs, values, beliefs, and views of the community as well as of the counseling profession. In summary, the philosophy of the school and guidance program will indicate the direction of the program as well as set the tenor of the counselor's job description.

Using Information from Learned Societies

It is important to examine and consider the view of counseling professionals regarding the counselor's role and function. You will find this review to be helpful in preparing a job description. The primary authority on the role of school counselors is their professional organization, the ASCA (1990). It defines the school counselor as

> a certified professional educator who assists students, teachers, parents, and administrators. Three generally recognized helping processes used by the counselor are counseling, consulting, and coordinating: 1) Counseling is a complex helping process in which the counselor establishes a trusting and confidential working relationship. The focus is on problem-solving, decision-making, and discovering personal meaning related to learning and development; 2) Consultation is a cooperative process in which the counselor-consultant assists others to think through problems and to develop skills and make them more effective in working with students; 3) Coordination is a leadership process in which the counselor helps organize and manage a school's counseling program and related services. (p. 1)

The literature abounds with definitions of the counselor's role and function. We believe that most such statements could be classified under the three C's above. Even so, we highly recommend that you review the literature carefully before writing a job description.

Sample Job Description

Without assuming any special needs or a unique philosophy of a given school, we offer the following sample job description to give you an idea of how one might read. You are cautioned against attempting to adopt the statement for your school. Rather, we hope it will serve as a reminder of some of the factors you might consider in developing a job description.

Counselor's Job Description

The counselor is responsible for the organization, management, and evaluation of the guidance program and counseling service provided in this school. The counselor, with the assistance of the guidance committee and the administration, will organize a program that is consistent with the philosophy of the school, and based upon the developmental needs and interests of the students. Minimally, the program will provide activities that will assist students, teachers, parents, and administrators as well as other school personnel. The counselor will manage the program based upon stated objectives and in a manner consistent with management practices of the school. Program evaluation will be based upon the success of meeting stated program goals and objectives, as well as an ongoing accounting of counselor activities.

COUNSELOR FACILITIES

Physical facilities are important in determining whether you will have the opportunity to do the job you are hired to do (Gibson & Mitchell, 1990). Therefore, planning for facilities should be given primary consideration in the organization of the program. Our broad definition of *facilities* includes space, equipment, audio-/ videotapes, films, books, kits, materials, and any other physical item that may lend support to the program. Here, however, we discuss primarily the use of space.

Planning for appropriate facilities may involve adding to a room or converting space in an established building. It may also entail designing a complete facility within a new building. Either way, planning the space, as well as selecting equipment and materials, is a continual process and should be given a high priority in the organization and day-to-day management of the program.

Factors to Consider

The nature of the facility may vary with the size and grade level of the school. The facility under discussion here is meant for middle or elementary school counselors working in a building of 200 to 350 students. In planning a facility, three factors should be considered regardless of school size or special program needs: amount of space, location, and equipment.

Amount of Space. The minimal amount of space should include enough square feet to allow for a private office and a reception-secretarial room. The office should contain 100–120 square feet and be soundproof and visually private. Many counselors prefer to have a door in their private office that opens directly into a hallway. The reception area should be large enough for the secretary's desk, file cabinets, display areas, and seating for those waiting to see the counselor. Other practical areas are a group room that could double as a conference room, a play media room, and a storage room. Additional factors to consider are lighting, ventilation, heating, and decoration. Attractive facilities contribute to a positive psychological climate. If at all possible, consult an interior decorator.

Location.

Location with Regard to Other School Facilities. Your office should not be located outside the main building, but reasonably close to the offices of other specialists within the school, the administrator's office, and the classrooms. Access to other professionals is important to the normal operation of the counselor's work.

Accessibility. Not only should your office be accessible to students, teachers, the administration, and other school personnel, it must—by law—be accessible to disabled persons. When designing a new facility, be sure the architect understands the current legislation as it pertains to accessibility. The same laws apply to remodeling an existing facility.

Select a location where congestion will be kept to a minimum. Locate and arrange the reception area so that persons waiting for an appointment will not be able to see directly into your office. The group or conference room, if you are fortunate enough to have one, will serve many purposes and should be convenient to your office as well as the storage room and reception area.

Obtaining the ideal space in the ideal location may seem impossible. However, many counselors receive excellent facilities in a new building by making their needs known to the right person at the right time. In a remodeled facility, some recommended changes cannot be achieved. However, counselors—with the help of the guidance committee—should submit a list of needs in priority order.

Equipment. Needed in the counselor's office are

> an attractive and functional desk, and a comfortable desk chair;
>
> two to four comfortable chairs for office visitors, one or two for small children;
>
> two lockable metal file cabinets;
>
> a telephone, including a system for communicating with the secretary;
>
> a computer and printer with appropriate software;
>
> a wall clock;
>
> an audiotape recorder and a videotape recorder with a monitor; and
>
> access to a filmstrip and 16mm film projector.

The room should include bookshelves, either built in or free-standing, as well as display racks and tables.

The reception-secretarial area should include

a secretary's desk and chair;

several comfortable chairs for visitors;

a computer and printer;

a typewriter;

a telephone with intercommunication system;

lockable file cabinets;

bookshelves;

display racks;

calculator;

bulletin board; and

a clock.

Since this area will serve all who use the counselor's service it should provide a comfortable, pleasant atmosphere for those times when a wait may be necessary.

HINTS FOR PROGRAM IMPLEMENTATION

We have found that counselors who are employed for a minimum of ten months—giving them at least two weeks at work before school starts—usually have the most success in organizing and implementing their program. Successful program implementation depends to a large degree upon how well the program philosophy is developed, understood, and accepted. In addition, establishing program and activity goals that are based upon a carefully carried out needs assessment will enhance the possibility of program success. Whether you are initiating a new program or revising an old one is not as important as how you go about the implementation process.

Before School Begins

Some hints are more appropriate for a new program than for an existing one, and vice versa. As you review the list, give special attention to those that best fit your situation.

1. Spend some time getting acquainted, or reacquainted, with the physical facilities of the school. If you are new to the school, learn where various offices and activity areas are located. Sometimes changes are made during the summer, so even returning counselors should make a quick survey to determine what changes have been made.

2. Begin the development, or redevelopment, of your relationship with the administration. Offering to help with transfer and special-needs students will not only help develop the relationship, but will assist you in getting better acquainted with students.

3. Spend some time reviewing school policy handbooks, school curriculum, student record systems, and the testing program including the utilization of results. To make a maximum contribution to the education of the students, you need to be on the cutting edge of policies, curriculum, and other important matters.

4. Survey or review student status. This is a good time to take a look at the students' socioeconomic status as well their overall ability and achievement. Sometimes this information is readily available; in other instances a study will be needed.

5. Begin the process of reviewing, developing, or revising program objectives and activities. Some of this cannot be completed in a new program until after the guidance committee convenes; but before school begins is a good time to make preliminary plans.

6. Review and/or prepare the program's budget. It is extremely important that the guidance program have a budget. Before school begins is an opportune time to become familiar with it, and if one is not available, to begin budget development.

7. Prepare or update program inventory. Take an inventory of books, audio- and videotapes, kits, equipment, and any other materials or supplies listed under the guidance program.

8. Prepare requests for any needed program equipment, materials, or supplies. Although it is better if equipment, materials, and such are ordered at the end of school, budgets may be tight at that time, or a piece of equipment may be overlooked. Be sure to follow school policy and procedure in making requests and/or placing orders.

After School Begins

1. Continue to enhance the counselor-principal relationship. During the first few weeks of school, take a few minutes each day to visit with the administration. This will help the administrator to better understand your goals. Keeping administrators informed will be a positive step toward a good working relationship.

2. Get acquainted, or reacquainted, with the teachers and other school staff. Be sure to introduce yourself to new faculty, and find out if they have any immediate needs that you could help satisfy. Go to classrooms and informally visit with all the teachers. Spend some time talking with other school staff, including lunchroom personnel, secretaries, maintenance engineers, health personnel, psychologists, speech therapists, and social workers. This is a good time to get their impressions of the new school year and what they see as important needs during the early part of the year.

3. Get to know as many students as possible. Early in the school year is an optimum time to get to know or become reacquainted with students. In the elementary school, going to the playground during recess or other free time will provide an informal opportunity to talk with students. Eating in the lunch-room is another good place to make contact. Also, as soon as possible, visit all classrooms. Include a brief and imaginative presentation with regard to counselor activities, how to see the counselor, and the like. If clerical assistance is available and the budget will allow, prepare to send each student a birthday card. This is helpful in establishing rapport with students and parents.

   4. Begin the process of getting to know the parents. Talk with parents whenever possible. If any parent groups are scheduled to meet, see if you can participate. Hold parent coffees and invite parents to come to your office for get-acquainted sessions. Early in the year, prepare a short counselor newsletter explaining your role and send it home with the students.

PUBLIC RELATIONS

Public relations (PR), as it pertains to your work, has been defined as an organized effort to obtain information about the existing guidance program, including its philosophy, objectives, and its needs; and to communicate this to administrators, faculty, staff, parents, students, and others in the community (Hollis & Hollis, 1965).

   The effectiveness of the guidance program or any counselor activity will depend upon the extent to which the objectives, goals and purposes are understood by the school and community. Public relations is the vehicle through which this information can be provided. Through PR, persons within the school community and beyond are able to receive information that will assist them in utilizing and understanding the guidance program, and the counselor's service.

Ways of Conducting Public Relations

Hollis and Hollis (1965) state:

> Public relations activities are conducted through (1) mass media—publications of various kinds, radio and television broadcasts, and the like, and (2) group techniques—meetings, projects, guest-speaker programs, and other means by which information can be transmitted to or obtained from a number of people at one time. (p. 52)

To organize a meaningful PR program, whether it be through mass media or group presentations, you need to collect and disseminate information in an objective manner. Public relations should not become a high-pressure selling activity, but rather a way of providing objective information that will enable students, parents, faculty, and others in the community to actively participate in the guidance program.

Public Relations Hints

1. Be sure PR efforts are honest, both in intent and execution.
2. PR should be simple and easy for the public to understand.
3. PR is more than telling what has happened or what is about to happen. Have a long-range plan.
4. All efforts should include reference to the total school program.
5. PR is a continuous process.
6. Make sure the guidance program PR is in accord with school policy.
7. All PR releases should be made through the proper school channels.

Techniques used to implement PR will depend upon who is to receive the information and why the information is being released. In other words, select the technique that will be most useful in fulfilling the original purpose. Many techniques have proven successful if used appropriately, including

group meetings

reports

newsletters

bulletins

radio and television

news releases

giving talks at assemblies, in classrooms, at clubs, and other social events

How the information is transmitted is not as important as whether the content is clear and satisfies the purpose of the release. Marketing the counseling and guidance program involves analyzing the school's needs, then developing a PR plan that stresses program benefits. The plan can then be carried out through appropriate techniques and targeted toward specific audiences.

PROGRAM EVALUATION

Counselors are asked by school administrators, local boards of education, and state departments of education to be accountable and to provide data that can be used to determine the success of their work. Unfortunately, too often counselors at all levels have not carried out accountability studies, claiming that they are too busy. This is no longer acceptable. As Myrick (1987) states: "Accountability is an essential part of a developmental guidance and counseling program" (p. 432). In the last few years—and for the foreseeable future—the pursuit of excellence in education at all levels has been on the front burner and proposed changes are being heard from all corners. According to Myrick (1987):

> School counselors can play important parts in shaping the nature of their work and the future of their profession. But, this requires a sound

rationale for guidance and counseling programs, a clear understanding of their job potential and roles, and a willingness to accept the challenges and changes which will affect them. (p. 433)

The overall goal of evaluation is to provide counselors and administrators at the local and state levels with meaningful data that can be used to improve the school's guidance program (Gysbers et al., 1992).

Purposes of Evaluation

Evaluation of guidance programs may be done for different reasons in different schools. Therefore, local schools must identify the purposes for which they are evaluating. Below we suggest some that may be considered.

1. To measure the effectiveness of the total guidance program, as well as each of the activities included in it. The evaluation should include the efficiency with which the activities are being provided, and determine the extent to which program objectives are being met.

2. To collect data that, after interpretation, will be meaningful in determining what program modifications are indicated. Evaluations serve to bring together data on various activities so that comparisons may result in recommendations for changes in the direction or goals of the program.

3. To determine the level of program acceptance and support from students, staff, parents, and the community as a whole. Collecting data that can be used to determine program acceptance will be helpful in determining which program delivery systems are in need of modification.

4. To obtain information that can be used to inform the public about the guidance program. Good PR is essential to the success of the program. Collecting and disseminating information that keeps the public informed about the program is a necessary aspect of PR.

5. To collect data that will become an important part of the counselor's evaluation. Counselors are responsible for the organization, management, and evaluation of the program. Certain data collected as program evaluation will provide information that can be used to determine the counselor's effectiveness and efficiency. This should not, however, be the only means of evaluating the counselor.

6. To analyze the program budget and compare expenditures to future program needs. Budget review will assist in determining how effectively program allocations are being utilized, and will reveal where the budget needs to be increased or decreased in the future.

Collecting Data

There are many methods of obtaining data that will be meaningful in the evaluation of the guidance program and of those who are responsible for it. How to collect data, and what to collect, should be a part of planning the evaluation system. In making these decisions, keep in mind that it is important to involve the guidance committee, and that collection methods and techniques will in part depend upon available resources and individuals. Following are some methods of obtaining evaluation data.

1. Developing an experimental design. Much of the program evaluation will be determined by how well the objectives of the program are met. Therefore, before the year's program is implemented, objectives can be stated in measurable terms, and evaluation criteria levels set, so that when data are collected the extent of success will be revealed. In designing research it is often difficult, if not impossible, to control all of the variables that may come into play. You should not let this discourage you from evaluating activities designed to have a measurable effect upon students. Instead, carry out the study and state the uncontrollable variables as limitations. This way you will be recognizing the other factors while at the same time collecting results that can be attributed to program activities.

2. Utilization of surveys, checklists, questionnaires, structured interviews, responses to open-ended questions, and published evaluation instruments. These instruments offer evidence of the attitude various program consumers hold toward the counselor and the program. Whatever the technique used, the study should include students, both past and present; faculty and other school staff; and parents and other members of the community. It is seldom possible to reach all of these persons. Therefore, the study can be carried out on a random sample basis. In preparing for this kind of evaluation, research the literature to find current commercial materials available, and review instruments being used by counselors from surrounding schools.

Record Keeping and Reports

Keeping track of your time and submitting written reports will serve not only to evaluate the program but you as a practitioner as well. We suggest that as a part of record keeping, record the number of individual and small-group counseling sessions. Consultation sessions with parents, teachers, special school personnel, outside agencies, and the administration should also be recorded. Keep track of the number, kind, and grade level for classroom guidance presentations. Make notes and keep records of the time involved in testing, public relations, staffing, observation and program evaluation activities, and any other aspect of your work. We suggest that you submit a summary report to the building administrator on the first of each month. At first glance this might appear extremely time-consuming; however, it is possible to simplify the process. Figure 12.2 is a form designed to save time and simplify record keeping. Figure 12.3 is a form for submitting monthly reports to the administration with regard to the number of conferences held. It should be supported by a written summary of the other activities you were involved in during the report period. Included in the written summary will be the number and nature of classroom guidance sessions conducted, and an accounting of all other activities, such as parent education groups, assessment, public relations activities, and the like.

Before using the two forms found in figures 12.2 and 12.3, it is important to follow some simple directions. First, prepare a generous supply of copies of

DAILY RECORD OF COUNSELING & CONSULTATION SESSIONS						
Month of _____ 19 ___						
STUDENTS			FACULTY & STAFF		PARENTS & OTHER	
Name	Gr	Date	Name	Date	Name	Date
1.						
2.						
3.						
4.						
5.						
6.						
7.						
8.						
9.						
10.						
11.						
12.						
13.						
14.						
15.						
NOTE: keep track of group counseling sessions on back of sheet.						

FIGURE 12.2   Daily record of counseling and consultation sessions

the daily counseling and consultation form (Figure 12.2). Keep enough in your desk drawer to get you through a month. The rest can be filed away. Then, each time you have a session with a student, a faculty or staff member, or parents and others, record an entry on the form. For example: If the first counseling session during a given month was with Jim Strobe, a fourth-grader, you would write his name in

MONTHLY SUMMARY OF COUNSELING AND CONSULTATION

For month of _____ 19 ____

STUDENT CONFERENCES

    Number of students _____

        Total number of conferences _____

    Comments:

FACULTY & STAFF CONFERENCES

    Number of students _____

        Total number of conferences _____

    Comments:

PARENT & OTHER CONFERENCES

    Number of students _____

        Total number of conferences _____

    Comments:

TOTAL NUMBER OF INDIVIDUAL CONFERENCES _____

GROUP COUNSELING SESSIONS

    Number of students involved _____

        Total number of sessions _____

FIGURE 12.3   Monthly summary of counseling and consultation

the first space, put a 4 in the grade column, and enter the date of the month in the top left box ("Date"). If you should see Jim again during that month, record the date in the next box; and so on. It is possible to record four sessions per person, per month. By the end of the month you will have likely filled several sheets with students' names. Therefore, you may want to provide a space in the upper left-hand corner to note the page number for this particular month. The form is easy to use, and if done consistently after each session, will provide the means to prepare the monthly summary form found in Figure 12.3. The summary form can then be submitted to the administration on or about the first of each month. It should be accompanied by the written summary that was discussed earlier.

SUMMARY

Few topics are as important to school counselors as how to organize, manage, and evaluate their school guidance program. This chapter covered techniques for carrying out these tasks. We stressed that organizational goals and objectives should be based upon the needs of the students, and suggested some ways of determining needs as well as converting needs into program activities. We emphasized the importance of your relationship with administrators, teachers, parents, and support personnel. Included in the chapter is information on how to develop a job description based upon school and program philosophy, as well as information from learned societies such as the ASCA. We detailed what is needed for counselor facilities and equipment. We provided a list of hints for program implementation as well as public relations. We presented program evaluation as an important aspect of the guidance program, and discussed the importance of collecting data and keeping records. Finally, we included two forms that we believe will assist you in your evaluation efforts.

REVIEW

1. Why should the guidance program focus primarily on felt or expressed needs?
2. List several techniques for determining needs, and discuss the steps for converting needs into activities.
3. What is meant by *management by objectives*?
4. How do counselors go about developing and maintaining positive relationships with administrators, teachers, parents, and school support personnel?
5. Discuss how the school's philosophy should be reflected in the guidance program's philosophy and the counselor's job description.
6. Prepare a schematic drawing of desirable physical facilities for the counselor.
7. Make a list of activities you would engage in to bring about smooth program implementation.
8. Prepare a 10-to-15-minute talk, aimed at a group of community leaders, that outlines your work as a counselor.
9. Using information found in this chapter and other sources, prepare a comprehensive program evaluation strategy for a one-school guidance program.

REFERENCES

ASCA. (1990). *Role statement: The school counselor.* Alexandria, VA: Author.
Coleman, J. C. (1960). *Personality dynamics and effective behavior.* Chicago: Scott, Foresman.

Collison, B. B. (1982). Needs assessment for guidance program planning: A procedure. *The School Counselor, 30,* 115-121.

Gibson, R. L., & Mitchell, M. H. (1990). *Introduction to counseling and guidance* (3rd ed.). New York: Macmillan.

Gysbers, N. C. (1990). *Comprehensive guidance programs that work.* Ann Arbor, MI: ERIC Counseling and Personnel Services Clearinghouse.

Gysbers, N. C., Hughey, K. F., Starr, M., & Lapan, R. T. (1992). Improving school guidance programs: A framework for program, personnel, and results evaluation. *Journal of Counseling and Development, 70,* 565-570.

Hollis, J. W., & Hollis, L. U. (1965). *Organizing for effective guidance.* Chicago: Science Research Associates.

Maslow, A. H. (1954). *Motivation and personality.* New York: Harper

Monnette, M. L. (1977). The concept of educational need: An analysis of selected literature. *Adult Education, 28,* 116-127.

Myrick, R. D. (1987). *Developmental guidance and counseling: A practical approach.* Minneapolis, MN: Educational Media.

Rye, D. R., & Sparks, R. (1991). *Strengthening K-12 school counseling programs: A support system approach.* Muncie, IN: Accelerated Development.

Stone, L. A., & Peer, G. G. (1970). *Implementing a functional elementary school guidance program.* Topeka, KS: State Department of Education.

chapter 13

Guidance in the Middle School

OUTLINE

INTRODUCTION

In 1894 the Committee of Ten, which was charged with reviewing the status of public education, recommended that secondary education begin at grade 7 (Howard & Stoumbis, 1970). This recommendation was to introduce the "solid" academics at an earlier age. As a result, the most popular organizational structure for school became the 6-3-3 arrangement, wherein the first six grades comprise the elementary school, the next three constitute the junior high school, and the last three represent the senior high school. James Conant (1960) strongly criticized the existing school structure, which relied on junior high to educate the middle graders, and called for a restructuring. In the 1960s the literature continued to question grade structures that treated the middle grades either as part of the high school or elementary school.

The middle grades are unique and separate from those preceding or following. Young people at these age levels are characterized as the in-between-agers (Alexander et al., 1968). Similarly, Eichhorn (1966) considers this age period "the stage of development which begins prior to the onset of puberty and extends through the early stages of adolescence" (p. 3). Traditionally, ages 10 to 14 have not been adequately addressed in public school education (Alexander et al., 1968). The advent of the middle school in the late 1960s to early 1970s was intended to specifically address the needs of this in-between group. This chapter aims to acquaint you with the purpose and nature of the middle school as a unique structure.

THE MIDDLE SCHOOL CONCEPT

Alexander et al. (1968) define the middle school as "providing a program planned for a range of older children, preadolescents, and early adolescents that builds upon the elementary school program for earlier childhood and in turn is built upon by the high school's program for adolescents" (p. 5). Ideally, the middle school is housed in a separate building, apart from either the elementary or high school, and joins one or more of the elementary grades with one or more junior high grades (Educational Research Services, 1965). It replaces the junior high school and necessitates a restructuring of both the elementary and high school. Educators generally agree that the ninth grade should be excluded from the middle school.

Beyond a simple restructuring, the middle school concept calls for a change in educational philosophy. The rationale for middle schools developed from three foundation points (Alexander et al., 1968):

1. Individual differences present in the in-between-ager. Because of the wide variation among young people during this time, the middle school places emphasis on the individual with two considerations in mind (Alexander et al.,

1968): first, the in-between quality of these young people and how they differ from elementary or senior high students; second, the tremendous variability among young people, which adds to the complexity of teaching young people during this time. One way to address these issues is through a flexible curriculum.

2. Providing continuity across the K–12 educational experience. Clearly, the middle school is a transition between the elementary and high school. Since junior high school has been regarded as being too similar to high school, the middle school becomes a developmentally appropriate buffer, smoothing the transition from elementary to high school. The issue of continuity is difficult when you consider how variable young people are at this time, and then factor in the orientation toward a nongraded curriculum. The education of children and adolescents has been regarded as a ladder approach, wherein students move up the rungs as they move through the grades. Continuity, then, becomes a K–12 issue, not just a problem of the middle school. There needs to be close planning at all levels with consideration for what precedes and follows in the educational schema.

3. Introducing innovations in instruction and curriculum to accommodate the new organizational structure. As Alexander et al., (1968) indicate, innovation is more easily accomplished when restructuring takes place. Unfortunately, at times, restructuring occurs for reasons other than educational innovation to meet the needs of young people. It may be a factor in matching enrollments with facilities, arranging levels to establish acceptable class size, or some other reason that may or may not impact the delivery of quality education.

After 25 to 30 years of operation, the middle school concept is under review. The Task Force on Education of Young Adolescents of the Carnegie Council on Adolescent Development (cited in *Turning Points Revisited: A New Deal for Adolescents,* 1993) makes a number of recommendations.

1. Schools should become small learning communities, wherein students and teachers are joined together as teams, forming schools-within-schools. This would be a team effort consisting of as many as 5 teachers and 150 students.
2. A core academic program should be provided that will promote literacy. This curriculum would encourage children to think critically, lead a healthy life, act ethically, and become responsible citizens in today's complex pluralistic society.
3. All achievement level tracking should be removed to stimulate students to experience success in their educational endeavors.
4. Schools should utilize teachers who are specifically trained to teach young adolescents, rather than the typical practice of staffing the middle school with teachers who often are simply placed in this environment.
5. Schools should encourage health and fitness as a means of impacting student academic performance in a positive direction.
6. Schools should involve families in the education of their middle-grade children. Many professionals currently believe that the key to children's success in school is the engagement of parents in the process of education.

7. Students should establish school/community partnerships to create a connection between the school and "real world" of the community. Through this partnership the responsibility for the education of children would be shared and learning could be carried out of the school building and into the community. (pp. 2–3)

These recommendations have been advanced only in the past four or five years, and represent the latest view of the middle school. What is most noteworthy about the middle school concept is that different approaches are necessary to meet the needs of young people during this period of their growth.

THE MIDDLE SCHOOL CHILD

To address the curricular and guidance needs of young people in the middle grades, primary consideration must be given to the middle graders themselves. The middle school years are often thought to start at grade 5 and last through grade 8. Kohut (1976) notes that ages 10 to 14 comprise a distinct stage of development wherein young people possess similar physical, emotional, social, and mental characteristics. Thornburg (1970) regards this age range as an awkward time that bridges the gap between childhood and adolescence. He indicates that young people at this time are difficult; teachers find them uncooperative; and parents find them annoying. In general, he feels it is easier to work with young people who are either younger or older.

Research has demonstrated that the years from 12 to 15 are very stressful for young people (Search Institute, 1990). These youngsters gain increased freedom from their parents, have greater mobility, confront their emerging sexuality, and face the issues of alcohol and drug use.

Any attempt to address these difficult in-between years must start with their developmental characteristics. Eichhorn (1966) describes in-betweeners as *transescents,* or young people in a state of transition. Foremost about them is their uniqueness and considerable variability. They are experiencing a series of changes in their physical, emotional, social, and intellectual characteristics, and there is no uniformity among these young people.

Physical Characteristics

These center around the arrival of puberty and the growth spurt; both boys and girls grow at a greater rate than at any time since infancy (Milgram, 1992). Girls develop approximately two years earlier, but there is great variation within either sex: Some youngsters will be advanced by several years, while others will be delayed. Another aspect of the growth spurt is the restlessness apparent in both the classroom and in social interactions—middle schoolers seem to constantly bump one another. They are very concerned about their appearance. Since some parts of the body grow faster than others, these young people may be awkward and self-conscious. Generally, girls are more concerned about appearance. However, members of either sex are inclined to feel bad about some part of their bodies, and their self-esteem is fragile (Milgram, 1992).

Intellectual Characteristics

Middle schoolers exhibit curiosity about a broad range of topics. These students may not function intellectually at a greater level of abstraction; but they have received greater exposure to the world through various media than have their age-mates at any other point in history (Alexander & George, 1981). They want answers to questions that have particular meaning to them and their relations with their peers (Klingele, 1979). They have short interest spans and respond to experiential learning activity. Because of the broad-based exposure, their attitudinal changes render them vulnerable and unstable (Klingele, 1979).

Social Characteristics

Middle schoolers tend to be conformists as they seek the acceptance of their peers. Peer influence and pressure have a significant effect on the social environment of these students. Peers are important because they provide familiarity and reassurance (Klingele, 1979). Young people of this age doubt themselves a great deal and are frequently searching for an identity through the peer group. Middle schoolers seek out peers who are much like themselves. This association provides a sense of security in the midst of a great deal of confusion and turmoil (Alexander & George, 1981). At the same time middle schoolers are pulling away from parents and other significant adults in an effort to gain independence, autonomy, and freedom. There is some evidence that middle schoolers who are close to their parents have less need to conform and yield to peer pressure (Milgram, 1992).

In friendship patterns, gender tends to be the most important factor (Milgram, 1992). In spite of developing interest in members of the opposite sex, middle schoolers have the strongest attachments to same-sex friendships, and will maintain this until later adolescence. Same-sex friendships have a significant role in the socialization of middle schoolers.

Emotional Characteristics

Like their physical state, middle schoolers' emotional state is in upheaval. It is likely that during the middle years young people experience the greatest period of emotional intensity so far (Milgram, 1992). They are a picture of emotional contrasts. At one moment they might be close to their parents, and at another act as if they were ashamed of them. They may strongly desire to participate in some activity, but decline because of how others might view them. They are emotionally and physically too old for childhood and too young for adulthood. In the main, they do not know how they are supposed to feel. Although they are emotionally unsure of themselves during the middle school years, they will achieve some stability once they are into adolescence. This frequently is a time of emotional struggle between middle schoolers and adults, particularly parents. One reason for this struggle is that people of this age do not see the world the same way as adults. They have a tendency to overdramatize events, and adults find it very hard to see the world through their children's eyes. These youngsters are still dependent upon adults; regardless of their search for emotional autonomy, they really are not ready to be emotionally independent (Milgram, 1992).

Middle schoolers experience mood swings and display inconsistent behavior (Klingele, 1979). Since their world is changing rapidly, they are confused by their physical changes and by their quest to understand and order their social environment. They exhibit a wide array of fluctuating emotions. There is a constant push/pull between childhood and more mature adolescent behavior. For the most part, they are searching to understand their emotions and are experiencing an overload. The interaction between the physical changes and companion emotions is very confusing to these young people.

Psychological Characteristics

The psychological characteristics of middle schoolers provide something of a synopsis of the physical, intellectual, social, and emotional characteristics. Key goals for middle schoolers are individuality and independence, which they pursue with zeal, while at the same time expressing a need for the security of behavior guidelines provided by adults (Klingele, 1979). These youngsters vacillate between childhood behavior and adult roles. Middle schoolers are decidedly between these two worlds.

Because of physical and emotional changes, middle schoolers are hypersensitive. But, as they advance through this stage of development, they "mellow out" and become more stable. They worry about the future, which can manifest itself in a pessimistic view of life (Klingele, 1979). Since their world seems upside down much of the time, they search for personal meaning in the events around them and strive to develop a consistent view of their place in the scheme of things.

In summary, middle schoolers are experiencing a period of intense change and struggling to understand and keep up with these changes. They are moving toward greater freedom, autonomy, and self-direction with a mixture of confusion, excitement, and fear.

MIDDLE SCHOOL STRUCTURE

The middle school is built around the 1–12 grade-level divisions. Once these divisions are determined, the structure of the curriculum and roles of the staff are considered. What follows is a brief discussion of grade-level structure, with a broad examination of the nature of the curriculum.

Grade-Level Structure

Historically, grade divisions resulted in eight years of elementary school and four years of high school. In the early 1900s the junior high school appeared, and the 6-3-3 division was instituted (Howard & Stoumbis, 1970). This popular structure continued until the middle school came into being in the 1960s. In a 1964 NEA survey, only 20 school systems out of 433 reported middle school structures. By 1967 there were 599 middle schools in place; by 1968 this had grown to 1,101, and by 1970 there were 2,298 schools (Kohut, 1976).

The appearance of the middle school gave rise to several structural arrangements. The main point of division was to separate the ninth grade from the lower grades, either leaving it with the high school or as a free-standing unit. In most cases the ninth grade remained a part of the high school. Variations in the division between the elementary grades and the middle school have been the subject of much debate. Kohut (1976) reported that in 1969, approximately 60 percent of schools used a 6-7-8 grade structure, while 30 percent employed a 5-6-7-8 structure, and the remaining 10 percent used other variations. In 1976, 50 percent of all middle schools used the 6-7-8 structure, 37 percent the 7-8 structure, and 13 percent the 5-6-7-8 structure (Kohut, 1976).

Apparently, the 6-7-8 grade structure is the most appropriate for middle schools: Fifth-graders are generally immature, while sixth-graders are more like seventh-graders than fifth-graders (Kohut, 1976); and ninth-graders are more like tenth-graders than eighth-graders in terms of overall maturity (Meyers, cited in Kohut, 1976).

Curriculum Structure

Alexander and George (1981) divide the curriculum into three overlapping units: personal development, skills of communication and learning, and major knowledge areas (p. 56). Lounsbury (1991) identifies broad components in the middle school curriculum: the basic program, the exploratory program, a separate physical education element, and the guidance program (pp. 14–15). Eichhorn (1972) clusters the curricular elements into three groupings: knowledge, learning processes, and personal development (p. 41). These systems share strong similarities and slight differences. Conceptually, we see three broad components: a core knowledge program, an exploratory program, and a personal adjustment program. Health and physical education are important curricular elements, which are included but not specifically identified with any of these programs. We discuss each of these areas to highlight its function in the school.

Core Knowledge Program.   Typically the core has been the foundation coursework that has always been taught at these grade levels. Included are the basic tool subjects of math, English, science, and social studies. The difference lies in the approach taken to these subjects. Much like traditional programs, grade-level continuity is maintained in the core program, so that sixth-, seventh-, or eighth-grade students are separated. Within the grade-level configuration students may be grouped by ability or heterogeneously. When there are sufficient numbers of students, middle schoolers are often grouped by ability in math and reading. In other subjects, separation by ability is not considered particularly important. The core is the element of the curriculum that is designed to provide a broad knowledge base for middle schoolers. Because of the maturational variation among these young people, core subjects are often team-taught. This interdisciplinary approach enables a blending of subject matter, and addresses the differences in young people through individualized instruction.

Alexander et al. (1968) identify three considerations in developing the core curriculum: first, continuity within subject areas and across grade levels to provide academic experiences that address developmental differences in students; second, flexibility in the curriculum, which may relate to the amount of time available to address certain subjects or to the use of resources or content variation; and third, provision for individualizing subject matter.

These suggestions are conceptually sound but appear somewhat variable in practice. We have observed most frequently the use of team teaching, and interdisciplinary efforts to address differences among students through individualized instruction. Team teaching may combine the expertise of teachers of a single subject to maximize the talents of each teacher; or it may be interdisciplinary in nature, bringing together teachers from several areas to blend their subject matter and provide students with a more comprehensive approach.

Exploratory Program.   Exploratory courses are designed to acquaint young people with a variety of topics and skill areas. Toepfer (1992) identifies the purpose of this program as assisting students to apply facts and skills learned in core curriculum in projects and activities in their exploratory courses. According to Lounsbury (1991), this component of the curriculum clearly addresses the nature and needs of the age group. Frequently included here are courses in graphic arts, performing arts, industrial arts, home economics, outdoor education, and various areas of technology. Exploratory courses may be oriented toward enrichment; interest-centered minicourses may augment standard exploratory courses (Lounsbury, 1991). Presently, many middle schools have exploratory laboratories where students can sample a number of different areas in a short-course format.

Another aspect of this program is the infusion of exploratory courses into the core knowledge base. Since middle schoolers may fail to see the relevance of academics, hands-on experiences serve to stimulate their involvement in core subjects. As Toepfer (1992) notes, middle schools assist young people to consider the usefulness of academics in their world. Exploratory activities are an excellent means with which to link school and life.

Personal Adjustment Program.   This addresses the wide array of maturational differences. The guidance of young people in this age group is extremely important. The means and methods of approaching these issues lie both within and outside the classroom. Alexander et al. (1968) view personal development as fundamental to the middle school curriculum. They regard personal development as consisting of counseling, both individual and group; the development of values; health and physical development; and exploration of interests.

The focal point of the personal adjustment program is the *home-base* or *teacher/advisor program*. This has been a fundamental part of the middle school from its inception. Alexander and George (1981) note that each middle school student should have one adult to whom he or she can turn. In this curricular unit the teacher functions much like a counselor, providing individual and group guidance to students and acting as a liaison between young people and the school counselor. The program can assist students in educational decisions and matters of normal or typical school adjustment. It does not replace counseling but augments it, making for a more effective counseling program and collaboration between counselors and teachers. Although the most desirable arrangement for this is as a part of the daily schedule, students generally meet with their teacher/advisor several times a week for approximately 25 minutes. (The teacher/advisor role is difficult for many teachers, and frequently this time is not used effectively.)

Although it has been proposed that teachers assume extensive responsibility for guidance (Alexander et al., 1968), without special training most teachers feel ill equipped to do so. Toepfer (1992) assures that guidance activities serve to assist students in their decision-making process regarding educational choices, career development exploration, and emotional adjustments to the widespread changes that middle school youth are experiencing. Counselors, school psychologists, and social workers should assume responsibility for intensive guidance work with young people in their respective areas of expertise. Particular emphasis needs to be placed on providing all students with information on alcohol, drugs, and sex education.

Health and physical development are usually managed through separate courses and activities, such as intramural competition between home-base groups, and participation in clubs and interest groups. Lounsbury and Vars (1978) point out that this area is vulnerable to distortion by the competitive mind set rampant in the high school. Care must be taken to ensure that these programs afford students the opportunity to be successful participants rather than winners or losers.

PROFESSIONAL STAFF

The professional staff of the middle school is crucial to its effective functioning. To this day, many states do not mandate unique academic preparation for middle school administrators, teachers, and counselors. These professionals receive training geared for the elementary or senior high school (Alexander et al., 1968; Eichhorn, 1966; Howard & Stoumbis, 1970; Klingele, 1976; Kohut, 1976). Because of the uniqueness and widely varied needs of middle schoolers, it is important to consider the characteristics of the professionals who work with them on a daily basis.

Administrators

Building principals are the administrative and educational leaders of the school. Kohut (1976) states that with the advent of the middle school the role of the principal has changed dramatically. The principal should take on activities and educational roles beyond managing personnel and finances—functioning as the community liaison and acting as parent-relations specialist. It is entirely appropriate that the principal serve as a member of the teacher-advisor cadre and even participate in team teaching. Probably the most important characteristic of the middle school principal is the ability to understand the uniqueness of middle schoolers and to create an atmosphere that will allow them to muddle through the trials and tribulations of this in-between age.

Teachers

Teachers of middle schoolers are not generally trained to work with this age group; they often find themselves in the middle school because a position was available. Klingele (1979) identifies two characteristics of the middle school teacher: the ability to relate to students at this age level, and the ability to develop and carry out an instructional plan appropriate to the needs of this group.

We believe the middle school teacher should be part counselor, part teacher—and part saint. To work with these young people day in and day out, teachers must be extremely patient, flexible, sensitive, supportive, and persistent. They must also provide sufficient boundaries to allow students freedom to explore and grow, while imposing an appropriate structure that gives children a sense of "grounding" about acceptable and unacceptable behavior. We have long admired teachers who choose to work with middle schoolers because they like these children and find their work rewarding.

One of the most important qualifications is a thorough knowledge of the development of young people between the ages of 10 to 14. This understanding leads to meaningful interpersonal relations and instructional strategies. Beyond an understanding of the student, teachers need personalities that will invite positive student-teacher interaction (Klingele, 1979). Important traits include tolerance, flexibility, a sense of humor, and a sensitivity to the uniquely human nature of middle schoolers.

Effective middle school teachers need a balanced approach to young people. Respect for these students is essential, because it is a base upon which teachers can organize and conduct their classroom in a democratic fashion. The democratic classroom teaches students to acquire a sense of self-direction and responsibility. It also provides students with a sense of dignity and self-worth that is highly important to this age level. The tolerance displayed by teachers in this setting gives students a sense of affirmation—despite the feeling that they are out of phase with most of the world around them—and encourages them to be more tolerant of others.

Since middle school teachers usually assume the role of teacher/advisor and are in charge of a home-base program, they will function more effectively if they possess the ability to facilitate the affective development of students. This is a problem area, because teachers generally are not trained to work with students on intrapersonal and interpersonal development. You will most likely provide in-service training and consultation to assist teachers in carrying out this role.

Because of the nature of middle schoolers, teachers must be willing to adapt instructional techniques to the mercurial needs of the students. As Klingele (1979) indicates, "teachers become intermediaries between students and their environment" (p. 44). In effect, they are constantly interpreting the world to their students, who in turn can identify with the material and see its relevance.

Counselors

Middle school counselors pay particular attention to the uniqueness of the setting and population. Throughout this chapter we have emphasized the distinctive characteristics of middle schoolers. To address these characteristics we believe that counselors must possess the same basic qualities that we have identified for teachers and administrators: patience, tolerance, flexibility, empathy, and adaptability.

GUIDANCE ACTIVITIES

Guidance in the elementary and middle school is developmental in nature, fostering healthy development while preventing adjustment difficulties from arising. To meet the needs of middle school students requires a team effort, with the teachers and counselor as its primary members.

Klingele (1979) notes that early in the middle school movement, one of the primary issues regarding the teacher's involvement in the guidance program was "who is to do what," while "what's to be done" was a secondary concern (p. 283). Many writers in the field believe the teacher has a fundamental and far-reaching role in the guidance of middle school youth (Alexander et al., 1968; Costar, 1988; Klingele, 1979; Kohut, 1976). Although the teacher's role is important, it is not pivotal because teachers rarely possess the training to be fully effective. We believe teachers function in direct and indirect roles. In the direct sense, teachers staff the home base and provide guidance through their teacher/advisor role. Some of these activities are planned and used by all teachers/advisors in home base, and other activities are individualized to meet the specific needs of a home-base group. Individual activities are frequently planned with input from the counselor. Teachers are often uncomfortable with affective material; therefore, the most valuable guidance role of the teacher may be indirect: Their sensitivity and support form the basis for their interaction with young people. The best teachers, from the students' perspective, are those who show they understand and care about young people.

From a broader guidance and counseling perspective, Klingele (1979) appropriately proposed that the program should be based on the needs of middle school youth. To meet these needs he identified four areas of concentration: character development, mental health development, career development, and physical development (p. 284). These points of emphasis are similar to those of the elementary school counselor as identified in chapter 2. We have chosen Klingele's schema because his categories best represent the guidance and counseling needs of middle schoolers. Our approach recasts Klingele's terms to more accurately represent current nomenclature.

Personal Development

Klingele (1979) used the term *character development* to represent what we regard as the personal development of middle school youth. Under consideration in this area is a focus on the development of interpersonal skills through peer interaction, the development of problem-solving and decision-making skills, the enhancement of relationships with adults, and the development of responsibility through independence and self-direction.

Much of the activity in this area will come in the form of individual counseling and small-group activity, either through home-base programs or small-group counseling. Young people need to learn decision-making skills, and programs have been developed to systematically work through problem situations (Clabby & Elias, 1986; Vernon, 1989). Another area that deserves attention is peer interaction, including peer pressure (Kaplan, 1987). This subject could be addressed by classroom guidance or home-base programs. Keep in mind that peer relations cannot be taught in single-session activities; effective skills are developed over time.

Personal Adjustment

Although Klingele (1979) referred to this as *mental health development,* we consider the emphasis to be on intrapersonal functioning. Students are encouraged to engage in realistic self-analysis and evaluation to promote an improved self-concept. Underscoring this effort is the need to help students adopt a sense of self-worth, integrity, and an understanding and appreciation of their physical selves in the midst of rapid change.

Helpful activities in this area focus directly on self-concept and may be used in the home-base program or other classroom guidance groups. Materials have been developed for the classroom and for use by parents. These can easily be adapted for a variety of settings and with various age levels (Berne & Savary, 1987; Borba & Borba, 1978; Clark, Clemes, & Bean, 1980; McKay & Fanning, 1987). Self-esteem programs are often verbally based. They focus on adult supportive behavior and offer exercises that help young people identify their strengths and realistically accept the areas in which they perform well.

Career Development

Some time can be meaningfully spent on career exploration, but students often do not have clearly defined interests: They like everything or nothing. Therefore, interest patterns are only beginning to develop, and activity in this area should be exploratory. Activities can focus on self-understanding and developing interests. (Self-understanding activities are addressed under the topic of personal adjustment.) Interests can be explored through discussions of academic and leisure-time preferences.

Physical Development

Without discounting the health value of physical activity, our concern lies with an appreciation for the physical self and an understanding of the abuses of the body through the use of alcohol, other drugs, and sexually transmitted diseases.

Activities to promote physical development start with helping young people to understand their physical selves. This can be enhanced through health classes and home-base discussion of hygiene and grooming. Generally, adults believe—without much justification—that young people understand their bodies and know how to care for themselves. Once hygiene has been addressed, attention can be turned to the use of alcohol and other drugs. Prevention approaches are based on communicating with young people about the physical and psychological effects of these substances. Particular emphasis might be placed on tobacco use. Middle schoolers are inclined to experiment with tobacco, which is clearly a "gateway" substance. Most of the work in this area will be through small groups, either through the home-base program or counselor-initiated activity. Young people who are involved with abusive substances require an approach focusing on their behavior; the process is one of intervention.

Sex education is purported to be uniformly addressed in most school curricula. Unfortunately, this material is often treated lightly or incompletely. Information about sexual development should be provided to both girls and boys in the middle school, and focus on sexually transmitted diseases, including AIDS. Health teachers can provide much of this information if all students participate in a health course. Alternative approaches are through the home-base program, where more general information may be disseminated, or through the counselor.

Guidance activity for middle schoolers is divided among group activity in the home-base environment, counselor-led classroom guidance or small-group counseling, and individual counseling interviews. Activity may be structured and programmatic or unstructured and tailored to the individual or group. A complete guidance program will address all four of the areas we have discussed above: personal development, personal adjustment, career development, and physical development issues.

At the middle school level you are more likely to engage in individual and small-group counseling than at the elementary or high school levels. Some time is spent in consultation with teachers and parents, though not enough with the latter. Parents are clearly in need during these years; they have not distanced themselves to the extent that will be seen in the high school years. They still have the opportunity to moderate the natural tendency to draw away from young people who are creating distance between them.

SUMMARY

This chapter presented an overview of the middle school to provide you with a sense of the differences in working with students of this age compared to younger individuals. Middle schoolers experience sweeping changes and are extremely vulnerable.

We discussed the nature of the middle school and its curricular programs. The watchwords of the school are flexibility and interactive experiences. Teachers need to allow for student variability and will be more effective if they can address students' immediate needs. The academic curriculum needs to address the students' physical, intellectual, social, emotional, and psychological characteristics, accounting for differences among students and between middle schoolers and the levels that precede and follow.

The professional staff in the middle school must possess sensitivity and tolerance to serve—and survive—this age group. From administrator to counselor, all need to be well versed in the developmental characteristics of the various ages of young people in the middle school.

We concluded this chapter with guidance suggestions for working in the middle school. Although we did not provide specific activities, we did identify the general realm of work and indicate the focus of the guidance personnel who work with middle schoolers.

REVIEW

1. Distinguish among the middle school, junior high school, and high school.
2. Describe typical middle schoolers in terms of their physical, intellectual, social, emotional, and psychological characteristics.
3. Present your perception of the most desirable middle school grade-level structure.
4. Explain how exploratory courses can serve the development of middle schoolers.
5. Describe a common trait of effective middle school administrators, teachers, and counselors.
6. Identify two guidance activities that can serve the personal development of middle schoolers.

REFERENCES

Alexander, W. M., & George, P. S. (1981). *The exemplary middle school.* New York: Holt.
Alexander, W. M., Williams, E. L., Compton, M., Hines, V. A., & Prescott, D. (1968). *The emergent adolescent.* New York: Holt.

Berne, P. H., & Savary, L. M. (1987). *Building self-esteem in children.* New York: Continuum.

Borba, M., & Borba, C. (1978). *Self-esteem: A classroom affair.* San Francisco: Harper.

Clabby, J. F., & Elias, M. J. (1986). *Teach your child decision making.* New York: Doubleday.

Clark, A., Clemes, H., and Bean, R. (1980). *How to raise teenagers' self-esteem.* Los Angeles: Price, Stern, Sloan.

Conant, J. (1960). *Education in the junior high years.* Princeton, NJ: ETS.

Costar, J. W. (1988). *Focus on improving your middle school guidance program.* East Lansing: Michigan Association of Middle School Educators.

Educational Research Services, American Association of School Administrators and Research Division. (May 1965). *Middle schools.* Circular No. 3. Washington DC: NEA.

Eichhorn, D. H., (1966). *The middle school.* New York: Center of Applied Research in Education.

Eichhorn, D. H. (1972). The emerging adolescent school of the future—now. In J. G. Saylor (Ed.), *The school of the future—now.* Washington DC: ASCD.

Howard, A. W., & Stoumbis, G. C. (1970). *The junior high and middle school: Issues and practices.* Scranton, PA: Intext Educational Publishers.

Kaplan, L. S. (1987). *Coping with peer pressure.* New York: Rosen Publishing Group.

Klingele, W. E. (1979). *Teaching in middle schools.* Boston: Allyn & Bacon.

Kohut, S. (1976). *The middle school: A bridge between elementary and high schools.* Washington DC: NEA.

Lounsbury, J. H. (1991). The middle school curriculum—Or is it curricula? In J. Capelluti and D. Stokes (Eds.), *Middle level education: Policies, programs, and practices.* Reston, VA: National Association of Secondary School Principals.

Lounsbury, J. H., & Vars, G. F. (1978). *A Curriculum for the middle school years.* New York: Harper.

McKay, M., and Fanning, P. (1987). *Self-esteem.* Oakland, CA: New Harbinger Publications.

Milgram, J. (1992). A portrait of diversity: The middle level student. In J. L. Irvin (Ed.), *Transforming middle level education: Perspectives and possibilities.* Boston: Allyn & Bacon.

Search Institute. (1990). Teenagers' search for new connections. *Source, 6*(2).

Task Force on Education of Young Adolescents of the Carnegie Council of Adolescent Development. (1993). *Turning points revisited: A new goal for adolescents.* Washington, DC: Carnegie Council on Adolescent Development.

Thornburg, H. (1970). Learning and maturation in middle school age youth. *The Clearing House, 45*(3), 150-155.

Toepfer, C. F. (1992). Middle level school curriculum: Defining the elusive. In J. L. Irvin (Ed.), *Transforming middle level education: Perspectives and possibilities.* Boston: Allyn & Bacon.

Vernon, A. (1989). *Thinking, feeling, behaving: An emotional education curriculum for adolescents, grades 7-12.* Champaign, IL: Research Press.

chapter **14**

Current Issues in Counseling

OUTLINE

Review

References

INTRODUCTION

This chapter addresses a plethora of issues arising from an increasingly complex society. Among these are the pressures on the school to provide social and emotional support and training to young people; the increased frequency of crisis situations; abuse of alcohol and other drugs; students who find little meaning and success in school and have been labeled at risk; the need for renewed emphasis on career development in an increasingly technological society; a rise in sexually transmitted diseases, especially AIDS; the increased presence of children of divorce; more frequent reports of child abuse; and the dramatic upswing in suicide among young people. A decade ago these problems were less in evidence and less frequently the province of the school.

We also discuss ethical concerns specifically related to the school counselor. We feel it is important to consider these areas, but recognize that a great deal is yet to be learned. The information presented will likely be foundation, at best, with updates flowing from the current literature.

THE STATE OF AFFAIRS IN SCHOOLS

Reform Movements

Throughout the twentieth century, society has experienced periodic reform movements designed to change the focus or improve the efficiency and quality of public education. Since counseling in the schools is relatively new, the reform movement has touched our profession twice. First, in 1958, the passage of the NDEA provided the impetus for the growth of the profession. Second, the 1983 publication of Gardner's *A Nation at Risk: The Imperative for Educational Reform* generated considerable reform effort and spawned widespread interest in improving the quality and rigor of education and imposing accountability on the schools. Although counselors and counseling are rarely mentioned in the proposals, any change in this country's educational system has the potential to dramatically impact counseling. This most recent movement has produced an emphasis on the social-emotional development of young people and quality performance assessment (QPA) or outcomes-based educational efforts. The role of counselors in children's social-emotional growth is a constant and a given; their involvement in QPA is variable and less clear.

Reaction.   The social-emotional emphasis in the reform movement has created a stir among some parents and religious groups, who regard this as an exclusive province of family and church. Therefore, some counseling activities are coming under increased scrutiny by these conservative groups. Although classroom guidance has been the most closely examined, the overall sensitivity raised by this reform advocacy has brought to the forefront a consideration of all counseling activity in the elementary and middle school. How far this movement will go is yet to be known, but we urge you to be attentive to the forces in your community that may raise concerns over your guidance and counseling program.

Expectations of Counselors

With the advancing complexity of society and the greater numbers of troubled children in the schools, counselors are being called upon to do more, and do it more quickly. When a desperate teacher exhorts you to "fix" kids and send them back tomorrow, we suggest you ask him or her how you should go about fixing such a child. This is intended to encourage the person making the demand to think realistically about the difficulty of your task. You might also ask this teacher how long he or she thinks it has taken the child to develop the problem behaviors. Through these efforts you can help the teacher understand that a child is a "finished product," and it will take time to change the child's behavior. The frustrated teacher or administrator should stop and think about the scale of your task. Once these professionals can separate themselves from their involvement with the troubled child, or depersonalize the problem, they can reasonably appraise the magnitude of the situation and understand that altering a child's behavior takes time.

Counselors complain about the difficulty of securing cooperation from teachers. If teachers will not allow you to take children out of their class, ostensibly because of loss of classroom learning time, you may (as a moderator) point out that you wish to make the classroom situation more pleasant and productive, and that by working with the child maybe some information can be gained to move in this direction. When all else fails, you must honor teachers' wishes and work with children whose teachers are more cooperative. Your abiding hope is that resistant teachers will eventually see the value of your efforts and soften their stance.

One effective technique in developing positive relations with teachers came from one of our former students. This individual created a coupon similar in size and shape to Monopoly money that says "Stress Reducer—Go back to your room, relax and take five. I'll cover your duty because I have some extra time" (B. Letcher, personal communication, November 9, 1993). This coupon would be given at sporadic times when the counselor had some free time and could easily release a teacher from his or her extra duties, such as lunchroom or recess monitoring. The counselor discovered that this simple act of courtesy was clearly a means to building a cooperative relationship with her teachers.

CRISIS INTERVENTION

With increasing frequency, schools are faced with situations that arrive unexpectedly. These disasters impact everyone in the school. Your school's response will have polar positive or negative outcomes, with rarely an in-between resolution.

In the worst case, it will leave a negative residue that will occupy more of your time than you could ever imagine. This section is designed to provide you with an effective approach to facing such a crisis.

The Crisis Situation

What constitutes a crisis? Jay (1989) divides crises into acts of nature or human nature. The former might include tornadoes, floods, hurricanes, earthquakes, or blizzards; the latter, suicide, drug overdose, theft, vandalism, AIDS, driving accident, teacher strikes, scandal involving faculty or other staff, in-school injury, or bomb threat. The Chinese representation of crisis is composed of two words, *danger* and *opportunity* (Jay, 1989). We hope to provide you with an improved chance of overcoming the danger and using the opportunity.

A Crisis Plan

All of us remember fire drills and, in some parts of the country, tornado or hurricane drills. But how often have you experienced a fire at school, or a tornado or hurricane (Siehl, 1990)? Now, schools should prepare for other crises. Because as counselor you are involved with a variety of people within the school and have contact with vital community resources, you are in a prime position to help develop a crisis plan.

There are two aspects of the crisis plan: development, including the preparation of the school staff to use the plan, and implementation.

Plan Development.   Develop the plan using a team approach wherein the members represent a cross section of the school and community. Usually the team will include you as the counselor, an administrator, the school psychologist or social worker, volunteer teachers, possibly a member of the law enforcement community, mental health agency representatives, parents, a member of the news media, possibly older students, possibly a member of the clergy, and a member of the superintendent's office. These team members will meet to draft the plan and will assist in the preparation of the staff to implement the plan. Once the plan has been developed it should be presented to the school board for approval.

The plan should include a procedure for handling the crisis, with a precise sequence of steps and the identification of who is involved in each activity. Although each situation will require some variation in approach, the general points in a crisis management checklist are similar. We have developed a process based on several of these lists from the literature (Kelly, Stimeling, & Kachur, 1989; Petersen & Straub, 1992):

1. bring together the crisis team;
2. establish a crisis headquarters;
3. collect and verify the facts;
4. adapt the plan to fit the particular crisis;

5. announce the crisis to the school;
6. identify the responsibilities of the teachers;
7. determine the counselor's responsibilities;
8. enumerate the administrator's responsibilities;
9. manage the media, including the selection of a spokesperson;
10. evaluate the crisis plan; and
11. bring the crisis to a close.

In-service training is the most practical means to prepare the staff to use the plan. These programs are conducted for teachers and support personnel—such as bus drivers, cafeteria staff, custodians, and playground supervisors. This training course consists of a walk through the plan, with emphasis on the primary pressure points and how to handle those affected by the disaster. The roles of each staff member should also be addressed. The sequence of steps should be clearly delineated and the personnel involved in each step identified. A discussion of each element follows.

1. Bring together the crisis team. Initiating the plan when the crisis occurs is usually the responsibility of the principal, who brings together the crisis team. The team often consists of an administrator, counselor, school psychologists, teachers, mental health professionals, and uniquely trained professionals suited to the crisis situation.

Generally, members of the crisis team are notified through a preplanned telephone chain. At the same time, the superintendent should be notified so that she or he can prepare for reactions from the media, community, and parents. The crisis team provides direction for all intervention efforts outlined in the plan. Sorensen (1989) notes that this meeting should address the nature and intensity of the crisis, determine the emotional needs of students and staff, and identify the high-risk population in the school and the nature of parent involvement. Further, Sorensen thinks decisions about intervention strategies should be made collectively by the team.

2. Establish a crisis headquarters. When a crisis occurs, structure is important in stabilizing the situation. A necessary effort in this direction is to establish a crisis headquarters from which to coordinate all activities. The crisis center can be either the administrative offices or the counseling office. It is preferred to leave the counseling offices available to serve the needs of individuals and small groups of students.

3. Collect and verify the facts. This is the next essential step to prepare the team to inform staff, students, parents, and the media. This will help the team to confirm the nature of the circumstances, and to minimize rumors and misinformation.

4. Adapt the plan to fit the particular crisis. Team members lay out their approach to the crisis, addressing the unique feature of the situation. Included in the plan will be meetings with teachers to determine classroom activity, counseling activity with individuals and small groups, parent meetings, and briefing the press.

5. Announce the crisis to the school. This will begin with a meeting of the faculty to brief them on the situation. The purpose of this meeting is three-fold: to inform the faculty of the situation, provide facts to reduce rumors and misinformation, and set in motion the activities of the school to manage the situation (Siehl, 1990). Every effort should be made to maintain the regular school day as a part of stabilizing the situation.

6. Identify the responsibilities of the teachers. Teachers will have a checklist or sequence of steps to follow in addressing the crisis. They should present the facts in a manner appropriate to the age levels of the children, and avoid overdramatization by the students. Moreover, the situation should be discussed with the students to clarify what has happened. Teachers should inform students of the availability of counseling services and then return to the regular classroom routine as soon as possible. Some students may show extreme emotional reactions to the crisis; they are to be referred to counseling. Some young people may need to be excused from school because of their emotional response and because they may feel more secure at home. In the days that follow, teachers should remain alert to residual reactions by students and apprise you of their behavior.

7. Identify the counselor's responsibilities. Individual and small-group counseling should be available immediately after the crisis subsides, and should continue for some time. All counseling activity should ensure privacy and be easily accessible for students, staff, or parents who desire this assistance. Quite possibly, the length of time necessary for counseling services will be determined by the frequency with which the service is used.

8. Enumerate the administrator's responsibilities. The administrator will likely chair the crisis team and act as liaison between the team and the super-intendent's office. Further, this individual will provide periodic informational updates to the faculty and will be responsible for any adjustments in the school's schedule and activities. The administrator should also work closely with the media spokesperson to dispel rumors and avoid misinformation.

9. Manage the media. Coordination of media activity is vital. This includes the selection of a spokesperson to maintain ongoing contact with the media and act as the liaison between the school and community. The media spokesperson will meet with the media early in the crisis and present an honest, accurate account of the situation. This form of reporting can dispel rumors, correct misinformation, and set the tone for a positive outcome by inviting the media to work in partnership with the school. Also, as necessary or desirable, establish a media headquarters to provide space and a means for close cooperation between the school and the media. These efforts will help enlist the help of the media.

10. Evaluate the crisis plan. The effort to evaluate the effectiveness of the plan should begin before the crisis ends and continue after it has subsided. Initial efforts can be undertaken with the crisis team. A discussion among team members will take place, with someone recording the observations for later use. Questionnaires may also be given to faculty, parents, and community members. This effort will help improve the process of managing subsequent situations.

11. Bring the crisis to a close. When the emergency situation has subsided, try to bring closure to the disaster and return to normal. Recognize that some students and staff will need assistance long after the immediate crisis has ended. Closure may be brought about through a media summation, a meeting of the school staff, and classroom meetings with students.

We recognize that each crisis will be different. Therefore, the plan presented here is a broad-based guideline for managing these situations. Once your plan is established, your team formed, and staff have received in-service training on the nature of the plan, then you have done about all you can to be prepared for the situation.

ALCOHOL AND OTHER DRUGS

Abuse

Although alcohol and other drugs are not usually viewed as a problem in the elementary school and are considered isolated problems in the middle school, the abuse of these substances is becoming more prevalent in both. More frequent is the use of tobacco, particularly in the middle school years. The gateway substance of tobacco can lead to experimentation with alcohol and then other drugs. Usually tobacco is introduced by peers as a means of imitating adult behavior. Available data on elementary and middle school alcohol and drug use are limited and scattered, but the signs are clear: These young people are experimenting, and some are abusing. Hawley (1990) states first-time drug experimenters are between the ages of 11 1/2 and 13. Further, he reports increasing numbers of children in grades 6 to 8 who are experimenting with drugs. Borton (1983) reports peer pressure has brought half of all seventh-graders to try marijuana. Inhalants are also a significant problem among elementary school children. These are considered a gateway substance for elementary schoolers.

Research cited in a 1987 issue of the *Weekly Reader* (Wilmes, 1988) indicates that elementary school children report significant pressure from peers to try alcohol as early as fourth grade, with 36 percent saying they felt pressure from peers (p. 31). This study also indicates that the number of fourth- to sixth-graders who believe that some or many of their age-mates had tried alcohol increased from 79 percent in fourth grade to 93 percent in sixth (pp. 31–32). Johnston et al. (1987), in one of their national surveys, report that alcohol and other drug use begins by sixth grade for 8.8 percent of the respondents and 22.6 percent of seventh- and eighth-graders. Stevens et al. (1991) report that alcohol use is a serious problem. In a survey of 1,190 fourth- through sixth-graders, Stevens et al. found that 56.4 percent had tried alcohol and 6.3 percent reported drinking at least once a month. Benton and Benton (1992) report 28.4 percent of female students in grades 4–6 use alcohol, while 30.2 percent of males the same age use alcohol. Clearly alcohol is a problem in the elementary and middle school grades, although not to the extent of the later grades. Repeated findings indicate that drinking behavior in the later years is largely developed in earlier years

(Brook et al., 1986; Hill et al., 1990; Jones & Bell-Bolek, 1986; Miller, Smith, & Goldman, 1990). Clearly, this points to the need for schoolwide preventive efforts and intervention.

Prevention

"Just say no" just does not work. It is a simplistic and narrow approach to a complex problem. Helping young people faced with temptation to experiment or pressure to abuse runs the gamut from education to prevention. The school is an ideal place to implement programmatic efforts.

What is the difference between education and prevention? Essentially, education is an effort to better inform those in the school about the dangers of alcohol and other drugs. Often these efforts are superficial, short term, and periodic. By contrast, prevention is a comprehensive effort extending across the year and involving all members of the school community—students, teachers, support personnel, and parents.

Prevention begins with the establishment of a districtwide statement of philosophy and policies regarding alcohol and drug use. An excellent source for both is Anderson (1987). The philosophical and policy statements are developed by a core committee consisting of key members of the school and community, and are ultimately approved by the school board.

Once the philosophy and policies have been developed, they are to be articulated to the faculty, staff, and parents. Hawley (1990) notes that schools must be prescriptive and descriptive about the alcohol and drug problem: prescriptive in that all school personnel must be in agreement with one another and aligned with existing philosophy and policy. To be effective the school must have complete faculty and staff support, as well as the support of the community. This may be a tall order if the community does not view alcohol use as a problem, but only as matter of discretion and control. If teachers and community members at least pay lip service to the district policies, the prevention program might garner reasonable support.

Resources. At the elementary level, the primary focus will be on prevention through self-esteem development and on addressing the effect of parental abuse of alcohol and other drugs on children. A number of good resources address self-esteem development. *Substance Abuse Prevention Activities for Elementary Children* (Gerne & Gerne, 1986) is organized by grade levels with specifically designed activities: feelings for grades K and 1; making choices for grades 2 and 3; the effect of smoking for grade 4; alcohol and its effects for grade 5; and positive peer pressure for grade 6. At each level the activities focus on substances that may be misused.

Other approaches focus on intrapersonal feelings, problem solving, and interpersonal relations. For a representative example of well-developed general programs, see Daugherty, Newman, & O'Bryan (1985); McDaniel & Bielen (1990); Newsam (1992); and Vernon (1989a, 1989b).

Other approaches to prevention can be easily developed to fit the uniqueness of your situation by adapting the above material, using a committee approach within your school, or using your own creativity. Since prevention is best managed as a year-long program, we strongly recommend involving others and trying to provide some means of rotating committee members, as we have discovered that burnout comes all too easily.

Intervention

Intervention naturally increases in frequency as one moves from elementary to middle to high school. First consideration is given to school-related signs that young people are abusing alcohol or other drugs. These may include lack of interest, poor academic performance, and self-imposed isolation from classmates. At the elementary level these indicators may be barely visible. If you observe such factors in combination over time, further investigation is warranted.

Interpersonal elements include relations with peers and family. Unquestionably, young people face pressure to conform to a peer group. Interestingly, some have said the issue is not one of peer pressure as much as peer selection. Young people's choice of associates places them in situations where they may be vulnerable to pressures and exposed to drug abuse.

Factors in the home include parental use of alcohol and other drugs, lack of supervision, dysfunction, and abuse or neglect. A correlation seems to exist between child abuse and parental abuse of alcohol or other drugs. This does not mean that one necessarily causes the other; only that there is often a connection between the two. Therefore, a powerful moderator is the relationship between parents and children. Logically, time spent in supportive interactive relationships seems to have ameliorating effects on children's substance abuse.

Intervention is a difficult and time-honored process because substance abusers are high on denial and resistant to change. Some insist that any confrontation regarding abusive behavior constitutes intervention (D. Engel, personal communication, February 1993). Duke Engel and Otto Schultz (D. Engel, personal communication, November 29, 1993) refer to these spot interventions as "flashing your brights." The implication is that young substance abusers are like drivers without headlights: They cannot see where they are going. After many such interventions, expressed with concern and empathy, the young abusers will acknowledge your sincerity. Another method has a school team trained in group confrontation meet with the young abuser and collectively confront his behavior (Schaffer, 1987).

Following a successful intervention, programming can begin to help young people develop interpersonal skills in areas of communication, problem solving, decision making, assertiveness, and relationship building. Once acquired, these skills will help young people to consider their situation and redirect their behavior. Newsam's (1992) student assistance program provides examples of activities to help young people develop more effective daily living skills. The road back to normality from highly abusive behavior is long and risky. Widespread opinion in the treatment field is that approximately 50 percent of all young people who enter rehabilitation will experience a brief relapse in the first 30 days after treatment, and 80 percent will do so during the first year.

Children of Alcoholics

A relatively new counseling category is children of alcoholics (COA). Over the past decade these young people have come to the forefront in the mental health field. Recent research indicates that young people are concerned about their parents' drinking habits. Benton and Benton (1992) found that among children in grades 4-6, 17.3 percent of the boys and 8.3 percent of the girls were concerned about their mothers' drinking. Regarding fathers' drinking behavior, 31.6 percent of the boys and 25.9 percent of the girls expressed concern. Anderson (1987) reports the typical estimate is that 25 percent of all young people in school have at least one biological parent who is an alcoholic. Elementary school children are creatures of the significant adults in their lives, namely, parents and teachers. Children of problem drinkers are at increased risk for becoming problem drinkers themselves. These figures strengthen the possibility that COAs represent the largest single problem you will face in the area of substance abuse.

Robinson (1989) points out that the single largest pitfall in treating COAs is finding them. This group is relatively hidden, and your attempts to help COAs will be hindered by being one step removed—working with the child and not the adult.

Who are the COAs and what characteristics do they display? They are difficult to spot because they do not readily reveal the deep-seated family secret about the drinking parent (O'Rourke, 1992). Black (1981) has identified three rules that protect the family of an alcoholic: Don't talk, don't trust, and don't feel. Anderson (1987) adds *don't know,* meaning remain ignorant about alcoholism or other drug abuse.

The research is mixed on the effects of parental alcohol abuse on children's behavior and performance in school (Anderson, 1987). In the absence of methods to identify COAs, you can observe and make inquiries of the children who raise your concern. Sometimes you can use anonymous questionnaires to allow children to identify problems in school and at home.

Once you have identified the COA, what can you do? Robinson (1989) recommends a child-centered approach, which assumes you can help the children to understand their feelings and ultimately change their behavior—even without the parents' involvement. Mainly, these children are assisted in support groups with other COAs. To help children of alcoholics the following points are emphasized (Robinson, 1989):

1. recognize that alcoholism is a disease;
2. everyone gets hurt in these families;
3. COAs are not alone;
4. they are not responsible for the parent's problem and they can't change it;

5. they can take care of themselves in other ways;
6. expressing feelings helps things to be better;
7. in safe settings it is OK to talk about parents' drinking;
8. COAs are high-risk themselves;
9. these children need to identify a trusted support system away from home; and
10. there are many ways to solve problems and live with the alcoholic parent.

It is important that you help other school staff to be sensitive to the COA. These children may be unusually tired or emotionally withdrawn. Since they are difficult to identify, convincing teachers of their need for special treatment and sensitivity may be difficult. One possible approach is to conduct a faculty in-service on COAs and the ramifications of their lifestyle on their ability to learn. Teachers need to be innovative in their work with these children (O'Rourke, 1992). They may require special arrangements to update school assignments and obtain supplies when the home situation is in disarray.

CONTEMPORARY CONCERNS

At-Risk Children

Today's at-risk child was yesterday's potential dropout. Most frequently these young people are identified by their academic struggles. They have repeated one or more grades, have failed two or more subjects, are behind two or more grade levels in assessed achievement, or appear as social isolates in the school. Retention is ineffective beyond kindergarten or first grade because of the social stigma it promotes. As an alternative, we favor classroom approaches that use heavy doses of encouragement from significant adults and peers. There is no such thing as too much encouragement. Encouragement is best modeled by teachers so that children and parents can observe and learn its application. A review of DUSO-2 (Dinkmeyer & Dinkmeyer, 1982) or STET (Dinkmeyer, McKay, & Dinkmeyer, 1980) will provide the rudiments of the encouragement process.

Other techniques include peer tutors and "study buddies"—classmates who provide assistance and support to the struggling student. This approach has the added value of increasing the social interaction between the struggling student and those who have experienced success in school. We have observed that the best tutors or buddies are students who are just a cut above the student you are trying to help.

Dysfunctional families are another source of at-risk students. They may harbor a physically abusive parent and/or one who is abusing alcohol or other drugs. In these homes, support for the child is minimal or nonexistent. Often the parents are out of the home for a significant period of time, and neglect the supervision of their children. This results in a reduced opportunity for children to develop self-directed responsible behaviors. We firmly believe all young people need the guidance of adult supervision and monitoring. There is no substitute for spending time with young people, regardless of age.

Career Development

Why place career development in a section on contemporary issues? Actually, we assert that almost everything you do as an elementary school counselor provides career development counseling because you focus on the development of self-esteem, which is essential to surviving in a competitive society. Directly or indirectly, you engage children in career activities by focusing on their adjustment to the school environment and the acquisition of healthy work habits. If you don't directly address career choices, children can readily observe the work activities around them.

The career education movement of the 1960s and 1970s (Hoyt, 1993) and the more recent National Career Guidance Guidelines (NOICC, 1989) identify stages of career development for school-age youngsters. Hoyt (1993) regards career awareness as the focus for grades K–6; NOICC (1989) identifies competencies for each level built around self knowledge, educational and occupational information, and career planning. At the elementary level, NOICC guidelines emphasize the child's developing self-competence and relationships with others, recognition of the value of education and the child's place in the educational realm, nascent understanding of the world of work, and the initial acquisition of planning skills for decision making.

Awareness.   Both Hoyt and NOICC place initial emphasis on awareness of self, the world of work, and planning. Career awareness starts with self-awareness to help children become more realistic about their strengths and limitations. A balanced understanding of these two elements is imperative in determining what young people are best suited to do in life. Children should also develop a sense of themselves as workers in the school.

Exploration.   This begins somewhere in the middle school years with a rudimentary exploration of work activity and a broad introduction to careers. The intention at this level is to help students understand career clusters and begin to relate their interests to particular careers.

Planning.   This is centered in the high school years. Sudents learn more about specific careers and appraise themselves in relation to career requirements (e.g., training and job demands). High school students should begin to look at the intangible qualities related to success, such as work attitudes.

Elementary school counseling and career development are as much a matter of attitude as focus and content. If we begin to relate self-awareness and interpersonal skills to the work people do every day, we will further the holistic development of our children.

Children of Divorce

The current statistic has 50 percent of all marriages ending in divorce. Similarly, it is estimated that one out of every three children will live with one parent before they graduate from high school. In a longitudinal study, Wallerstein (1989) reports that children may require as long as ten years to adjust to divorce. Children of divorce often experience difficulties that affect their schoolwork. Among the frequent emotional problems are distractibility, impulsivity, acting out, lowered academic achievement, and aggressiveness (Kelly & Wallerstein, 1977). These statistics clearly underscore the need for divorce adjustment support groups in the school.

Yauman (1991) proposes that group counseling is the most effective means to address divorce adjustment issues because counseling groups provide children with a feeling of inclusion. Children should be grouped by age to address developmental similarities. This does not mean that an age span cannot be present, but the range should probably not extend beyond three years. We consider these groups to be developmentally oriented support groups rather than remedial experiences. They should assist the child in making a transition from the divorce to a new family structure. Gaver (1987) suggests that divorce groups focus on

1. providing information about divorce and its impact on all members of the family,
2. creating a supportive caring environment to stimulate sharing,
3. helping members acquire positive coping skills,
4. giving encouragement to members during times when they are feeling low, and
5. communicating to members that they are not alone in this situation.

Groups may be structured around print materials, media, and board games as stimulus materials (Yauman, 1991). An early work written to help children address divorce is *The Boys and Girls Book about Divorce* (Gardner, 1970), followed by *The Boys and Girls Book about One Parent Families* (Gardner, 1978). Another source focusing on particular grade levels is *Children of Divorce* (Stolenberg, Camplair, & Zacharias, 1991), which is designed for grades 3 through 6.

Also available are complete programs for children experiencing divorce. Although there is security in using a packaged program, we recommend that you select materials that make sense to you and seem most appropriate to your group. There is no magical approach to helping children move through this adjustment period. When you encounter children experiencing pervasive and intense adjustment difficulties, individual counseling or referral is the best course.

Yauman (1991) suggests that groups be made available for custodial parents. Although programs for parents are important because their adjustment impacts their children's, this is not your primary responsibility. An alternative approach to leading parent groups would be to enter into a partnership with a social worker or with staff from the local mental health center. If you can collaborate with another professional you will avoid having your time consumed by one activity.

You will also develop a collegial relationship with this professional, wherein each can support the other. A good resource for parents is *The Parents Book about Divorce* (Gardner, 1977).

Acquired Immune Deficiency Syndrome (AIDS)

The issue of AIDS is relatively new in our society but it has dramatically impacted our social institutions, social consciousness, and public information (Holcomb, 1990). ASCA suggests that counselors' primary responsibility is to educate children about AIDS—particularly how to avoid exposure—and to create a favorable atmosphere for AIDS education in the school. Unquestionably, AIDS evokes strong reactions of fear, myth, and controversy. In spite of these reactions, we cannot ignore or avoid our obligation to inform young people of the threat of AIDS. High school and college students, in spite of their awareness, are far less concerned about AIDS than is prudent; young people have the feeling that it can't happen to them. This underscores the need for accurate information. Holcomb (1990) asserts that AIDS education should be included in the curriculum beginning at about fourth grade. Further, he recommends you use survey data collected from the students regarding their knowledge and attitudes about AIDS, provide accurate information, assist teachers in managing student anxieties, conduct groups for parents to reduce their concerns, conduct classroom groups that address fears, and start groups for children who are worried about AIDS (pp. 89-90).

How should you respond when a child is diagnosed with AIDS? To manage school and community reaction, initiate a crisis policy and procedure. To assist a child diagnosed with AIDS, you need to inform teachers and other members of the instructional staff of the side effects of medical treatment and the impact of this treatment on the child's school performance.

Try to allay concerns about the presence of the AIDS victim. Addressing the concerns of others in the school about this individual should follow much the same pattern as providing general education about AIDS. Support groups for children and parents should also be included.

Child Abuse and Neglect

On one level, managing the issue of child abuse and neglect is simple: It must be reported to the authorities. The simplicity stops there. Child abuse is one of the most underreported crimes in our country. Hollander (1992) points out that unless the degree of abuse is unmistakable and the police are involved, this heinous crime goes undetected and continues uninterrupted.

Your role in child abuse is basically twofold: identification and prevention. Once the abuse has been verified, you might have a reduced role, deferring to social workers and focusing on school-related issues in the treatment of the victim.

Identification, however difficult, begins with definition. *Physical abuse* is the intentional harming of a child by hitting, biting, kicking, shaking, blows with objects, or other similar physical acts. Physical signs may be obvious. *Emotional abuse* results from verbal humiliation, threats, and attacks. Victims of emotional abuse may be difficult to detect; watch for hypersensitivity to criticism, aggressive acting out, a high degree of distractibility, and possible substance abuse in older children. *Sexual abuse* involves inappropriate touching, sexual contact, using children as subjects in sexual films, profuse obscene language, and physical exposure. Physical signs of sexual abuse may be injury or redness around the genitals. Emotional signs can include extensive and unusual knowledge about sex, extreme fatigue, or disclosures about being mistreated or abused. *Neglect* is parental lack of supervision and guidance, and failure to provide for the child's emotional and physical needs. Signs include frequent evidence of dirty and disheveled clothing or improper dress for the time of year. Neglected children may display consistent fatigue, constant hunger, and untreated medical problems. In almost all cases, definitive evidence is difficult to obtain. If you suspect abuse, investigate the situation through observation and consultation with teachers and other school personnel. It is generally unwise to intensively interview the child without experience in this area because improper interviews can taint the child's later report to authorities. Once abuse or neglect begins, it generally continues until an intervention is made. If the signs are there—even if you have doubts—report this to the proper authorities.

Your primary function here is prevention, usually by educating children and adults about the nature of abuse and the steps necessary to safeguard children. A number of commercial programs are available. A good example is *Body Rights* (Baird & Kile, 1986), whose DUSO format has high appeal to small children. Often, local mental health agencies will serve as a resource for schools to present programs or provide consultation and materials for counselor-led programs. Keep in mind that supportive services should be available whenever an abuse prevention program is presented, as children will need help talking through the situation due to the painful issues that will be raised.

Suicide

Until recently, suicide among children was almost nonexistent, and adolescent suicide was rarely reported as such. Times have changed dramatically. The suicide rate among young people between the ages of 15 and 24 has increased threefold in the last 30 years (Rosenbert et al., 1987). After auto accidents, suicide among adolescents is the second leading cause of death. Hunt (1987) reports that most teen suicides occur between 4 P.M. and midnight. It has been thought that the most stressful time in the household is between 3 P.M. and 11 P.M., as this is the time when the entire family is likely to be home together. Most available data refer to adolescents; we simply do not have the same information about younger people. In one attempt to identify the risk factors at the elementary school level, Nelson & Crawford (1990) conducted a counselor survey. In the study, counselors identified causes of suicide attempts in children and noted that family problems are the primary reason, followed by peer pressure and academic pressure. The counselors listed depression; suicide threats; and aggressive, rebellious, or disobedient behavior as the specific behaviors demonstrated by children who attempted suicide (Nelson & Crawford, 1990). Crespi (1990) notes that there is no single predictor of suicide. The factors identified by Crespi are very similar to those of Nelson and Crawford (1990). Remley and Sparkman (1993) note that it is impossible to predict future suicide attempts. Because this phenomenon is so difficult to isolate, we can point only to signs of stress that may lead to suicidal ideations. Omizo, Omizo, and Suzuki (1988) have identified the stressors for elementary school children. These stressors are, in order,

1. family problems, including parental disapproval, fighting, and divorce;
2. feeling different, such as inferiority feelings, nonacceptance of self, lacking the material belongings of others, and a perceptual lack of strengths and limitations;
3. discipline, a fear of punishment, extremely critical significant adults, and severe or inconsistent punishment;
4. exaggerated concerns over doing something wrong, feeling that something dreadful will happen or that something is scary. (p. 269)

The stressors for middle schoolers are similar, with an emphasis on peer relations, family problems, learning problems in schools, and a generalized lack of control (p. 269). These stressors, paired with the suicide indicators, provide a picture of potentially suicidal children.

Prevention and Intervention.   Nelson and Crawford (1990) have identified your primary role in prevention as occurring through in-service of teachers, parents, and programs for students. Teacher in-service is the most critical need because teachers are the front-line contacts for students and have the greatest potential to identify symptoms of problem behavior. The next area of need is programs for students, followed by in-service for parents. Nelson and Crawford (1990) describe the teacher in-service on suicide prevention as including myths about suicide, warning signs, and suggestions of teacher-led classroom activities.

Programs for parents are essential in suicide prevention. These should include concepts of child behavior, suicide warning signs, myths, and what parents can do when they are concerned about their children (Nelson & Crawford, 1990). In particular, parents should be familiar with community resources.

Programs for students should begin at about fifth grade and focus on the same topics as those for teachers and parents. The difference lies in helping students understand what to do when they are concerned about their friends or themselves.

Finally, Nelson and Crawford (1990) suggest that you coordinate the development of guidelines for teachers to follow when they observe students displaying suicidal behavior. These guidelines provide encouragement for the teachers to act when they become concerned about children in their classroom.

Once school personnel, parents, and students have received input on suicide, the school is in a position to act when concerns arise. Poland (1989) believes the entire school has a role in prevention. This involves making efforts to detect suicidal young people, assessing the level of severity of the behavior, notifying the parents, working with the parents on obtaining the needed assistance, and monitoring the student following initial assistance. The treatment of the suicidal student is best left to those trained to counsel in this area (e.g., clinical staff in community mental health centers)

Remley and Sparkman (1993) point out that counselors face a dilemma when they recognize a potentially suicidal student. The distinction between acting in a timely fashion and overreacting is never a clear one. When you suspect that a student is suicidal, act quickly but with caution. To immediately contact the parents and mobilize community resources may be premature. Probably the best reaction is to take seriously any suicidal ideation. Remley and Sparkman (1993) recommend that you exercise your professional judgment and meet with the students to further appraise their behavior and attitudes. Discuss their thoughts and actions to determine the severity of the ideation or behavior. If, after a session with a student, you believe he or she is suicidal, consult with a colleague. Based on your collective judgment, determine whether the parents should be contacted. This is one case where confidentiality is abridged. Your actions should always be guided by sound professional judgment, and only after the case has been thoroughly examined. Suicide prevention is never an easy proposition; but common sense, professional judgment, and consultation with others will provide the best informed response possible.

ETHICAL PRACTICE

Areas of Ethical Concern

We conclude with emphasis on the key ethical principles. We focus on the ASCA Ethical Standards for School Counselors (1984) because we believe they highlight the most relevant issues for you. The ASCA standards were developed to complement the ACA ethical code, not to replace it. We highlight six ethical responsibilities: to pupils, parents, colleagues and other professionals, the school and community, yourself, and the profession.

Students.   The welfare of the student/client is primary because we believe that you function as an advocate of the child. Furthermore, all ethical codes stress the allegiance of counselors to their clients unless the latter are in danger of harming themselves or others. The relationship between yourself and your young clients is of paramount importance to your effectiveness, and confidentiality must be maintained unless the issue of harm or violation of the law comes into play.

Parents.   As a counselor, you need to make a concerted effort to involve parents in your work. Such a partnership dramatically increases the likelihood of effectively impacting young people.

Professionals.   In coordinating and collaborating with others, your primary responsibility to other professionals is to fulfill this role. With related professionals (i.e., teachers, administrators, and other staff), a primary concern is with helping these individuals to understand and appreciate the confidential relationship between counselors and their student/clients.

Aggregate School and Community.   Your responsibility as a counselor is to represent student interests in educational programming within and outside the school. Also, you must constantly work to articulate the role and function of the counselor, since their nature is frequently misunderstood. Finally, it is in the best interest of young people to promote collaboration between the school and community agencies that are meaningfully involved with young people. Agencies that are most pertinent in the community are governmental social service agencies, the court system, public health agencies, law enforcement agencies, and mental health agencies.

Yourself.   Among your professional obligations to yourself are to function within the boundaries of your competence and recognize the effect of your personality and personal power on those you serve. You are also responsible for continuing your professional development.

The Profession.   Participating in professional organizations and behaving in a professional manner are worthy endeavors. But, most important, we believe in strict adherence to ethical standards and in separating your professional and personal life. Finally, we all have the obligation to report others who act in violation of the ethical principles of our profession.

ASCA Ethical Standards for School Counselors[1]

Preamble

The American School Counselor Association (ASCA) is a professional organization whose members have a unique and distinctive preparation, grounded in the behavorial sciences, with training in counseling skills adapted to the school setting. The school counselor assists in the growth and development of each individual and uses his/her specialized skills to ensure that the rights of the counselee are properly protected within the structure of the school program. School counselors subscribe to the following basic tenets of the counseling process from which professional responsibilities are derived:

1. Each person has the right to respect and dignity as a unique human being and to counseling services without prejudice as to person, character, belief or practice.

---

[1] Ethical Standards for School Counselors was adopted by the ASCA Delegate Assembly, March 19, 1984. This revision was approved by the ASCA Delegate Assembly, March 27, 1992. Reprinted by permission of the American School Counselors Association.

2. Each person has the right to self-direction and self-development.
3. Each person has the right of choice and the responsibility for decisions reached.
4. Each person has the right to privacy and thereby the right to expect the counselor-client relationship to comply with all laws, policies and ethical standards pertaining to confidentiality.

In this document, the American School Counselor Association has specified the principles of ethical behavior necessary to maintain and regulate the high standards of integrity and leadership among its members. The Association recognizes the basic commitment of its members to the Ethical Standards of its parent organization, the American Counseling Association (ACA), and nothing in this document shall be construed to supplant that code. The Ethical Standards for School Counselors was developed to complement the ACA standards by clarifying the nature of ethical responsibilities for present and future counselors in the school setting. The purposes of this document are to:

1. Serve as a guide for the ethical practices of all professional school counselors regardless of level, area, population served, or membership in this Association.
2. Provide benchmarks for both self-appraisal and peer evaluations regarding counselor responsibilities to students, parents, colleagues and professional associates, school and community, self, and the counseling profession.
3. Inform those served by the school counselor of acceptable counselor practices and expected professional deportment.

A. Responsibilities to Students
The school counselor:

1. Has a primary obligation and loyalty to the student, who is to be treated with respect as a unique individual, whether assisted individually or in a group setting.
2. Is concerned with the total needs of the student (educational, vocational, personal and social) and encourages the maximum growth and development of each counselee.
3. Informs the counselee of the purposes, goals, techniques and rules of procedure under which she/he may receive counseling assistance at or before the time when the counseling relationship is entered. Prior notice includes confidentiality issues such as the possible necessity for consulting with other professionals, privileged communication, and legal or authoritative restraints. The meaning and limits of confidentiality are clearly defined to counselees.
4. Refrains from consciously encouraging the counselee's acceptance of values, lifestyles, plans, decisions, and beliefs that represent only the counselor's personal orientation.

5. Is responsible for keeping abreast of laws relating to students and strives to ensure that the rights of students are adequately provided for and protected.

6. Avoids dual relationships which might impair his/her objectivity and/or increase the risk of harm to the client (e.g., counseling one's family members, close friends or associates). If a dual relationship is unavoidable, the counselor is responsible for taking action to eliminate or reduce the potential for harm. Such safeguards might include informed consent, consultation, supervision and documentation.

7. Makes appropriate referrals when professional assistance can no longer be adequately provided to the counselee. Appropriate referral requires knowledge of available resources.

8. Protects the confidentiality of student records and releases personal data only according to prescribed laws and school policies. Student information maintained through electronic data storage methods is treated with the same care as traditional student records.

9. Protects the confidentiality of information received in the counseling relationship as specified by law and ethical standards. Such information is only to be revealed to others with the informed consent of the counselee and consistent with the obligations of the counselor as a professional person. In a group setting, the counselor sets a norm of confidentiality and stresses its importance, yet clearly states that confidentiality in group counseling cannot be guaranteed.

10. Informs the appropriate authorities when the counselee's condition indicates a clear and imminent danger to the counselee or others. This is to be done after careful deliberation and, where possible, after consultation with other professionals. The counselor informs the counselee of actions to be taken so as to minimize confusion and clarify expectations.

11. Screens prospective group members and maintains an awareness of participants' compatibility throughout the life of the group, especially when the group emphasis is on self-disclosure and self-understanding. The counselor takes reasonable precautions to protect members from physical and/or psychological harm resulting from interaction within the group.

12. Provides explanations of the nature, purposes, and results of tests in language that is understandable to the client(s).

13. Adheres to relevant standards regarding selection, administration, and interpretation of assessment techniques. The counselor recognizes that computer-based testing programs require specific training in administration, scoring and interpretation which may differ from that required in more traditional assessments.

14. Promotes the benefits of appropriate computer applications and clarifies the limitations of computer technology. The counselor ensures that (1) computer applications are appropriate for the

individual needs of the counselee, (2) the counselee understands how to use the application, and (3) follow-up counseling assistance is provided. Members of underrepresented groups are assured of equal access to computer technologies and the absence of discriminatory information and values with computer applications.

15. Has unique ethical responsibilities in working with peer programs. In general, the school counselor is responsible for the welfare of students participating in peer programs under her/his direction. School counselors who function in training and supervisory capacities are referred to the preparation and supervision standards of professional counselor associations.

B. Responsibilities to Parents
The school counselor:

1. Respects the inherent rights and responsibilities of parents for their children and endeavors to establish a cooperative relationship with parents to facilitate the maximum development of the counselee.
2. Informs parents of the counselor's role, with emphasis on the confidential nature of the counseling relationship between the counselor and counselee.
3. Provides parents with accurate, comprehensive and relevant information in an objective and caring manner, as appropriate and consistent with ethical responsibilities to the counselee.
4. Treats information received from parents in a confidential and appropriate manner.
5. Shares information about a counselee only with those persons properly authorized to receive such information.
6. Adheres to laws and local guidelines when assisting parents experiencing family difficulties which interfere with the counselee's effectiveness and welfare.
7. Is sensitive to changes in the family and recognizes that all parents, custodial and noncustodial, are vested with certain rights and responsibilities for the welfare of their children by virtue of their position and according to law.

C. Responsibilities to Colleagues and Professional Associates
The school counselor:

1. Establishes and maintains a cooperative relationship with faculty, staff and administration to facilitate the provision of optimal guidance and counseling programs and services.
2. Promotes awareness and adherence to appropriate guidelines regarding confidentiality, the distinction between public and private information, and staff consultation.

3. Treats colleagues with respect, courtesy, fairness and good faith. The qualifications, views and findings of colleagues are represented accurately and fairly to enhance the image of competent prefessionals.
4. Provides professional personnel with accurate, objective, concise and meaningful data necessary to adequately evaluate, counsel and assist the counselee.
5. Is aware of and fully utilizes related professions and organizations to whom the counselee may be referred.

D. Responsibilities to the School and Community
The school counselor:

1. Supports and protects the educational program against any infringement not in the best interest of students.
2. Informs appropriate officials of conditions that may be potentially disruptive or damaging to the school's mission, personnel and property.
3. Delineates and promotes the counselor's role and function in meeting the needs of those served. The counselor will notify appropriate school officials of conditions which may limit or curtail their effectiveness in providing programs and services.
4. Assists in the development of: (1) curricular and environmental conditions appropriate for the school and community, (2) educational procedures and programs to meet student needs, and (3) a systematic evaluation process for guidance and counseling programs, services and personnel. The counselor is guided by the findings of the evaluation data in planning programs and services.
5. Actively cooperates and collaborates with agencies, organizations, and individuals in the school and community in the best interest of counselees and without regard to personal reward or remuneration.

E. Responsibilities to Self
The school counselor:

1. Functions within the boundaries of individual professional competence and accepts responsibility for the consequences of his/her actions.
2. Is aware of the potential effects of her/his own personal characteristics on services to clients.
3. Monitors personal functioning and effectiveness and refrains from any activity likely to lead to inadequate professional services or harm to a client.
4. Recognizes that differences in clients relating to age, gender, race, religion, sexual orientation, socioeconomic and ethnic backgrounds may require specific training to ensure competent services.
5. Strives through personal initiative to maintain professional competence and keep abreast of innovations and trends in the profession. Professional and personal growth is continuous and ongoing throughout the counselor's career.

F. Responsibilities to the Profession
The school counselor:

1. Conducts herself/himself in such a manner as to bring credit to self and the profession.
2. Conducts appropriate research and reports findings in a manner consistent with acceptable educational and psychological research practices. When using client data for research, statistical or program planning purposes, the counselor ensures protection of the identity of the individual client(s).
3. Actively participates in local, state and national associations which foster the development and improvement of school counseling.
4. Adheres to ethical standards of the profession, other official policy statements pertaining to counseling, and relevant statutes established by federal, state and local governments.
5. Clearly distinguishes between statements and actions made as a private individual and as a representative of the school counseling profession.
6. Contributes to the development of the profession through the sharing of skills, ideas and expertise with colleagues.

G. Maintenance of Standards
Ethical behavior among professional school counselors, Association members and nonmembers, is expected at all times. When there exists serious doubt as to the ethical behavior of colleagues, or if counselors are forced to work in situations or abide by policies which do not reflect the standards as outlined in these Ethical Standards for School Counselors or the ACA Ethical Standards, the counselor is obligated to take appropriate action to rectify the condition. The following procedure may serve as a guide:

1. If feasible, the counselor should consult with a professional colleague to confidentially dicuss the nature of the complaint to see if she/he views the situation as an ethical violation.
2. Whenever possible, the counselor should directly approach the colleague whose behavior is in question to discuss the complaint and seek resolution.
3. If resolution is not forthcoming at the personal level, the counselor shall utilize the channels established within the school and/or school district. This may include both informal and formal procedures.
4. If the matter still remains unresolved, referral for review and appropriate action should be made to the Ethics Committees in the following sequence:
   • state counselor association
   • national counselor association
5. The ASCA Ethics Committee functions in an educative and consultative capacity and does not adjudicate complaints of ethical misconduct. Therefore, at the national level, complaints should be submitted in

writing to the ACA Ethics Committee for review and appropriate action. The procedure for submitting complaints may be obtained by writing the ACA Ethics Committee, c/o The Executive Director, American Counseling Association, 5999 Stevenson Avenue, Alexandria, VA 22304.

H. Resources

School counselors are responsible for being aware of, and acting in accord with, the standards and positions of the counseling profession as represented in official documents such as those listed below.

Code of Ethics (1989). National Board for Certified Counselors. Alexandria, VA.

Code of Ethics for Peer Helping Professionals (1989). National Peer Helpers Association. Glendale, CA.

Ethical Guidelines for Group Counselors (1989). Association for Specialists in Group Work. Alexandria, VA.

Ethical Standards (1988), American Association for Counseling and Development. Alexandria, VA.

Position Statement: The School Counselor and Confidentiality (1986). American School Counselor Association. Alexandria, VA.

Position Statement: The School Counselor and Peer Facilitation (1984). American School Counselor Association. Alexandria, VA.

Position Statement: The School Counselor and Student Rights (1982). American School Counselor Association. Alexandria, VA.

SUMMARY

This chapter addressed some of the unique issues that counselors face today. Many of these are dealt with in collaboration with others within and outside the school. This chapter emphasized that the lives of today's young people are more complex than at anytime before. It also pointed to the changes in our society where crisis, the threat of abuse, the presence of alcohol and drugs, potential violence, the discouragement young people feel from school failure and disrupted home life, and where young people feel pressure from peers are all ever present and unyielding. Much more of your time will be spent on these issues unless you can use developmental counseling in the lower grades to prevent problems from arising and assist parents in coping more effectively with a society that at times appears out of control.

REVIEW

1. Describe how the counselor's role in school reform has become a source of controversy.
2. Develop two approaches to improve relations between counselors and teachers.
3. Create a hypothetical school crisis and then develop two teacher-led classroom activities to address this situation.

4. Through the use of examples, differentiate among drug abuse education, prevention, and intervention.

5. Children of alcoholics constitute a special population. Develop a humanistic approach to addressing this issue with COAs.

6. Defend or refute the inclusion of career development in your elementary school counseling program.

7. Distinguish between the counselor's role in developmental support and in therapy for children experiencing divorce.

8. Using the ASCA ethical standards as your focal point, select the counselor responsibility that you consider to be the most noteworthy. Indicate what makes this responsibility important.

REFERENCES

Anderson, G. (1987). *When chemicals come to school: The student assistance program model.* Greenfield, WI: Community Recovery Press.

American School Counselor Association. (1992). *Ethical standards.* Alexandria, VA: Author.

Baird, K., & Kile, M. (1986). *Body rights.* Circle Pines, MN: American Guidance Service.

Benton, S. A., & Benton, S. L. (1992). *Trends in rural Kansas students' alcohol/drug use.* (Paper presented at the Fourth Annual Conference of Regents Drug Abuse Prevention Consortium). Lawrence, KS.

Black, C. (1981). *It will never happen to me.* Denver, CO: M.A.C. Printing.

Borton, T. (1983, April 25). Pressure to try drugs, alcohol starts in early grades. *Weekly Reader.* Middletown, CT: Xerox Educational Publications.

Brook, J. S., Whitman, M., Gordon, A. S., Nomura, C., & Brook, D. W. (1986). Onset of adolescent drinking: A longitudinal study of intrapersonal and interpersonal antecedents. In *Advances in alcohol and substance use, 5,* pp. 91-100.

Crespi, T. D. (1990). Approaching adolescent suicide: Queries and signposts. *The School Counselor, 37*(4), 256-260.

Daugherty, R., Newman, D., & O'Bryan T. (1985). *Talking with your kids about alcohol.* Lexington, KY: Prevention Research Institute.

Dinkmeyer, D., Sr., & Dinkmeyer, D., Jr. (1982). *Developing understanding of self and others—2.* Circle Pines, MN: American Guidance Service.

Dinkmeyer, D., Sr., McKay, G. D., & Dinkmeyer, D., Jr. (1980). *Systematic training for effective teaching.* Circle Pines, MN: American Guidance Service.

Gardner, D. (1983). *A nation at risk: The imperative for educational reform.* Washington, DC: U.S. Department of Education.

Gardner, R. A. (1970). *The boys and girls book about divorce.* New York: Bantam.

Gardner, R. A. (1977). *The parents book about divorce.* New York: Bantam.

Gardener, R. A. (1978). *The boys and girls book about one parent families.* New York: Bantam.

Garver, C. (1987). Group counseling program helps students deal with divorce. *National Association of Secondary School Principals Journal, 71*(499), 32-34.

Gerne, T. A., & Gerne, P. J. (1986). *Substance abuse prevention activities for elementary children.* Englewood Cliffs, NJ: Prentice-Hall.

Hawley, R. (1990). The bumpy road to drug-free schools. *Phi Delta Kappan, 72*(4), 310-314.

Hill, D. J., White, M., Pain, M. D., & Gardner, G. J. (1990). Tobacco and alcohol use among Australian secondary school children in 1987. *Medical Journal of Australia, 152,* 19-22.

Holcomb, T. F. (1990). Fourth graders' attitudes towards AIDS issues: A concern for the elementary school counselor. *Elementary School Guidance and Counseling, 25*(2), 83–90.

Hollander, S. K. (1992). Making young children aware of sexual abuse. *Elementary School Guidance and Counseling, 26*(4), 305–317.

Hoyt, K. (1993). Comprehensive career education model. *Youth Policy, 15*(6 & 7), 15.

Hunt, C. (1987). Step by step: How your schools can live through the tragedy of teen suicides. *The American School Board Journal, 174*(2), 34, 37.

Jay, B. (1989). Managing a crisis in the school—Tips for principals. *National Association of Secondary School Principals Journal, 73*(513), 14, 16–18.

Johnston, L. D., O'Malley, P. M., & Bachman, J. G. (1987). *Drinking by America's high school students, college students, and young adults, 1975–1987.* Rockville, MD: National Institute on Drug Abuse.

Jones, C. L., & Bell-Bolek, C. S. (1986). Kids and drugs: Why, when and what can we do about it? *Children Today, 15,* 5–10.

Kelly, D., Stimeling, W., and Kachur, D. (1989). Before the worst, have your crisis plan ready. *Executive Educator, 11*(1), 22–23.

Kelly, J. B., & Wallerstein, J. S. (1977). Brief interventions with children in divorcing families. *American Journal of Orthopsychiatry, 47,* 23–39.

McDaniel, S., & Bielen, P. (1990). *Project self-esteem: A parent involvement program for improving self-esteem and preventing drug and alcohol abuse, K–6.* Rolling Hills Estates, CA: Jalmar Press.

Miller, P. M., Smith, G. T., & Goldman, M. S. (1990). Emergence of alcohol expectancies in childhood: A possible critical period. *Journal of Studies in Alcohol, 51,* 343–349.

Nelson, R. E., & Crawford, B. (1990). Suicide among elementary school-aged children. *Elementary School Guidance and Counseling, 25*(2), 123–128.

Newsam, B. (1992). *Complete student assistance program handbook.* West Nyack, NY: The Center for Applied Research in Education.

NOICC: National career development guidelines: Local handbook for high schools. Washington, DC: Author.

Omizo, M. M., Omizo, S. A., & Suzuki, L. A. (1988). Children and stress: An exploratory study of stressors and symptoms. *The School Counselor, 35*(4), 267–274.

O'Rourke, K. (1992). Young children of alcoholics: Little people with big needs. *Journal of Alcohol and Drug Education, 37*(2), 43–51.

Peterson, S., and Straub, R. (1992). *School crisis survival guide: Management techniques and materials for counselors and administrators.* West Nyack, NY: The Center for Applied Research in Education.

Poland, S. (1989). *Suicide intervention in the schools.* New York: Guilford Press.

Remley, T. P., & Sparkman, L. B. (1993). Student suicides: The counselor's limited legal liability. *The School Counselor, 40*(3), 164–169.

Robinson, B. E. (1989). *Working with children of alcoholics: A practitioner's handbook.* Lexington, MA: Lexington Books.

Rosenberg, M. L., Smith, J. C., Davidson, L. E., & Conn, J. M. (1987). The emergence of youth suicide: An epidemiological analysis and public health perspective. *Annual Review of Public Health, 8,* 417–440.

Schaffer, D. (1987). *Choices and consequences: What to do when a teenager uses alcohol/ drugs.* Minneapolis, MN: Johnson Institute Books.

Siehl, P. (1990). Suicide postvention: A new disaster plan—What a school should do when faced with a suicide. *The School Counselor, 38*(1), 52–57.

Sorensen, J. (1989). Responding to student or teacher death: Preplanning crisis intervention. *Journal of Counseling and Development, 67*(7), 426-427.

Stevens, M., Youells, F., Whaley, R., & Linsey, S. (1991). Prevalence and correlates of alcohol use in a survey of rural elementary school students: The New Hampshire Study. *Journal of Drug Education, 21,* 333-347.

Stolenberg, A. L., Camplair, C., & Zacharias, C. W. (1991). *Children of divorce.* Circle Pines, MN: American Guidance Service.

Vernon, A. (1989a). *Thinking, feeling, behaving: An emotional education curriculum for children, grades 1-6.* Champaign, IL: Research Press.

Vernon, A. (1989b). *Thinking, feeling, behaving: An emotional education curriculum for adolescents, grades 7-12.* Champaign, IL: Research Press.

Wallerstein, J. S. (1989, January 22). Children after divorce: Wounds that don't heal. *The New York Times Magazine,* pp. 19-21, 41-44.

Wilmes, D. (1988). *Parenting for prevention: How to raise a child to say no to alcohol/ drugs.* Minneapolis, MN: Johnson Institute Books.

Yauman, B. E. (1991). School-based group counseling for children of divorce. A review of the literature. *Elementary School Guidance and Counseling, 26*(2), 130-138.

Index